Traveling in the footsteps of the ~~~~~ Velvel Zbarzher, who s~~~~~ ~~~~~ and Yiddish, Jill Culiner ~~~ p~~~~~~~ an intense, powerful yet breezy narrative that is extremely unusual in that it is at once a work of history, biography, and memoir. On her long and often difficult research journey through the old Pale of Settlement (Belarus, Lithuania, Moldova, Poland, parts of northern Ukraine, Latvia and Russia), Culiner's first-rate eye allows her to render the world of the shtetl, past and present, with more intimacy, complexity and telling detail than anything else I have read. Zbarzher, considered a heretic by the religious Jewish community, fled to Romania in 1845 and spent the last twenty-five years there singing, writing poems, and carousing. It is the measure of the strength of Culiner's work that her own journey is as fascinating as that of her subject.

Robert A. Rosenstone, *Emeritus Professor of History, California Institute of Technology author of The Man Who Swam into History*

The lucky reader of A Contrary Journey makes the acquaintance of two great iconoclasts: Velvel Zbarzher and Jill Culiner, the author herself. Culiner's intrepid pursuit of the elusive troubadour and the lost world from which he emerged enriches us with a double depiction of the turbulent times and places of the bard's era and the galloping commercialization of our own. Like a chef who manages to document great recipes before they disappear, Culiner serves us an utterly delicious feast of flavours we do not want to lose.

Robin Roger, *writer, reviewer, Associate Publisher, New Jewish Press 2016-18*

Invited by Culiner to join her travels to find Velvel was a gift in isolated pandemic times. Part history, part biography and part literature, the writing poetically transfixed. Train rides, villages, and Velvel's life move between magical realism and extraordinary insights into Jewish history generally missing in heritage tourism.

Daniel J Walkowitz, *Emeritus Professor of History, Social & Cultural Analysis, New York University, author of The Remembered and Forgotten Jewish World*

A Contrary Journey is a captivating romance, a thrilling mystery, a fascinating walking/train tour back and forward in time, and much more. Culiner takes us out of the contemporary fast-paced, digital society and superbly redraws the contours of the shtetls of Eastern Europe via one remarkable itinerant Jewish existence: the unjustly forgotten Hebrew poet Velvel Zbarzher, a significant precursor of Yiddish theatre that moved from Galicia to Romania, to the Russian Pale of Settlement. A breathtaking read!

Dana Mihailescu, *Associate Professor of American Studies, University of Bucharest*

What a beautiful book! The writing is clear and direct, and the characters are lively and realistically portrayed. It's a good piece of reporting, and was entirely successful in wafting me to another time and place.

Barrington James, *former foreign correspondent for the Herald Tribune and UPI, author of The Musical World of Marie Antoinette*

A Contrary Journey

With Velvel Zbarzher, Bard

JILL CULINER

Claret Press

CLARET PRESS

Library and Archives Canada Cataloguing in Publication
Copyright ©Jill Culiner
The moral right of the author has been asserted.
www.jill-culiner.com

ISBN paperback: 978-1-910461-43-3
ISBN ebook: 978-1-910461-52-5

A CIP catalogue record for this book is available from the British Library.
This paperback or the ebook can be ordered from all bookstores and from Claret Press, as well as eplatforms such as Amazon and ibooks.
Front cover photo with courtesy from, The Memorial Museum of Hungarian Speaking Jewry, Safed, Israel http://www.hjm.org.il/

Book cover and interior design by Bernard Tisserand
www.bernard-tisserand.

www.claretpress.com

Contents

Part One: Prologue   1
  Introduction: *Lost Places, Lost Love*   3
  Chapter I: *Paris*   11
  Chapter II: *Cologne*   15
  Chapter III: *The Haskalah*   23
Part Two: Looking for Velvel   31
  Chapter IV: *The Shtetl*   33
  Chapter V: *Zbarazh*   43
  Chapter VI: *The Wedding*   53
  Chapter VII: *The Road*   59
  Chapter VIII: *Czernowitz*   65
  Chapter IX: *Romania*   75
  Chapter X: *Botoșani*   87
  Chapter XI: *Inns*   97
  Chapter XII: *Fame*   103
  Chapter XIII: *Expulsion*   113
  Chapter XIV: *Brody*   123
  Chapter XV: *Lemberg*   131
  Chapter XVI: *Return to Zbarazh*   139
  Chapter XVII: *Vienna*   151
  Chapter XVIII: *Itinerancy*   161
  Chapter XIX: *Return to Czernowitz*   169
  Chapter XX: *Malkele*   183
  ChapterXXI: *Constantinople*   189
  Chapter XXII: *After*   197
Part Three: The Russian Pale   203
  Chapter XXIII: *Dubno*   205
  Chapter XXIV: *Lutsk*   215
  Chapter XXV: *Harry's Story*   221
  Chapter XXVI: *Svinich*   227
  Chapter XXVII: *Poritsk*   237
Part Four: The New Country   245
  Chapter XXVIII: *Pickering, Ontario*   247
Bibliography   257
Acknowledgements   269
About the Author   271

Tell me, you beautiful moon,
You look everywhere when all is still
And covered with a black shroud
You shed your light
Everywhere at night,
There surely must
Be some haven for the just!
But the moon has gone behind the clouds,
Ashamed she moans, 'There is none.'

Velvel Zbarzher

Eastern Europe, 1870

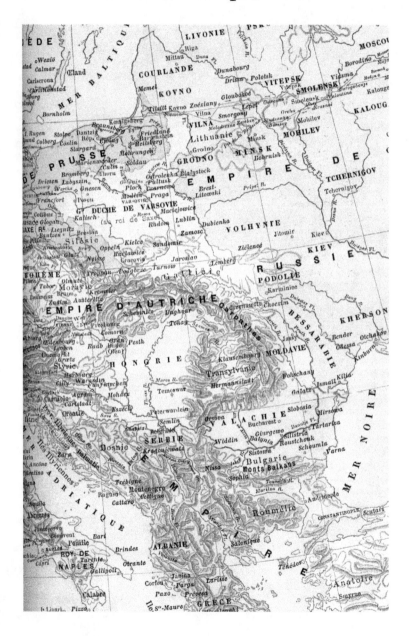

Part One:
PROLOGUE

Introduction
Lost Places, Lost Love

All journeys have secret destinations of which the traveller is unaware.

Martin Buber

I fell in love with Velvel Zbarzher one hundred and thirty years after his death. Sol Liptzin introduced us. In his History of Yiddish Literature, Sol wrote that Velvel (Benjamin Wolf Ehrenkranz) was born in 1826 in Zbarazh, Galicia; that he wrote scoffing Hebrew and Yiddish verse; that he was considered heretical by the conservative Jewish community; that he fled to Romania in 1845 and spent the next twenty-five years singing, writing poems, and carousing (a magic word that conjures up all manner of romantic excess). Then, in his fifties, he married his great love, Malkele the Beautiful, in Constantinople and died three years later.

What turned mere acquaintance into love? One dazzling sentence:

Zbarzher...might well have attained the pinnacle of fame...if he had not squandered his talent in disreputable Rumanian inns and Turkish coffeehouses.

Doesn't that make imagination reel? Wake up longing? (Love often begins with more banal catalysts: 'Would you like a beer?' 'What a beautiful dog!' 'Do you know the time?')

I began making plans—let's not tackle Malkele the Beautiful yet: just push her aside like any cumbersome mate in an illicit affair. Together, Velvel and I will flee Galicia and wander along Romania's pitted lanes; together, we'll idle and squander in low bars. I'll cheer him on, poke his ribs with a jocular elbow when his mood slides into its recurrent gloom; or pinching his ear between thumb and forefinger, I'll tweak him back to joy.

Unless I'm inventing a cheerier me. What will happen when the romance of the highway wears thin? Will I evolve into a harridan, thin-lipped and sour? The sort who chastises a brilliant love for his drunken bouts, for his loose-fingered relationship to cash that leaves our couple ever dependent upon charity? How will we know if we don't give it a whirl?

***

*M*y grandmother Machla had a large painting, one she took with her no matter how often she moved. It was (to me) a banal rural scene: a lush meadow and, deep in the scrabble of a copse, the suggestion of a wooden hut. That picture reminded her of a particular place near the townlet where she was born—Poritsk, in the former Russian Pale.[1] It was one of the few things she ever told me about the Old Country, the only hint that something had been lost or traded in. Further questioning only met with, 'That won't interest you.' But she was wrong. It would have. Even back then, I was on the lookout for the old days, for images from a world just out of sight. And I wanted to know how she got from there, that remote secretive place, to here, a flat Ontario landscape.

By the end of the nineteenth century, Jewish women in

---

[1]   The Russian Pale of Settlement (1791-1917) included all of today's Belarus, Lithuania, Moldova, Poland, a large part of northern Ukraine, and some sections of Latvia and White Russia.

the Old Country were being nourished on the new secular literature, on tales of true love and equality. The most courageous had begun refusing arranged marriages to pious men. How was I to know my grandmother had once been a firebrand, an anarchist, one of the radical women of her time? Only a few years ago did Helen, an old family friend, mention the hard-headed debates, the demands for social justice, the passionate activism out at the Workmen's Circle Colony in Pickering, Ontario.

By the time I knew her, Machla had given up the fight. The Workmen's Colony had evolved into a comfortable family cottage world where, during those yellow heat-soaked summer days, retired folks tended to vegetable gardens and prepared pickles. Dry and caustic, Machla expected conformity from her four sons and her grandchildren: we were to do well in school, be popular, successful, meet suitable mates, live in big houses, wear gold, and have clever children—the usual. To me, such goals seemed dull. With a liberating disregard for rules, I planned to meet malcontents, iconoclasts, people who didn't fit in, those who had escaped familial, social, and religious pressure. And I dreamt of far-away places.

I started wandering late at night. By the time I was fourteen, I was climbing through my bedroom window and shinnying down the drainpipe. Sticking to the shadows, learning to be invisible, I lurked in backyards all over the city, peeked into windows, saw how others lived. There wasn't much of interest: people watched TV or, perfectly immobile, stared at nothing. Sometimes they talked or sat until late with friends. But out in the cold dark, or up in the branches of a tree (to see the higher floors), I experienced the secret thrill that gives voyeurs and peepers their *raison d'être*.

Dreamy, secretive, a poor student ever ready to lie, I had a freedom other, more obedient children didn't. I travelled alone, learned every bus and streetcar route in Toronto, every far-flung corner of the city. The back-and-forth rides through the paltry twelve stations of the subway gave me a special kick. By seventeen, I was gone for good, slipping over the American border and heading for New York with a precious five-dollar bill safe in my pocket. There was a whole exciting world to be discovered.

***

*H*ow places and sounds have vanished, taken uniqueness with them. I've seen it happen. As a social critical artist and teller of tales in modest settings—front rooms, back kitchens, open fields, public halls, and many low bars—I've always chosen itinerancy over comfort and security. I've been shifting across the earth's surface for well over half a century now and doing it on the cheap: no soulless or chic hotels, no tourist venues for me. Just sleeping in open fields, or cars, or crumbling castles, or down-at-heel inns; crossing much of Europe on foot; lurking in unsavoury places; tasting life in French, German, English, Dutch, Hungarian, Latvian, Lithuanian, Polish, Greek, and Turkish villages.

And believe me, we've lost a lot: virtuoso spoon players in English miner's pubs; Bulgarian store-front bars where women sang in high-pitched traditional tones while their moustachioed lovers watched with cynical eyes; grim Hungarian back rooms where proud Gypsy musicians played cimbaloms, violins, violas, bass fiddles while garlic fried on a hot plate; German villages where roads were unpaved, the sun heated sweet straw, and ruddy folk squeezed accordions; Austrian country inns where stranger-hating men tickled zithers; dusty French towns undisturbed by tourism where house façades were neglected and hurdy-gurdies whined of fallow fields; wooden cottages on shore-lapping North American lakes where men sawed at violins and bears snuffled around the vegetable patch; seaside villages where frame houses sagged and wind-pushed screen doors made music of another kind.

Those spoon players, the fine moustachioed men, the singers with their high-pitched tones, and the hurdy-gurdies have all vanished. Lakes are churned by speeding boats. European towns are bland and tidy, housing developments have spread like relentless fungi, and traditional musicians have been humiliated out by youths screaming, 'Get modern.'

Today's cultural references demand a break with the past, and little has survived the onslaught of commercial noise, mass entertainment, bling, cement, and polyvinyl chloride. Reason and observation have been replaced by canned laughter, binge-watching, must-have products, and the star or victim of the moment. Gone are sounds, smells, and feelings. In their place are 'historical' reconstructions, touchy-feely interactive museums, atmosphere candles, world music, sound and light shows—all as authentic as any Disney creation. We didn't value what we had, we didn't cherish or preserve it, and we'll never get it back, despite designer determination.

I'm just another silver-haired crock tilting backward? Certainly not. A critical sense should be the essence of the present-day spirit; change, ever vaunted as progress, must be weighed before acceptance.

***

*T*ravelling into the past means abandoning preconceived ideas. Did the cosy, welcoming *shtetl*[2] ever truly exist? It's the one promoted to tradition-thirsty heritage travellers and a sitcom-nurtured society: a family-friendly fantasy world where solidarity, kindness, love, and pious warmth reigned. But doesn't such unity depend upon conformity and obedience? On submitting to the rules, on biting your tongue and accepting values not yours? It means tolerating superstition and fearing gossip; it means mistaking duty for love; it means terror of the big wide world just outside your door. It's refusing to take the road less trodden.

---

2 A shtetl was the Jewish section of town within a larger town.

The nineteenth century. What a time of violence and change, of cultural wealth, questioning, experimentation, and discovery. It was a century of brilliance in art, music, science, literature, and architecture. It was a time during which old social orders were challenged and overthrown, when it seemed that observation and reason might triumph over obscurantism. When some found the courage to defy society, accept banishment, risk imprisonment and death.

In Eastern Europe, the nineteenth century saw the end of serfdom. A peasantry, heretofore ignorant and subjugated, could now demand schooling and justice; and a handful of aristocrats, those able to rise to the challenge of a new order, could—and did—help usher in progressive change. In the Jewish world, the Enlightenment, the *Haskalah*[3], begun in Germany a century earlier, was challenging the religious stranglehold in Galicia, Romania, and the Russian Pale, and opening the door to secular education.

Despite popular belief, not all Jews who abandoned their villages were economic exiles. There were others, iconoclasts like Velvel Zbarzher, who rejected the status quo and sought freedom of thought and movement, the right to read and create modern literature, to play and enjoy music, to create and analyse art, to question belief or refuse it altogether. Most gathered in cities, although that choice usually meant poverty

---

3   Haskalah is from the Hebrew word sekhel, 'the intellect,' and refers to general knowledge and secular learning.

and factory slog; others changed continents and helped build railways, searched for gold and silver, carved out homesteads in deep forests, started pioneering farms, or opened new schools. Not a few became actors, musicians, teachers, and writers, and were responsible for a great outpouring of symphonies, novels, short stories, poems, essays, and plays. All knew the exile's misery. But they did have one thing in common: they were starting anew, abandoning frustration.

**

*B*ut enough! Time to step back two centuries, find my dearest Velvel and begin our glorious romance. I want to learn the colour of his eyes and the fineness of his hair (tell me: is Malkele the Beautiful really so beautiful? Really? How beautiful?). With Velvel, my life will again change. I'll escape modern sterility, video clips, flat-screen televisions, cell phones, thump noise, Ski-doos, Sea-doos, quad bikes, telephone hawkers, and speedways.

With Velvel, I will slip out of community grasp, head for the border, journey into the Old Country and see what remains of another century. I will, once again, become a thrilled peeper, observing unseen, sniffing out shadows.

I need no tour guide with a pre-selected venue for I'll be shepherded by the first-hand experience of Velvel's letters from Galicia, Romania, and Turkey, by the men who knew him: Professor Doktor Meir Weissberg, Doktor Moses Fried, David Yeshaya Silberbusch; and by others who lived through and wrote about that time: Joseph Margoshes, Yekhezkel Kotik, Echiel Levin Benzion, Karl Emil Franzos, S. Ansky, Joseph David Yeshaya, even my grandfather Harry.

Let all who want a glimpse into the past join me. We'll take to the road, bump along with Velvel and the other rebels.

Chapter I:
Paris

A meowing cat can't catch mice.

Yiddish proverb

*T*hese Paris train stations, once beautiful examples of neo-classical architecture and decorated with murals, are being converted into shopping centres and fast-food emporia. Only the façades remain. I'm in the Gare du Nord, hanging around on the platform, waiting for my train to depart. A ticket controller, also lolling out here, isn't averse to a complaining conversation.

'This is the Third World. Just last night there was a gang war: blacks against Arabs. They had machetes, axes, broken bottles. Happens all the time now. On the train, you'd better be careful too; at the Belgian border, the train stops for five minutes, and that's when the thieves get on, help themselves. Sure, there are plainclothes police on the train, but they're only there for immigration control. What a century!'

Why blame the century? The Gare du Nord, Gare de l'Est, Gare de Lyon, their surrounding streets have seen it all. Over a hundred years ago, Jewish refugees fleeing Eastern

European's pogroms and charges of blood libel, stepped into France here and, believe me, flat broke as they were, a plethora of no-goodniks were ready and waiting to exploit them: baggage thieves, unscrupulous landlords, pimps, sellers of bogus tickets to nowhere. Here were those who would turn immigrants into slaves, for a third entered France illegally. No official papers? No rights. You can't tell the desperate something like that, though; all believed Paris would be paradise, a Latin Shangri-La, the capital of a benevolent country where equal rights guaranteed dignity and freedom from anti-Semitism.

Those who settled became France's first Yiddish-speaking community and, with their Old Country traditions, managed to turn the Gallic streets of the Marais, Belleville, and Clignancourt into ersatz Eastern European shtetlekh. Crowding several families into each apartment, most worked as tailors, hatters, junk dealers, ragmen, shoemakers, or peddlers. Others starved or went from house-to-house begging; their unruly children ran wild and turned to petty theft. Not a few, their dreams shattered, climbed the Bastille with its gilded statue brandishing the torch of civilisation and leapt into the afterlife.

Avoiding the established French Jewish community (considering them heretical and hardly Jewish at all) the immigrants formed *landsmanschaften,* benevolent societies named after former hometowns, and depended upon them for aid and social life. Of course, not all the new arrivals were conservative. Some were of quite another ilk: intellectuals, students, and radical socialists, those who had cut all ties with Jewish tradition.

Yet, religious or not, these Eastern European Jews were a shock to France's established community. French Jews, like their German and Austrian counterparts, were modern, urban, urbane, and assimilated. Possessing the same rights as non-Jews, some had become powerful businessmen, bankers, lawyers, university professors, officers in the army, and engineers. In their synagogues, prayers and sermons were held in French; the *bimah*[4] was now right up in front like any church altar; there were choirs and organs. Sure, the incomers were also Jews, but what did they have in common with Frenchmen? Those kaftan-wearing eastern cousins hailed from orthodox communities where life had stood still for centuries, and where religious injunction dictated thought and behaviour.

Tension mounted. French Jews feared their backward-looking relatives would kindle anti-Semitism, that unpleasant racial stereotypes would be applied to them as well. Yes, they were sympathetic to the suffering of their brethren—the recently created AIU (Alliance Israélite Universelle) even organised an aid centre in the Galician border town of Brody—but wasn't it better to send the newcomers elsewhere? Where?

Jewish communities in Marseille, Avignon, Macôn, Troyes, Toul, and Saverne refused them, pleading lack of funds and local antipathy; Toulouse, Nîmes, Versailles, Haguenau, Lixheim, and Lille accepted a few, but with little enthusiasm. Only emigration to North America seemed a good solution, and most soon set sail. By 1901, Paris counted a mere three thousand Romanian Jewish immigrants, one thousand Polish, four thousand Russian, and a handful of Hungarians. But, as feared, economic jealousy, coupled with the Church's religious intolerance, did foster hatred.

Medieval tales of Jews as carriers of disease were revived. Catholic right-wing newspapers such as *L'Authorité* claimed Jews, 'the dirtiest people imaginable', were carrying cholera bacteria in their baggage. Edouard Drumont, founder of the French Anti-Semitic League, proposed that the Jewish population—entirely comprised of rich bankers, Polish swindlers, and criminals—be excluded from society. Those of left-wing persuasion claimed an all-powerful Jewish bourgeoisie would sap France's strength through

---

4   An elevated platform for Torah readings that stands near the centre of traditional synagogues.

modernisation, and then betray the country to foreign enemies.

Soon, all Jews, even elite bankers, were on the receiving end of jibes, caricatures, and virulence. Any pretext—the Yiddish language, the Jewish physique, success, education, and way of life—was fuel for the anti-Semitic fire, and it culminated in the false charge of treason against the Jewish army officer Alfred Dreyfus. France's Great Rabbi Zadoc Kahn openly defended Dreyfus. So did the journalist Bernard Lazare, and prominent non-Jews such as Anatole France, Émile Zola, Henri Poincaré, and Georges Clemenceau. But not the established Jewish community. The future Jewish Prime Minister, Léon Blum, later wrote: 'The prevailing attitude was that Jews shouldn't get involved in the affair.'

***

*A*n ear-popping electronic beep signals the train's departure. I take my assigned seat and, despite my determination to time-travel backward, am firmly ensconced in the twenty-first century, pinned here by the monologue of the woman sitting across the aisle.

'I really wanted to go to Thailand for my holiday,' she whines to her companion. 'I mean, I just wanted to go to some exotic place, lie on the beach, relax, soak up the sun. Then I found out that all the places with beaches—every single one of them—cater to tourists. Can you imagine? That's not what I'm looking for. The whole world's been ruined by tourism! Cambodia and India, too. There's not a decent beach left anywhere.'

After that, she laments her mother's indifference; that all men are selfish and break your heart; that she has endless problems with a smartphone application. Her friend, a passive victim to this logorrhoea, struggles to keep her eyes open: she only wants to snuggle down, doze.

Defeated, I change train compartments to escape this century's nasal plaint.

Chapter II:
Cologne

Every thief has a good excuse.

Yiddish Proverb

*I*n the Kalk district of Cologne, I spend the night at the home of Paula and Attila (she's German, he's Hungarian.) Outside the house, the sidewalks are dotted with *Stolpersteine*—stumbling stones—little brass squares on which are engraved the names of those deported and exterminated because they were Jews, Roma, Sinti, Communists, homosexuals, Jehovah's Witnesses, disabled, or opposed to the Nazi regime. Seventeen thousand stones have been set into the sidewalks in German towns and villages. There are also Stolpersteine in Belgium, Hungary, Austria, and Poland. There are none in France.

'You can't go to Ukraine by yourself,' Paula says. She, one of those energetic, chatty women, is on the telephone, listening to the warnings of her son's Ukrainian friend. 'It's dangerous. There are thieves; you'll be robbed. The police are corrupt; they stop people on the roads and demand money. For a woman alone, it's a big risk.'

'There are normal people in Ukraine too,' I answer.

'And there's the conflict with Russia. What's so important about this poet-singer you're looking for? Does anyone remember him? Does anyone even know about him?'

'He matters to me.' Do I sound fatuous? No doubt. How to explain the past's magnetic pull, my desire to be in places once important? I don't dare mention Velvel's capacity for red wine or the disreputable inns I plan to haunt.

Paula sighs with defeat, but not conviction. 'Well, try to stay out of trouble.'

'She'll be fine.' Attila, a man of wide belly, proud moustache and luxuriant white beard, is a musician. Back in Communist days, he played to dour workers and informers in damp bugged cellars; to rowdy Eastern Bloc tourists and informers in drear, bugged hotels; to sneering politburo clones and their informers in glorious but bugged concert halls. He'd never warn me of dangers, largely imaginary.

He hands me a heavy photo album. 'This is what Galicia looked like not so long ago.' The photos were taken by Attila's father during the Second World War, when he was a soldier with the Hungarian army that was allied with Germany. Here are deep valleys and traditional architecture. Villages where half-naked Roma children salute the soldiers or trudge barefoot through the snow. Streets where houses sag into mud, and where Jews, Poles, Ukrainians, and Ruthenians[5] lived side by side until Jewish extermination and Polish banishment.

***

*W*hat do we know of that vanished world, the Old Country? Group heritage tours offer a reassuring peek from a secure seat; films and musicals give us a finger-snapping American image; personal memoirs conjure

---

5   Ruthenian, historically applied to eastern Slavs, can also refer to ethnic Rusyns, the inhabitants of historic Carpathian Ruthenia. With the emergence of Ukrainian nationalism, the term fell out of use.

up tightly knit, loving families; and sentimental yearning portrays shtetlekh as comforting places, peopled by poverty-stricken but open-handed and pious Jews. All these versions, inadequate and romantic, try to fill a vacuum left by our silent grandparents. 'The Old Country? Forget about all that,' they said. 'It's not interesting.' But did we pose the right questions? Shouldn't we have prodded more? Insisted? We didn't, and our history has escaped us.

***

*W*hy not start with the earliest times, summon up forgotten peoples and vanished empires in a region of dark forest, sucking swamps, and bleak moorland. Let's put modern life into perspective, acknowledge that, through intermarriage, rape, passion, abduction, slavery, conquest, and conversion, these folk are part of our genetic heritage: isn't it nice to find relatives?

Between 100 BCE and 300 CE, today's Ukraine was occupied by Lugii, Goths, Slavic Lendians, and Vandals of (exaggeratedly) bad reputation. The Dulebi arrived in the sixth century, followed by Volhynians, then Bug River Buzhans. A small Jewish population formed, descendants of Black Sea traders and Byzantines. But what was the origin of those Turkic-speaking nomads whose state stretched from the Caspian to the Black Sea? Their Khagan (king) and ruling class of Khazars adopted a simplified Judaism in 740 CE (all the while continuing human and animal sacrifice). When their empire was shattered in 970, many sought refuge in Eastern Europe.

Vladimir the Great and his Kievan Rus (Slavs or Vikings?) arrived in 981 and brought Christianity. Annexed by Poland in the twelfth century, this became the Rus principality of Galicia–Volhynia until swallowed up by Poland once again: it had to wait for over 600 years before becoming today's independent Ukraine.

Ask around: how many people know about the Polish–

Lithuanian Commonwealth? Few. Yet, after Poland and Lithuania united in 1569, that powerful bi-confederation stretched over Poland, Lithuania, Latvia, most of Ukraine, Belarus, and the Carpathians. Eager to attract the settlers and skilled artisans who would push beyond the fearsome primeval forests and exploit the region's natural wealth, Galician princes and Polish kings welcomed Armenians, Roma, Hungarians, Germans, and Austrians into the country, and they rubbed shoulders with local Ruthenians, Boykos, Huzuls, Poles, Ukrainians, and Slovaks. Jews, expelled from France, Spain, and Portugal, or persecuted in Moravia, Bohemia, Hungary, and the German lands also arrived. To avoid debilitating religious strife, the Commonwealth attempted (despite sporadic violence) relative tolerance— an acceptance that, by the mid-seventeenth century, had deteriorated under pressure from grasping nobles, German merchants, and Jesuit influence.

Little over one hundred years later, the Commonwealth came to an abrupt end. Prussia, Russia, and Austria, taking advantage of Poland's internal chaos and economic weakness, began carving the country out of existence and dividing the tasty slices amongst themselves. The first partition took place in 1772, the second in 1793. There was a desperate struggle to maintain independence under the Polish-Lithuanian military leader Tadeusz Kościuszko[6]—even Jewish soldiers participated in the light cavalry legion led by the Jewish merchant Colonel Berek Joselewicz.[7] The effort failed, and after Poland's third partition in 1795, former Poles found themselves residing in one of four different and separate areas: Prussia, Russia, Galicia in the Austro-Hungarian

---

6   Kościuszko fought on the American side in the Revolutionary War. In his will, his American assets were to be used for the education and freedom of the country's slaves, but this wish was never carried out.

7   Joselewicz formed an all-Jewish cavalry unit. Five hundred poor tradesmen and artisans formed the regiment known as the 'Beardlings' because they retained the right to have beards. The unit was almost totally wiped out in 1794, and Joselewicz joined Napoleon's campaign.

Empire, and Congress Poland[8] which was under Russian rule but retained the Constitution of the Kingdom of Poland.

Jews living in small towns and villages in Prussia and Congress Poland soon began moving to urban centres, adopting the modern lifestyle of their German counterparts. But Russian and Galician Jews remained as isolated, as traditional as ever. It was as if there had been no change in the regime. New borders, different masters ? Did it matter? They'd adapt. Business as usual. Yet, Galicians and Russians viewed each other with suspicion:

> *The Galician Jews looked down on the Russians as disenfranchised Jews and were unable to grasp how anyone could live and breathe under arbitrary rule, deadly pogroms, and random persecutions... For their part, the Russians despised the Galicians as backward, fossilized—an ignorant mass without culture or aspirations.[9]*

And, although Poland no longer existed, most still called themselves Polish Jews.

***

*T*he chunky youngish man sitting beside me at the Dortmund airport looks stressed. He's the one who starts the conversation: a German living in Budapest, he runs a tour company, brings many Jewish groups to Ukraine, to Romania, to Hungary.

'Will you be guiding tourists now? In winter?'

'No.' He stares at me, a trifle unsure, as if he needs to share a secret. Then decides I look innocuous. 'I'm going to Lviv to kidnap my son. Bring him back to Budapest.'

He'd been married to a beautiful Ukrainian woman,

---

8   After Napoleon's 1806 victory over Prussia, most of Prussia's share of Poland was allocated to Russia as the semi-autonomous Congress of Poland.

9   Ansky, *The Enemy at His Pleasure.*

but she'd only wanted his money and his nationality. Life had been hell; she lolled in bed all day, talking on her cell phone. When he was out of town, she spent the nights in discos, leaving their baby alone in the apartment. They had separated, and the court had granted him custody, but, after draining their joint bank account, she'd taken the child and gone back to Ukraine.

He loved his little son. The ex-wife was incapable of raising him. She only wanted to drink, party, get more money out of him. He'd paid detectives to find her whereabouts in Lviv, and he had his son's passport in his pocket. He wouldn't leave without him.

'There's just one problem: my wife knows I intend to kidnap my son. She's probably warned the Ukrainian police and, if customs officials find the child's passport on me, I'll be in big trouble. Look, could you do me a favour? Just take the passport, put it in your handbag, and go through customs. You're only a tourist. Why would anyone search you?'

He has to be joking. He has to be! I refuse. Of course, I do. Who does he think I am? Someone born yesterday? Someone still wet behind the ears? Why would I want to spend my days in a Ukrainian jail? What does all that have to do with me?

'Please,' he begs.

'No,' I answer.

'Too bad.' He looks utterly miserable. Resigned, too.

We board the small shivering plane for the (very cheap) flight to Lviv. The bulky man, sticking to me like glue, takes the seat next to mine.

'Many Jews go to Ukraine looking for their family roots. Is that what you're doing?' he asks.

I remain silent, unwilling to be part of a modern trend. He's not fooled. Fumbling in a briefcase, he pulls out a brochure he published: Jewish sites in Ukraine.

'Why are you so interested in Jewish history?' I ask.

'Because I'm Jewish.' His father had been a German Christian, but his mother is Jewish. His Latvian grandmother was one of the few who had survived the Holocaust. How?

He has no details. 'She always refused to talk about that time. But you see why family is so important to me? Why I'm kidnapping my son? I want to take him to Canada. There, we'll be safe. Canada will respect the court's custody decision. Are you sure you won't take in my son's passport?'

'I'm sure I won't.' I mean, honestly! And how much of this story can I believe?

He shrugs. Looks resigned again. Then resumes our conversation. How did I plan to travel? On local buses? Trains? Good idea. The roads are pot-holed and dangerous; private cars are stopped by the police who demand baksheesh. 'Be careful where you stay: backwoods hotels can be dirty, and sometimes there's only running water between eight and ten in the morning. And it's usually cold water.'

Not grim news to me, I assure him. 'I've known much worse.'

'I don't mind it either.' His grin is lopsided. 'I like the contrast. We take luxury for granted, so we need a certain amount of distress to keep our feet firmly on the ground.'

I'm beginning to like him (or perhaps he just has a good eye for easy prey.)

'Will you stay in Lviv?' he asks.

'No. I'm heading for many places: Lutsk, Brody, Czernowitz, Svinich, Poritsk.' The last two names mean nothing to him: tiny villages, insignificant.

'And Zbarazh,' I add.

'Oh, Zbarazh. Why there?'

'Because that's where Velvel Zbarzher was born.'

'He was, indeed.'

Now I'm gaping at him with slack-jawed astonishment. 'You've heard of Velvel Zbarzher? You've heard of the town of Zbarazh?'

'I certainly have. Why are you so interested in him?'

'I want to find the world he lived in.'

He nods as if my answer is perfectly reasonable. 'People in Romania still talk about Zbarzher. Someone mentioned his name quite recently. In Botoşani, I think it was.'

'No! Really?'

'Go see the Jews in Botoşani. Tell them I sent you.'

Is this a pretty line meant to soften me up? I'll never know. I'm grateful for his offering. Incredibly grateful (so I'm not on a wild goose chase after all). And because of it, I agree to take the child's passport.

After a horrifically bumpy landing on the pot-holed runway, we separate, although he keeps his eye on me from far ahead in the seemingly endless customs queue. As I wait, I listen to the businessmen behind me talking in German.

'Business isn't bad nonetheless,' says one.

'No, it isn't,' confirms the other.

I laugh. 'I haven't heard that in a long time.'

So they explain—one is German, the other Danish—that they have products made cheaply in Ukraine, sell them in Europe.

'Can't lose.'

In the end, the German is Jewish. And the younger man standing right behind the two businessmen says he's Jewish too; he's heading for a yeshiva in the Crimea. Jews returning to Ukraine? Why am I surprised? The European Jewish Congress puts the number of Jews now living in the country at 360,000 to 400,000.

I pass through customs easily, receive my official stamps. My new tour guide friend is right; officials aren't interested in me or in my belongings. Outside the airport, under the cover of night, I return his son's passport.

'I'll write, let you know what happens,' he promises as he slips into a car driven by one of his hired detectives.

'Yes, please do.'

But we never contact one another again.

Welvl Zbarier (fotografie inedită, descoperită de d.
Schoss-Roman într-un album de familie, la Roman.

Chapter III:
The Haskalah

*The Jews, as in the other countries of Europe, live insulated
amidst the nation to which they belong; and continue to
form a separate people, who will never mingle with any
other race. Self is their ruling principle, and private interest
their sole study. Without love for their sovereign, without
concern for their country, they are indifferent to everything
excepting money, which is the god of their idolatry.
Leading, wherever they are found, a wandering life, they
consider themselves as travellers than as citizens, whose
fortunes are dependent on the prosperity of their native
land.*

Frederick Shoberl, 1828

*T*his is the only image we have of Velvel, and I find
it troubling. Signed, dated, it's a magazine copy,
obviously retouched. The original was supposedly found
in a family album in the Romanian town of Roman almost

a century ago.[10] Here's the problem: Velvel was fifty-five[11] years old in 1881, had led a rough itinerant life, had been a hard-drinking man and was no longer in the best of health. Wasn't he then living in Constantinople and writing his poems in the coffeehouse belonging to Malkele the Beautiful, his second wife? They had little money: surely, he couldn't have been swanning about in Romania. The date might well have been added on by a 'fan' wanting to claim personal acquaintance, and there were many of those.

How about the photo itself: does it agree with descriptions of Velvel? One biographer, Dr Moses Fried,[12] had known him in Zbarazh, and he claimed Velvel was slender, clean-shaven, with an oval face, blond hair, and a wonderful roaring laugh. Another biographer, Dr Meir Weissberg[13], wrote that Velvel was sad, pale, and wore an ever-soulful expression. The writer David Yeshaya Silberbusch,[14] who met Velvel in Czernowitz in 1876, said he was short, with a round shaven face, small liquid eyes, and a steady fine smile. And the essayist Streitman[15] gave him a massive head with a few thick white hairs adorning his chin.

What do we see in the photo? A mild-looking man with a rounded face, plump chin, and large clear eyes. His hair is as thick and as dark as his moustache; his shoulders are narrow,

---

10   In 1869, Velvel wrote to his brother Meir, mentioned he'd had his photo taken in Lemberg, and that he would distribute copies amongst friends. Perhaps this one dates from that time.

11   No one seems to agree on his birth date. Some claim it was in the (unlikely) year of 1806, or 1812, or 1821, or 1823. On his tombstone, the year is 1826. It was, presumably, the date on his official papers.

12   *Biographisches über Benjamin Wolf Ehrenkranz*, Dr Moses Fried. Born in Zbarazh, Fried studied theology and philosophy in Breslau, and was appointed rabbi in Stockholm.

13   *Wölwel Zbarazer, der Fahrende Sänger des Galizische-Jüdischen Humanismus*, Dr Meir Weissberg was one of the last surviving leaders of the Galician Haskalah.

14   Silberbusch, *Mi-Pinkas zikhronotai.*

15   Streitman, *Adam.*

sloping, and he's well dressed: Velvel was said to be a dandy who favoured elegant black suits and a cylinder hat.

Here's another photo, that of Karl Emil Franzos, the Galician Jewish writer. He was twenty-five years younger than Velvel, had lived in Czernowitz, Vienna, Budapest, Berlin, and Graz, and had travelled throughout Eastern Europe. He had also been in Romania in the 1880s. Does he resemble the man in Velvel's photo?

So, is the first portrait really of Velvel? We do know he was an admired folk poet with a wonderful voice; that his songs were filled with love for his fellow man; that, warm and generous, he could also be unruly, difficult, moody, and uncouth. That, as a knight in the Enlightenment's battle, he was mocking, satirical, but never brutal, and that he has since been hailed as 'the father of Yiddish bohemian poets in Eastern Europe.'[16]

***

Much the same as the earlier eighteenth-century European Enlightenment,[17] the late eighteenth-century Jewish Enlighten-ment—the Haskalah—fought religious orthodoxy and abuse. Its advocates, known as

---

16 Reisen, *Leksikon fun der yiddisher literature,* cited by Roskies in, *Jewish Search for a Usable Past.*

17 The groundwork had been laid by two brilliant Jewish philosophers: Baruch Spinoza in seventeenth-century Amsterdam, and Moses Mendelssohn in eighteenth century Berlin.

Maskilim,[18] pointed to the need for transformation in a rapidly changing world. If Eastern European Jews had once enjoyed some measure of protection in Polish lands, now, after partition and with repressive Russian or restrictive Austrian rule, that security was gone. Jewish isolation had to end; the abject feudal Jew had to be vanquished. Jews needed to become fully integrated citizens of the modern centralised European states that were—or would eventually be—governed by enlightened rulers.

Religion could no longer direct thought and action. Outdated rituals needed to be replaced by universal education; reason and experience would vanquish superstition, prejudice, myths, and miracles. Modern dress had to be adopted, and modern European languages spoken. Jewish children must be allowed to learn science, geography, languages, history, mathematics, grammar, philosophy, and to read the new secular Hebrew and Yiddish literature. Jewish moral codes were to be preserved, but ancient texts required a rationalist interpretation.

Like Velvel Zbarzher, most Maskilim had been raised traditionally. Distinguishing themselves as prodigies in Talmudic learning, they had been groomed to become religious leaders and upholders of tradition. Yet, somehow slipping out of family and community grasp, they escaped from the shtetl's suffocating clamour, fled to the important Galician cities of Tarnopol, Brody, and Lemberg, or to Russian Odessa, and sought Haskalah leaders, writers, and teachers.

They discovered that life in the modern world was shockingly hard. Condemned as heretics, cut off by their families, and estranged from their communities, they were still confronted by anti-Semitism and official restriction. Forced into itinerancy, they knew aching poverty and life

---

18 The name came from Daniel 12:3 and meant men of wisdom. The first Maskilim were men like Israel Samoscz, Herz Homberg, or Simon Dubnow who described Eastern European Jews as 'a tribe of nomads lacking in historical feeling...whose lives are entirely in the present and who have neither a future nor a past.'

in squalid flophouses. But the compensations were great: heady stimulation; the companionship of other exiles met in libraries, cafés, and wine bars; and an intellectual freedom prohibited in traditional life.

**

*T*he early Haskalah was very much a men's movement. A Maskil could earn a living as a teacher or private tutor to the wealthy enlightened, work as a singer, a musician, or a player, but women were excluded from such spheres. Unable to read the revolutionary new Hebrew literature, for most knew only Yiddish, many rejected—or were forbidden to read–the contemporary progressive publications in Yiddish. Remaining fiercely protective and traditional, most wives and mothers fought modernity's incursions tooth and nail.

It was a confusing time, even for the Maskilim. Relationships between men and women had always been contractual, not emotional. One married, not out of love but as a social duty, for family status, religious obligation, sexual need, and to procreate. The new ideas of romance, emotional commitment, equality and shared intellectual stimulation were difficult to absorb. When writers and educators like Yitskhok Yoyel Linetski and Avrom Ber Gotlober introduced their wives to modern thought, the women were forced to return home and divorce such renegade husbands.

In the great French, Italian, Russian, Prussian, German, and Austro-Hungarian cities, things were very different. Bourgeois Jewish women held brilliant literary salons where forbidden literature and plays were read. But they were society's elite. Outside such gilded circles, women were certainly present as wives, daughters, friends, lovers, and mistresses of Maskilim, but they only make brief appearances in novels, biographies, and short stories. You can almost discern their presence in those smoky cafés where impassioned discussions lasted all night, and they were very present in the revolutionary movements at the end of the century. But as equals or leaders in the Haskalah? As Maskilot, female writers of the new Hebrew literature? For that, society had to wait until the enlightened men had their own families, provided their daughters with Hebrew tutors, and gave them the education necessary for participation in that literary world.[19]

***

The threat of change that comes with new ideas, scientific and technological innovation, always triggers a violent counter-reaction. Rational thought wakens its fearful opposite. Alongside the European Enlightenment were mystical revivalist movements: Quietism, the Old Believers, Great Awakenings, the Methodist Revival, and the Erweckung.

Jewish *Hasidism* was founded in the mid-1700s by Rabbi Israel ben Eliezer, also known as the Besht or the Baal Shem Tov, and who claimed to communicate with supernatural personages. Hasidism was impervious to the ideals of equality, the secular state, and modern schooling. Life was an illusion; Jewish suffering was due to the interplay of human and divine forces. The real world began after death when the souls of the pious were reunited with the original fathers and tribal mothers.

Characterised by charismatic leadership, religious ecstasy, praying with exuberance, shouting, skipping, and dancing, Hasidism's miracle-working *zaddikim* or *rebbes* were believed to have the ability to cure infertility and impotency, to successfully settle domestic and business disputes, to control natural law and stop ghosts or devils. Visitors to any Eastern European village were led to places where wonders had been worked, to synagogues where a cannonball would have wreaked terrible destruction if the rebbe hadn't ordered it to be captured in the wall.[20]

---

19 Apparently most of these women abandoned writing once they were married and had children to raise.

20 Similar stories are told about miracle-working priests in village churches.

In the Hasidic dynasties, power was transmitted from father to son, and famous rebbes lived like magnates, surrounded by servants, and court musicians. They went about the countryside in great carriages pulled by fine horses, and their bejewelled wives and daughters dressed ostentatiously in the latest fashions. Submissive kaftan-wearing followers left their families and travelled enormous distances to be in their presence, to lavish them with gifts, listen to their utterances, and snatch leftovers from their table. The Jewish (like the peasant) imagination, peopled with the living dead, werewolves, vampires, and the household imps—*shretelekh, lantekh,* and *kapelyushniklim*—now added fantastic Talmudic beings to the multitude: amorphous *golems, dybbukim* (devils), *gilgulim* (reincarnated souls), and the *lamed vov tzadikim,* the thirty-six hidden saints who prevented the destruction of the universe.

The established rabbinic authority (known as 'opponents' or *Misnagedim,*) considered Hasidism a dangerous sect and issued bans of excommunication, imprisoned its leaders, and destroyed pamphlets. Yet, less than a century later, Hasidism, a fortress of both zealotry and economic strength, had undermined the rabbinate's power.

Whether one of the Hasidim or the Misnagedim, the duty of a Jew was to serve God, and every aspect of daily life—eating, dressing, and behaviour—was ruled by the 613 commandments of Jewish religious law, *Halakhah.* Non-Jewish learning was forbidden; independent thinkers were threatened with moral rebuke, magical retribution, excommunication, and communal expulsion. When misfortune struck, heretics were sought out for punishment: one widow, who openly conversed with servants and drank mead in their company, was held responsible for a smallpox epidemic. And, even for petty lapses, justice was not necessarily even-handed:

Shabbes-guardians would exercise more pressure on the poorer classes than on the rich...it would not be a pretty sight to see how such a foolish 'kept' son-in-law on 'kest', would take it out on a poor miserable street-vendor because she would be out in the streets with her baskets a bit too late.

In those days there wasn't an underground sewage system yet. The women sat next to each other on the sidewalks over the whole length of the street with their feet dangling in the open gutters, trying to sell the few leftover grapes and other fruits that people need for the high holy days. Their merchandise was not of the best. It was overripe, and if they didn't succeed in selling it very soon it would not be worth a penny afterwards. But the young men started emptying out their baskets into the gutter.

A big tumult arose, the women cried and pleaded: 'Can't you see there are buyers standing over there, ready to take what we have got, just give us a minute.' But they did not listen to them.[21]

Hebrew, stripped of its literary aspects, was taught with no dictionary and no grammar books. There were no history books, only prayers for the victims of blood libels, and chronicles recounting expulsions and epidemics. Young boys (sometimes as young as three when families were large) attended the cheder, a dimly lit hut where, crowded on benches or on the dirt floor, rocking back and forth, they repeated the teacher's words in a screaming singsong.

Yes, Jewish children were literate, far more so than peasant children—in 1880, the illiteracy rate amongst all Galicians over the age of five was 77.1%[22]—but they were ignorant. The best-educated rabbis were masterly Talmudists but opposed to Western reason. Only the luckiest children profited from the few Haskalah writers and poets who managed to penetrate the traditional teaching world. But as soon as their liberality was discovered, such teachers were dismissed.

---

21 Kotik, *Journey to a Nineteenth Century Shtetl*. Russian Maskilim took pleasure in pointing to (and sometimes exaggerating) all that was negative and corrupt, particularly ignorant and violent teachers, and fanatical rabbis.

22 McCagg Jr., *A History of Habsburg Jews*.

Part Two:
LOOKING FOR VELVEL

Chapter IV:
The Shtetl

The appearance of Polish Jews is appalling...A weekly paper cooked into mush wouldn't disgust me more than the sight of those ragged and dirty figures...nonetheless disgust became compassion after looking closely at the pigsties in which they live, chatter, pray, haggle—and are impoverished.

Heinrich Heine, 1822

I'm on the wrong rusty minibus. The driver, a friendly roly-poly man, expert in dangerous driving, hawking and spitting, makes that clear. He and a few passengers explain with gestures and shouts that this bus doesn't go as far as Zbarazh—or I think that's what they're saying. Who knows? Do I care? Despite the lack of heating in this rotting vehicle, I've been lulled into contented passivity by the sight of snowy fields and frozen lanes ambling on to nowhere in particular...until the bus slithers to an uncontrolled halt and deposits me at an empty crossroads. I'm to do the last four kilometres on foot? Fine with me. Can anything be more exciting than walking into the shtetl where Velvel was born, where he grew up?

The flat Ukrainian plain has given way to gentle Carpathian foothills and snow-dusted conifers. Was this the very road Velvel took, going the other way, sneaking out of town in 1844? The idea puts a delighted bounce into my step and, with my cheap and trusty plastic camera, I snap pictures of the woods, misty hills, and the frozen dirt track for horses and carts running alongside this paved roadway. Until a sign announces I've arrived.

***

*W*hen he was in his mid-eighties, my paternal grandfather, told the young sociologist who interviewed him: 'I was born in Svinich, a small Jewish shtetl.' My grandmother who came from Poritsk, some ten miles away (six, over the swampland) said her village was also a Jewish shtetl. Where were those shtetlekh now? 'Wiped off the face of the earth,' they both answered. So no wonder we got things wrong. No wonder we thought whole villages and towns had vanished.

Communism ended. We began, quite easily, travelling to places almost impossible to reach before. And sentimental, determined to find the past, we discovered that what our grandparents had meant by shtetlekh were simply the Jewish sections of market towns or villages in Eastern Europe. In some municipalities, the Jewish population was large, sometimes even a majority, and there was at least one synagogue, one *mikveh* (ritual bath), a Jewish cemetery, schools, and a building for the officials responsible for religious and communal functions. But Jews were only part of the scene: Ukrainians, Ruthenians, Poles, Russians, Armenians, Germans, Romanians, Hungarians, and a few Muslim Tartars[23] were right there, too, in those same towns or villages, and all were held firmly in place by a rigid social structure. Aristocrats, priests, peasants, and Jews all had defined roles in this world

---

23   A misnomer. Tartars or Tatars were a tribe defeated by the Mongols on their westward sweep. They are, in fact, Cossacks, descendants of the Mongols.

of little social mobility, and boundaries were rarely crossed.

Nobles—Polish, Lithuanian, Podolian, Prussian, and Ruthenian—comprised eight to nine per cent of the population, and they were a powerful force, yet not all were equal. Magnates possessed vast stretches of land, many villages, forests, and tens of thousands of peasants; lesser nobles owned one or two villages and a few serfs; those lower down might own part of a village, but no serfs. At the bottom of the noble heap were poor yeomen who, although believing themselves inherently superior to common folk, lived in squat mud houses like the peasants, slept on stoves or wooden benches, wore clothing as rough as their manners, and worked their own land; others were servants to the rich. Yet nobility was not a completely inflexible status. Until 1764, peasants could be ennobled for valour in warfare, a noble title could be purchased, and wealthy baptised Jews could also join their ranks.

In the sixteenth century, despite their mixed origins, members of the *szlachta* (the Polish landed nobility) began cultivating a perfectly mythical belief in descent from the Sarmatians, an early Iranian confederation of the fifth century BCE. They affected dress of Persian origin, adopted exotic traditions and a pseudo oriental lifestyle...until the advent of the French Enlightenment. After that, French and Italian tutors were hired, French and Italian foods were served, French and Italian manners were copied (although in French society, such 'frenchified' nobles were mocked as costumed Tartars).

In church, nobles sat in places of honour, and the priest waited for their arrival before beginning the service; commoners moved to one side, bowed to the ground, and made the gesture of kissing the *pan's* hand when only his carriage passed. A noble could never be contradicted or questioned, and keeping the peasants ignorant and illiterate was one way of ensuring their servility.

Spoilt, dissipated, and slack, the wealthiest kept footmen, great stables of horses, and punctuated their lives with dances, feasts, hunts, gambling, travel, foreign luxuries, and debt. Thanks to travel and education, some did become excellent writers, brave explorers, and patrons of the arts who maintained orchestras, encouraged composers, artists, and craftsmen. Yet, their wealth ever depended on others: their labouring peasants, their serfs, and their trading Jews.

Most peasants were serfs. They paid taxes and compensation to both aristocrats and the clergy, provided both with labour, cannon fodder, vegetables, fruits, animals, and showed only submission, humility, and piety. The vilest owners could flog their serfs to death, brand them, torture them for amusement, send them into military service, or deport them. No lofty ideals of the French Enlightenment could soften the fate of these victims, and there were no tribunals to protect them. Children toiled alongside their parents, and there was no time for schooling: both the aristocracy and the Church needed obeisant beasts of burden.

Peasant women, subject to the authority of fathers, husbands, and sons, abused by landlords and overseers, by anyone with power, were even more oppressed and brutalised; they had no choice but submission, for it might result in an extra scrap of food for their families. But woe betide those unlucky enough to find themselves pregnant outside of wedlock. That resulted in ostracism, infanticide, and suicide.[24] Yet, despite oppression and poverty, the peasant community was tightly knit. As craftspeople, they produced the most exquisite handiwork and the finest vernacular architecture. Keepers of folk knowledge, they created songs, stories, music, musical instruments, local language, and dialect.

Between noble and peasant were the Jews. Most were shopkeepers, tailors, water carriers, hawkers, or those notorious *Luftmenschen* (air people) who, without any established occupation, survived by owning a few sheep,

---

24 Unless it could be proved that the child's father was a nobleman. This, sometimes, provided protective status.

goats, chickens, a cow or two, selling milk, manure, skins, and meat, but retaining the heads, legs, and other minor parts for personal consumption, by fattening geese, plucking fowl, baking bread and Passover matzo, renting a peasant's worked-out strip of land, strewing manure and planting potatoes one year, barley, oats or buckwheat the next, returning it when fertile and again ready for the peasant's soil-exhausting rye.

Because excluded from artisan guilds and land ownership, Jews had come to excel in commerce and money lending over the centuries. As negotiators and a source of credit, their job was to keep the nobles wealthy enough to maintain their exorbitant, often ruinous, lifestyles. Jews with international business contacts held high positions, administering estate finances, managing forests and town fishponds, selling lumber and distilling pitch, leasing orchards, milling flour, distilling alcohol, and leasing the noble's inns. And Jewish musicians played the polkas and mazurkas that kept the nobles dancing.

Although a negotiator's intelligence could allow for a certain social superiority, even the highest Jew was viewed with the contempt reserved for those able to make money, as illustrated by this conversation between one well-travelled nobleman and Chaimek, his Jewish agent:

> *'Chaimek,' spoke he, 'wert thou in Cracow?'*
>> *'I was not, serene lord.'*
>> *'Then thou art stupid.'*
>> *Chaimek bowed.*
>> *'Chaimek, wert thou in Rome?'*
>> *'I was not, serene lord.'*
>> *'Then thou art very stupid.'*
>> *Chaimek bowed again, but in the meanwhile he had made two steps forward. On his lips wandered one of those smiles common to the people of his race—clever, cunning, in which it is impossible to say whether there is humility or triumph, flattery or irony.*

'Excuse me, your lordship,' he said softly, 'has your lordship been in Szybow?'

The nobleman answered, 'I was not.'

'And what now?' answered Chaimek still more softly.[25]

The life in each shtetl, town, and village was woven into the next by marriages, market days, trade fairs, and those who travelled between them all: musicians, predicators, the *badkhonim* or wedding jesters, merchants, weavers, shoemakers, water carriers, drovers, roofers, sawyers, farmers, wagon drivers, wainwrights, blacksmiths, peddlers, and hawkers. Communities were small enough for all to be known by both their name and an often-brutal nickname: Clubfoot Yankel, No Underwear Schwarz, Stinking Avru, and Old Maid Chantzah.

As in any town or city everywhere in the world, some folks were friends, some were kindly, and some were wealthy with high status. Those at the bottom of the Jewish social barrel—water carriers or unmarried girls from poor families—were constantly reminded of their inferior status by vicious comments, mockery, and cruelties. Close to this low social grade were the so-called illiterates—the workers and craftsmen who, as adolescents, had been apprenticed or sent off to labour in factories. They didn't attend Talmudic schools; they were less steeped in religious knowledge; they mixed with Christians in the working world. As unpaid apprentices, they were beaten and humiliated by employers and forced to perform domestic chores. They were also discriminated against in religious ritual, allowed to participate only in additional readings after the Torah service.[26]

---

25   Orzeszkowa, *An Obscure Apostle*. Orzeszkowa, a leading Polish novelist nominated for the Noble Prize in Literature, was born into the noble Pawłowski family.

26   At the nineteenth century's end, workers made themselves heard through political action: Bundism, Socialism, and Zionism. Much later, in the interwar period, the *Handwerker Fereyn*, the Artisan's Union, sought to give the despised artisan more self-respect.

Some defiantly opened their own prayer groups (*minyans*); others chose estrangement and renunciation—a hazardous move. As in any tightly knit society where religion dictates the rules, those deviating from piety were the butt of merciless collective humour and the recipients of physical abuse. If considered dangerous to the community, a death sentence could be issued.

Jews and Christians differed in daily language. Jews used Yiddish for daily life and Hebrew for prayer. When dealing with authorities they used Polish; when dealing with peasants, they spoke Byelorussian, Russian, or Ukrainian, although all of these were usually simple pidgin versions of those languages. Non-Jews who dealt with Jews spoke pidgin Yiddish.

But, Christian and Jew, they were in it together, suspicious of each other, sometimes hating each other's guts, sometimes mingling and doing business, sometimes behaving with violence, sometimes falling in love, converting, and marrying. They heard each other's battles, smelled each other's cooking, and ate (with the exception of pork) the same foods: knishes, latkes (potato pancakes) with sour cream, sauerkraut (probably introduced by the Mongols), cabbage rolls, meat, beet or sorrel borscht with sour cream, rye bread, poppy seed rolls. Jewish challah is Ukrainian kalach; Pesach's (Passover's) matzo is Easter's paska.

All had grape vines and fruit frees—apple, cherry, pear, mulberry, and peach—all grew cabbages, carrots, potatoes, and beans in cottage gardens. They shared superstitions, feared the evil eye, told the same fairy tales (although the evil witch was a Jew in peasant stories and a peasant in Jewish ones), and they shared melodies. There were Christian and Jewish con men, beggars, and light-fingered children. And, in any not-so-distant copse, Christian and Jewish outlaw bands waited for their prey.

All lived in terror of aristocratic employers, feared floggings, humiliation, and shared the prayer: 'God protect me from (the noble's) evil dogs.' Girls kept themselves dirty and neglected so as not to attract the lord's attention and fire his lust. When armies were stationed in town, all homes became public places where soldiers drank themselves rowdy, hacked tables to pieces, and smashed glasses.

After the decline of Polish power in the nineteenth century, towns degenerated. Foreign travellers sneered at the heavy sour rye bread, the salt butter, the simple meals of eggs and fish, and at village wretchedness and low sanitary standards. But, this is a marshy country where folk were gnawed into misery by all manner of winged and crawling beasties; where, in the rainy season, horses sank to their bellies in mud and could only be pried out with heavy poles; where summer heat baked those same roads into hard miserable ruts, and winter drifts obliterated them entirely.

True, cows, pigs, goats, or fowl wandered where they would, and village streets were punctuated by reeking dunghills, slops, and sewage (those lacking primitive privies attended to their needs in the open.) True, water could be deadly, and rivers were fouled by night soil. And yes, such conditions are inconceivable in the face of today's fear of microbes, dirt, insects, birds, wildlife, odours, and even natural vegetation, but do you think conditions were better in western and southern Europe? In the new North American towns and cities? They weren't. That's just what life was like back then.

Here's what else it was like: there was a silence we don't know today, a calm that admitted voices from a neighbour's house, conversations on the street, taunts, laughter, sobs, the sagging sounds of those reeling tipsily along alleyways. There was the barking of dogs, the thud of horse's hooves on dirt lanes, the jingle of decorative horse bells, the rumble of wagon wheels, the singing of so many birds,[27] the rustle of leafy trees. People hummed, sang, or whistled as they worked; peddlers blew whistles and called out their wares

---

27 According to the European Bird Census Council, the farmland bird population has declined by 53 per cent in some areas, and by 70 per cent in others.

in a singsong. The streets were alive with hawkers willing to exchange salt, tobacco, matches, needles, and ribbons for eggs, meal, bones, bristles, feathers, fowl, pelts, mushrooms, and berries. There was the clang of blacksmiths and pot menders, the rasp of sawyers, the hammering of carpenters and roofers, the terrified cries of animals being slaughtered in roadways, yards, or on doorsteps.

And every Sunday, red-booted peasant girls and proud peasant lads would join arms, sing before the taverns and inns, stamp their feet on the earthen road, while musicians (blind musicians, Jewish klezmorim, pipers, or fiddlers) played until dawn.

The aroma of sun-heated grain floated on the air, mixed with the perfume of flowers and ripening fruit. There was the hot reek of seeds being pressed for oil, and you could smell feathers, animals, blood, rot, dust, black earth, grain, snow, wood smoke, filth, corn, sun, rain, storms, and all the different seasons.

Chapter V:
Zbarazh

*There is something wrong, for without good reason no
one would come to this place! There is some secret in it
which I must find out...All tell stories and make allusions
to strangers who had visited them in such and such a year;
jesters relate anecdotes about it, and they are not always
within the bounds of propriety; men twirl their beards and
smile; old women jokingly scold the jesters, angered and
laughing at the same time; young married women stealthily
look upwards with their drooping eyes, hold their hands
before their mouths and choke with laughter.*

Sholem Yankev Abramovich[28]

*L*ittle houses crouch along the road at Zbarazh's town
edge. Behind are barns, then the broad plain. I know that
peasants once lived out here, but these dwellings are the only
reminders of bygone days. Following them are a modern
gas station, rows of high-rise cement blocks, and a disused

---

28   The grandfather of Yiddish literature, better known by his pseudonym
Mendele Moïcher Sforim

communist bus station with boarded windows. Next to the immense church, sits an abandoned agricultural building. This is no longer a pleasant town laid out to plan by the Polish aristocracy. Even older buildings are of a nondescript more recent vintage. Zbarazh feels like a has-been.

With no idea where I'm going, I put my trust in personal radar assisted by the only town map I possess, one dating from the Austro-Hungarian Empire. Do I think I'll stumble upon some homey corner where time and tradition have stood still? Find myself surrounded by public buildings, noble residences, inns, Catholic and Orthodox churches, and the synagogue? Locate rows of small shops selling cloth, aprons, scarves, ribbons, tar, and resin? Usually Jewish-owned, such businesses were run by women who, sitting outside, jealously spied on a neighbour's commercial success. Men stayed home studying or gathered in study halls and backstreet prayer houses.

I stop in a square...of sorts. Can this have been the open market? Who knows? That bit of wasteland, just over on the next street, might have been a market square as well. What about this elegant but ruined and windowless building in front of me, now defaced by the usual semi-illiterate spray-painted squiggles? Large enough to have been a school or an important community building in the days of the Austro-Hungarian Empire, there is no clue as to its former purpose. I approach a scrawny woman shaking out an acrylic rug, but she mutters sullenly, sends me a dirty look before eclipsing into her lair and slamming the door. Does she think I'm a beggar? A sorceress selling amulets or incantations? A sneaky manifestation of the evil eye disguised as a foreigner in scuffed walking boots and a second-hand overcoat?

Were these middle-class streets? Everything has been badly modernised or partly knocked down. Other than one very fine old house, also ravaged, gutted, and abandoned, I find no trace of symmetrical grand dwellings with broad pillared porches and elegant windows, places where nobles, entrepreneurs, both Jewish and Christian, once resided. For, contrary to myth, a wealthy Jewish elite also existed:

When [the Jewish lumber merchants] came to town for Rosh Hashanah you would see fine carriages with excellent equipages and well-to-do people in fine clothes in the streets. They would bring their silver tableware and heavy silver candlesticks and they all tried to outdo each other in lifestyle, showing how rich they were by buying themselves the most coveted turns at the reading of the scriptures and putting the most expensive dishes on their tables. They brought banquets into fashion. They were not stingy with brandies and wines either.[29]

Up the road, some small, low bungalows could be older than they look. Their willow hedges and picket fences vanished long ago, but perhaps, buried under modern cement façades, there are still walls of wattle and daub. In such homes, families lived in one main room, sleeping, drinking eating, studying. Sausages and fruits hung drying in corners, bread was perched on two beams or poles, and barrels of sour beets or cabbage stood next to crocks of water, good and foul. Heat came from the *oyfen* or *pripitchik*,[30] the huge earthenware oven incorporated into one wall; on its top, was a stucco shelf, large enough to sleep on in winter.[31] Furniture was simple: wooden tables, benches, chests, and beds.

The poor slept covered by their coats, cloaks, or jackets; the well off had several rooms and fine bedding—feather

---

29 Kotik, *Journey to a Nineteenth-Century Shtetl.*

30 The Yiddish song, *Oyfn Pripitchik*, written by Mark Warshawsky (1848-1907) and describing a group of children learning Hebrew in the cheder, became a symbol of pre-Holocaust Jewish life.

31 Chimneys were of clay mixed with straw or hollowed-out tree trunks lined with clay: only in the last half of the nineteenth century did brick become common. The poorest hovels possessed no chimney, merely a hole in the roof to let out the smoke. In such places, walls were black with soot, and all sat on the ground so as not to be choked. But smoke also killed vermin in the dirty linen hung up on poles.

quilts, pillows, embroidered linen sheets—and they aired it ostentatiously, hoping to excite envy. In peasant homes, were icons; in Jewish, *mezuzahs* and a *menorah*.[32] And every respectable house possessed a hand-mill, a mortar to crack meal and linseed, a block to split wood. In winter, animals also lived in the main room: here, goats and cows were milked, and chickens nested where they could.

I know that Velvel's family lived in one of these houses, for I even have his address—one that is useless because everything has changed. Obstinately, I pound along bumpy back lanes, trying to reconcile the present with my one-hundred-year-old map (did I really think I would manage to do so?) before conceding defeat and returning to the town centre. Perhaps to find Velvel, I must locate the former synagogue. No longer functioning today—there are no Jews left in Zbarazh—the building, converted into a vodka factory in communist times, and recently reconverted into office buildings, stands on Sholem Aleichem Street. The street is easy enough to find, but not the synagogue. I appeal to two loutish, dark-alley types for help. Graciously enough, they lead me further along the road, then stop in front of a discouraging slap of urban architecture and point to a corrugated green barrier. Wave goodbye. Abandon me.

Where can a former synagogue be in this landscape of shattered brick walls, industrial waste, and warehouses? There's no one else to question—the bitterly cold streets are now deserted, and the light is waning. Behind the green barrier, famished guard dogs rage. What does such a street have to do with Sholem Aleichem, with his crooked, comical, universal characters? There's nothing of his laughter out here, not even tragic laughter. This is modern life with its harsh reality.

Then, quite suddenly, I see it. Way back behind the metal barrier, enclosed in industrial tackiness, disfigured by plastic windows and a coating of cement, is the completely inaccessible former synagogue.

---

32 Most frequently, the seven-branched candle stand.

I stand for a while shifting from one icy foot to the other, hoping something will happen, change. That there will be some way to charm those frothing three-headed Cerberuses and pass beyond the barrier. I want to sneak inside the synagogue, slip, unnoticed, beneath the old stairway. Stay in that secret hidey-hole and enter the past. For it was just in there that the young Velvel hid from the seekers of apostasy and indulged in the forbidden rationalist literature.

***

Zbarazh, like any place where humans have tapped their feet, has a bloody history. Early peoples—Pechenegs, Kumans, Avars, Iazyges, Anartes, Gepids, Huns, Rus, and Vikings—massacred each other here; Tatars burnt the place down in 1474; and during Khmelnitsky's 1648 uprising, his massed troops murdered the Jews, besieged the castle, then slaughtered or sold into oriental slavery the starving peasants who abandoned the safety of its walls. Partly destroyed during the Russo-Polish War of 1654–1667, and again by the Ottomans in 1675, Zbarazh knew another bloody Cossack uprising in 1768. Then, in July 1943, the three thousand Jewish residents were murdered just outside town. Yet, nestled snugly into the valley of the Gniezna River, when Benjamin Wolf Ehrenkranz was born here in 1826, this was a sleepy enough place. So sleepy, a sugar factory, installed in the once-glorious castle, went bankrupt, and the edifice sagged into apologetic decrepitude.

A high birth rate resulted in much poverty in Galicia, but considering the region a mere backwater, the Austrian government did nothing to develop its economy. Forty per cent of Zbarazh's 8,785 residents were Jewish; Velvel's father, Moses Ehrenkranz—a ritual slaughterer nicknamed Moschke Shochet[33]—was relatively well-off and able to support his family of two daughters (Channah and Chava) and four boys.

---

33 A Shochet is a ritual slaughterer

He was a witty man, too, ever ready with a smart answer, a talent for twisting a grim event into a merry one, even turning a peasant's attack into a wry joke: ('I knew he wanted to beat me up because he did.')

Moschke Shochet studied the Talmud religiously, passed his fervour on to all four sons, and his profession to two—Abraham and Joshua. The youngest, Meir, would eventually become an intellectual, a Hebrew teacher in Czernowitz.[34] But it was soon clear to all that the most brilliant of the family was the second son, Benjamin, nicknamed Velvele or little Wolf. Sent to the cheder to learn the five books of Moses, and Rashi's commentaries, Velvele, with his remarkable memory, became the school's star pupil and, by age ten, he had much Talmudic knowledge.

Like his father, Velvele possessed an incisive wit, one that forced his brothers into the shadow. Like jealous siblings anywhere, they reacted with fury and spite; he answered their attacks with perfectly apt, insulting names. One particularly virulent brother—an emotional lad who desired the limelight for himself—he dubbed '*Hengst*' (or Stallion, Stud, also Jackass). The moniker spread like wildfire throughout the community.

The aggrieved victim protested to their father, and he forbade Velvele to ever utter the nickname again, a triumph that only provoked further fraternal meanness. Again, Velvele took revenge, writing '*Hengst*' on the outside house wall for all to see. Called to order by his father, Velvele defended himself: he hadn't disobeyed the paternal injunction; he hadn't spoken the word aloud. But, was it his fault that his brother was such an idiot, even the house walls made fun of him? This was an Old Testament reference to the Book of Habakkuk: 'the stone in the wall cries, and the wooden beams answer.'

Proud of this dazzling little son, Moschke Shochet sent him to Tarnopol, twenty-three kilometres away, to study with

---

34 And the author of a booklet of Hebrew satires. His son became a poet.

a highly respected Hasidic rebbe, Yosef Babad (aka Sniatyner). Clearly, Velvele was destined to become a highly placed rabbi in an important community; all would seek him out, heed his advice. What goal could be greater? This was the height of fame for a Jewish boy, the greatest fortune a proud father could possess. But, to quote Schiller:

> *With the mighty powers of fate*
> *Good fortune is a fickle mate.*[35]

***

*T*rouble always foments in a rigid society that demands submission and imposes fixed rules. By the 1830s, the Haskalah had even managed to sneak into drowsy, feudal Zbarazh—wasn't Brody, that centre of secular Jewish education and humanism, less than a hundred kilometres away? Hadn't satirist and educator Joseph Perl founded the Deutsche-Israelitische Hauptschule, the School for Higher Jewish Learning in Tarnopol, fifteen kilometres distant?

Somehow, Velvel obtained a copy of Moses Mendelssohn's German Bible written in Hebrew letters and accompanied by a rationalist interpretation, the *Bi'ur* (the Explanation).[36] How? Was there some welcoming local home where modern folk met and exchanged ideas? Didn't the family of Mendil Lefin, father of the Galician Haskalah, come from Zbarazh? Hadn't town men worked in Joseph Perl's Tarnopol printing house before the Orthodox forced it to close? Or, perhaps while pursuing his studies in that city, Velvel came in contact with the enemy, the heretical Maskil.

Escaping scrutiny, Velvel began hiding under the synagogue steps of Zbarazh, teaching himself German,

---

35 Doch mit des Geschickes Mächten ist kein ew'ger Bund zu flechten, und das Unglück schreitet schnell, cited by Fried, *Biographisches über Benjamin Wolf Ehrenkranz.*

36 Written in an elegant High German so that Jews could learn a modern European language and assimilate.

studying the *Bi'ur*, and pursuing his forbidden (said to be life-threatening) course of study. He soon realised how much was missing from his education. Although imbued with the biblical poetry that would eventually fuel his own poetical instinct, he had no real knowledge of Hebrew, no appreciation of that language's beauty. And what about Jewish life? Weren't there injustices? Didn't traditionalists humiliate those who thought differently? Weren't gangs of children encouraged to harass, even physically attack or stone alleged heretics and nonconformists?

Yet Velvel didn't revolt openly. He remained a covert autodidact, studying the Talmud to please his father, making a show of living religiously. He was certain no one noticed the change in him, but how can you keep secrets in a small community where every nose is sniffing for a whiff of scandal? Where religious leaders are apostasy's gleeful assassins?

Rumours were flying soon enough, and they headed directly for Moschke Shochet's ears. He was shocked; he was bitterly wounded. How could his adult son, Velvel, his bright star so admired by all, be looked upon with disapproving eyes, by the community? No! This tergiversation had to be nipped in the bud; Moschke Shochet's honour had to be saved.

The solution? Marriage to a girl from a good family— that would do the trick. Velvel was eighteen years old, that was old enough to start a family, take on responsibility, behave like the devout and respected Talmudist he was supposed to be, waking at four in the morning, moving no more than eight paces before beginning to pray, and passing the day studying. Despite his suspected apostasy and penchant for secular knowledge, Velvel was still an excellent catch, handsome, charming, witty, a sweet-talker, and talented in religious discourse. Of course, it mattered little if a Talmudist were diseased, backward, deformed, or mean; pale, thin, studious men were preferred. And admired by society, they were treated with the respect due to any prince.

But, before Moschke Shochet could begin marriage negotiations[37] for the dowry, the *nadn*, the compensation paid to a learned youth's parents, and the *kest*, the obligation for the bride's family to provide the newlyweds with food, clothing, and lodging for three to eight years, he had to find a suitable bride. She had to be a virginal young woman, one who would be an excellent housewife and exemplary mother, who would cater to her husband, believe him wise, saintly, and learned. She also needed a character strong enough to keep Velvel firmly anchored.

---

37 Arrangements that could (and did) engender conflict, misrepresentation, even fraud.

Chapter VI:
The Wedding

A pretty little apple is delicious,
A chaste bride is a delight!
A juicy apple is very sweet,
An unclean bride is very ugly!

Marriage song[38]

*M*arriage was the only respectable state for a woman; spinsters were openly mocked. Even after modern ideas penetrated Jewish life, women continued to dream of traditional marriages for their daughters, and to sing lullabies warning of the dire consequences befalling those straying from the true path. Even though her future happiness was at stake, no girl dared defy her family or question their choice of groom: unions were destined by God. But arranged marriages were also the fate of Christian peasant women, and those who protested were beaten into submission.

Only a tiny minority of Jewish girls attended a few early years of cheder, the traditional elementary school. Most

---

38   Rubin, *Voices of a People.*

remained home, helping with household duties, raising younger brothers and sisters, learning the *Tekhines*, the Yiddish supplications, prayers, and religious obligations, and acquiring the skills necessary for running the family business: if she married a pious man, she would be the family's sole financial support. But such skills weren't enough. A desirable bridal candidate had to be full-figured, free of imperfection, and graced with pale skin that showed she had never laboured in the fields. Had she blemishes—moles (small moles were acceptable unless in the middle of the forehead), hairy moles, a broken or maimed limb, halitosis, breasts too far apart, a tendency to sweat excessively—a nuptial agreement could be annulled. Discovered after marriage, such flaws were grounds for divorce.

New husbands usually moved in with the bride's family, and if the groom were a pious man, therefore not a breadwinner, supporting him was a sign of financial success as well as a demonstration of religiosity, especially for merchants who had devoted themselves to making money. Only the unluckiest girls went to live in a husband's house, becoming menials, the slaves of tyrannical mothers-in-law. This was the fate of Christian brides, since sons lived in their father's house after marriage and took over the family plot of land.

Christian or Jew, compliance was a woman's lot. If a husband were unfaithful, she was to hide her suffering; physical violence, fuelled by alcohol, was just part of life. Wives were beaten by their husbands; children were beaten; animals were beaten; bloody street fights were common. And even though unions were destined by God, it was sometimes admitted they were less than perfect.

Eastern European Jews had a remarkably high rate of divorce, and the reasons cited were conflicts with stepchildren and in-laws, mutual hatred, childlessness, illness, depravity, domestic violence, conversion, poverty, and desertion. Only widows or women with no brothers and no living parents could be independent. Yet, independence was shunned; those who could, quickly remarried. In 1867, one-third of Jewish brides and grooms and one-quarter of Russian Orthodox and Protestant Christians married for a second time.

***

*M*oschke Shochet found two suitable bridal candidates for his son.[39] The beautiful Chawcia was the daughter of a colleague; the second aspirant was Nachman Knödel's daughter, the pug-nosed Niusiuniu who lived right next door. Surely, it had been Niusiuniu's mother, the feared and pushy busybody, 'Aunt' Genendel, who had thrust her less-favoured offspring into the ring.

As can be expected, Chawcia and Niusiuniu were bitter rivals, and it was decided that the choice between the two would depend on a cooking competition (is it possible that a lifelong mate could be chosen on such a basis? Perhaps, when deprived of higher learning, a talent at cooking or sewing just might be a deciding factor. It's also possible that all knew beforehand who the winner would be.)

Thus, when Pesach reached its end, the beautiful Chawcia, renowned throughout the shtetl for her gastronomic skill, came to prepare her *knödel* and *kügelech*[40] in Velvel's family kitchen. Right next door, in her own home, Niusiuniu was left to throw together her foodstuffs, ones she knew would be sadly inferior. She possessed no culinary talent...but she did possess cunning. To give herself a fighting chance, Niusiuniu decided to spice the epicurean event with a rather tasteless plot. (And Velvel? Where was he? Hiding from the clamour, the stress and fuss, and concentrating on the books in Nachman Knödel's library. Wasn't he vexed that his future happiness depended upon comestibles? Perhaps he was plotting an escape.)

---

39 Only older bachelors could choose for themselves.

40 Dumplings made from matzoh meal and schmaltz and a sweet or savoury casserole made of vegetables, fruit, potatoes, noodles, or other foods.

Then, just when everything, cooked to perfection, sat steaming and ready for judging, a dreaded shriek was heard from behind Velvel's house: 'Fire!'

Chawcia and her mother Perele raced to the safety of the street. Unseen, Niusiuniu slipped inside Velvel's house, replaced Chawcia's very fine offering with her own, far poorer one, and hoped for the prize. The unsavoury trick was promptly exposed when the dishes purportedly containing Chawcia's strangely insipid delicacies proved to be from Genendel's house. Thus, it was announced that Velvel would marry Chawcia. They would digest well, procreate, and live happily ever after. But Moschke Shochet had made a grave error of judgment. As the old expression went: he'd made up the bill without reckoning on the landlord.

***

*T*o reinforce contractual and emotional ties, wedding celebrations were highly visible events, and they sometimes lasted for seven days. Even at the most modest, guests indulged, ate all night, and drank until capable of little more than lolling about in the fields and feeling dismal. To partake in the poor people's meal, beggars came from miles around with their ravenous wives and voracious children in tow. There were also government officials to wine and dine, and they, their cronies and neighbours, were ferried to the spot in hired coaches. An important wedding day feast could mean the presence of some two hundred guests—a considerable number back then.

Big or small, held in a courtyard or a meadow, the wedding's central figure was the badkhn, the master of ceremonies. He was the one who led the show, from the cheery welcome ritual through the many meals. Some—simple jesters, buffoons, comedians with a talent for improvisation—employed satire and crude wit, moulding their well-worn repertory to each wedding; others, more poetic, recited sentimental verses in honour of bride and groom. The badkhn was the one who addressed the veiled bride, demanded she repent of her sins, reflect on life's fleeting nature, and her sad lot as a woman:

> *Bride, bride weep!*
> *The bridegroom sends you a pot of horseradish*
> *And you will snivel to your teeth*

He was the one who initiated the *broyges tanz* in which the new couple staged a mock fight and mothers-in-law quarrelled:

> *My in-law, dear in-law*
> *My daughter comes to you in a wig*
> *And if you're going to be a vicious, evil mother-in-law*
> *Well, my daughter's no treasure either.*

And right at the badkhn's side, sawing, puffing, and tapping away, were his musicians, the klezmorim.[41] It was the klezmorim's musical brilliance that set the tone, pulled in joy. It was the teamwork of badkhn and klezmorim that ran the merry dance. And it was a difficult job, indeed:

> *Musicians were beaten if they didn't know the tunes.*
> *Weddings comprised much dancing and the fiddler had the*
> *hardest job because he had to play without a break and he*
> *had to accompany the singers. If he dozed off, he could be*
> *whipped into wakefulness.*[42]

Was Velvel and Chawcia's wedding a bright, cheery, joyful affair or did something go terribly wrong then and there? Did Velvel's brilliant wit challenge the badkhn's coarser jokes? Did his doubt of stifling tradition seep through his pious façade? Perhaps he quailed when the wedding noise receded and daily life's tick-tock banality began. Here was the beautiful Chawcia, now shorn of her locks and decked

---

41 Kley from the Hebrew 'instrument' and zemer from 'song'.

42 Slomka, *From Serfdom to Self-Government.*

in a wig as tradition demanded; here was the new life as a little prince in the shrunken kingdom of an in-law's house. From now on, Velvel was bound to pious study and stability. How to survive a narrow life when irrevocably changed by secret inquiry? How to be content with a dutiful woman of no learning, and no modern knowledge? To please his father and allay community suspicions, Velvel had sacrificed himself, sabotaged his youth and his right to free will.

Only a short time after his wedding, he vanished, abandoning Chawcia, his family, his home, and his town. Attempts to find him met with no success. Only several years later, was it discovered, through a passing traveller, that Velvel was alive, well, and living in Romania.

Romania: believed to be a perfect haven for Jews eschewing tradition.

Chapter VII:
The Road

Why should I wander sadly,
My harp within my hand,
O'er mountain, hill, and valley?
What praise do I command?
Full well they know the singer
Belongs to race accursed;
Sweet Minne doth no longer
Reward me as at first.
Be silent, then, my lyre,
We sing 'fore lords in vain,
I'll leave the minstrels' choir,
And roam a Jew again.

Süsskind von Trimberg[43]

*W*hat doubts—if any—assailed Velvel as he journeyed south? Was he angry and determined, or excited? Did he ever hesitate, think of turning back? The open road is a heady place leading to the future and freedom, but fear is

---

43 Süsskind von Trimberg was a thirteenth century Jewish bard.

there too, treading clumsily on a traveller's heels, conjuring up all that was taken for granted back home—the slanting tree in the yard, the sun-dappled porch, the moist odour of springtime in one particular lane, an indefinable warmth—and creating a permanent longing in the soul, one never again quite satisfied. That's the exile's heavy baggage. It's also true that those unable to conform are doomed to wander, and Velvel was not the only young man of his time to abandon all, leave behind an *agunah*[44] a grass widow, and head for Romania, Ottoman Turkey, Prussia, anywhere else, to pursue studies and create a new life.

How did he travel? There was no train line yet, but the hard-packed dirt roads were lively with coaches, wagons, and riders. Did peasant carts carry him some of the way? Perhaps, as travellers were wont to do, he strode the tree-lined lanes with shoes around his neck to save the leather, and helped himself to ripe fruit.

There were many afoot: peasants, cattle drovers with five hundred beasts, homeless farmworkers with their families, runaway serfs, grain-loaded animals, intellectuals and students, bands of soldiers, ex-soldiers, deserters and mercenaries returning from already-forgotten battles, chained prisoners, discredited nobles, servant girls, gamblers, lackeys, women of pleasure, immigrants, tree sawyers, clock repairers, tailors, shoemakers, pot menders, merchants, Jewish peddlers with bundles or display counters on their backs. There were chimney sweeps with their accoutrements,

---

44 An agunah is a married woman whose husband has abandoned her, gone on a journey and not returned, disappeared in battle without reliable testimony to his death, or has refused to grant her a get, a divorce. According to Jewish law, an agunah cannot remarry, and any child she has with another man is illegitimate.

booksellers, casters of spells, swarms of beggars[45] and beggar children, tricksters, hucksters, and sharpies on the lookout for tenderfoots, petty criminals who had lost all right to settle, and those who'd lost all through illness, alcohol, betrayal, or foolishness.

Also on the road were pilgrims: great swells—sometimes a thousand or more—of Hasidic followers beating a path to their revered rebbe, itinerant priests, *maggidim*, the wandering orators who, in synagogues and study halls, exhorted sinners to repent. There were also those who'd shuffled along Europe's roads since the Middle Ages—singers, bards, Gypsy musicians, Roma herders and metal workers, Ruthenian and Ukrainian folk bards, *kobzari*,[46] with their lovely lute-like stringed *kobzyas* or *banduras*. And here, too, are our klezmorim with their badkhonim.

In the Middle Ages, the rabbinate discouraged music: Jews were to mourn the destruction of the temple, not imitate vulgar gentile revelling. Forced onto society's edge, Jewish musicians—klezmorim,[47] minnesingers, minstrels, bards both male and female—continued crisscrossing thirteenth and fourteenth-century Europe, singing troubadour's songs as well as church music and Teutonic folk melodies. Seventeenth-century religious fervour further dampened secular endeavour and banned women from public performance, but the klezmorim perdured, animating markets, fairs, taverns, alleys around synagogues and churches, leaping on carts to serenade travellers for a

---

45 There are many words for beggar in Yiddish, the most common are schlepper, schnorrer, and betler. Homeless beggars were medine geyer. In, *Fishke the Lame*, Sholem Yankev Abramovich mentions religious paupers, foot paupers, horse-paupers, bread paupers, field paupers, hidden paupers, and many others, including the luftmensch who 'lives on hope, and hope is often a liar.'

46 Persecuted during the Soviet era, many traditional kobzari were killed in Stalin's purges. Their traditional instruments were prohibited as part of the Ukrainian ethnocide.

47 Although the term Klezmer originally referred to the music, it came to mean the musicians who played it.

few snatched coins. When fetched by a noble's carriage and transported to a manor for a wedding or ball, they churned out mazurkas, bulgars, and waltzes, accepted payment in coins, or chickens, potatoes, and bread.

A musician's status remained low. Their itinerant lifestyle and lack of piety was frowned upon, and they were defamed as womanisers, gamblers, and drunkards who frequented the lowliest inns. Yet even gentiles preferred Jewish musicians because of their relative sobriety, their greater repertory acquired during centuries of displacement, also for their willingness to work long hours and accept little gain.

Wandering the mucky lanes frequented by bandits and myriad cranks was a risky business. Sleeping in frowsty barns, damp pastures, or drear inn corners was a public display of poverty; so was playing in courtyards for a few tossed coins. Yet, with no formal musical education, no notion of musical theory, and no scores, the klezmorim were highly talented craftsmen, weaving together devotional music, Ottoman and Hungarian harmonies, Romany melodies, Russian drinking songs, Romanian dances and shepherd's laments.

Alongside them were the brilliant sharp-witted badkhonim, ever on the lookout for employment, shifting between one ceremony and the next, one community to another, but also relegated to society's abject margin. Even the Maskilim despised them for their 'degraded' popular entertainment, their shameful Yiddish jargon, their crude slapstick and vulgar humour, their role in that hated institution, the arranged marriage. Yet, albeit rejected and mocked, it was the badkhn's agile tongue that provided the first Jewish actors and comic Jewish café performers, the Broderzinger, with a model of performance. It was badkhn poetry, newly printed in inexpensive pamphlets, that inspired the maskilic satires of traditional society.

So here they were, Velvel and everyone else, padding along the road, gathering in wayside inns at dusk, exchanging melodies, sharing tales, itching and scratching through the flea-bitten night on some terrible straw-covered floor, then heading out again at dawn, richer for the exchange.

Many pushed south, drawn by Romania's magnetic reputation. It was a new country; the economy was booming; the city streets were said to be paved with gold. Under Turkish hegemony, Romania welcomed Jews, and young, idealistic Romanian revolutionaries were demanding equal rights and freedom for all. What a rainbow! Velvel would start a new life there:

> *Driven from home*
> *Left in poverty*
> *Don't worry about such things.*
> *A wise person*
> *Will soon learn*
> *Everywhere is his home.*[48]

But surely the idea never crossed his mind that one day he, too, would sing for his supper; that he would become a badkhn...but a badkhn of quite another ilk.

---

48 Unless otherwise stated, all verses are those of Velvel Zbarzher.

Chapter VIII:
Czernowitz

Speed is only good for catching flies.

Yiddish Proverb

*I*n the company of Karl Emil Franzos, I take the train south from Lemberg (now Lviv) to Czernowitz in the historic region of Bukovina. Born in 1848 in Czortkow, a town halfway between Tarnopol and Czernowitz, Franzos was the grandson of an enlightened Jewish candle factory owner, and the son of a doctor steeped in Enlightenment ideals. His father taught him German, the language of daily life and, while attending the town's modern school in the Dominican monastery, Karl Emil also studied Latin and Polish.[49] Alienated from his Christian schoolmates because he was a Jew, he was equally alienated from the local Yiddish-speaking Jewish youths:

I was different. But I knew exactly what I was, my father made certain of that. I was a German and a Jew at the same

---

49   After power in Galicia was handed over to the Polish nobles in 1867, all middle class Jewish schoolchildren were expected to learn Polish.

time...When a Jewish youth threw excrement at me, cursed me, and called me a traitor, I was told 'He is your brother, don't condemn him! He knows not what he does.' Naturally, I couldn't get closer to this brother, and I had little desire to do so. Any attempt I made ended badly with these little kaftan wearers beating and mocking me. However, if I met only one of them, he always ran away.[50]

Thus, he was the new Jew, caught in the new Jew's dilemma.

Franzos became famous with his book, *Aus Halb-Asien*, and his descriptions of travel on the new train line through Habsburg lands in the 1870s.[51] Almost a century and a half later, with that same tome clutched in my hand, I search for his world. Take, for example, the restaurant in the Lemberg train station:

I have seldom seen such a neglected room as the [station] restaurant in Lemberg. And these sleepy waiters in their unspeakable clothing morosely slouching about! And these cups from which one must drink coffee! One fights with oneself until overcome by the need to have something warm in one's belly.

The people around us don't seem to be troubled with such scruples...the travellers are served by dirty rascals with oil-soaked hair. There sit boyars from Moldavia with dark, sly faces, heavy rings, and hanging watches, and with dirty hands. There sit fine, smoothly, elegantly dressed men who take three rolls, claim they've taken only one, then leave a one gulden tip. There are wonderful, dark-eyed women in heavy silk dresses and dirty underskirts. In

---

50 Franzos, *Der Pojaz*. Anti-Semitism at the century's end hindered Franzos' careers as teacher and judge. Although a successful writer, anti-Semitism prevented the publication of some of his works and was responsible for the heart trouble that caused his death in 1904.

51 Victor Ofenheim built the line to take advantage of profits to be had in the new country of Romania. The line from Przemysl to Lemberg, completed in 1861, reached Czernowitz in 1867, Jassy and Botoşani in 1870.

between the civilized German and English travellers are
emancipated Polish Jews who want nothing more than to
be Jewish Poles and choose only roast pork from the menu;
long-bearded Ruthenian popes in shinning oily kaftans,
elegant Hussar officers, faded coquettes who are headed
for Bucharest and Jassy to try their luck there. And all are
eating, à la carte, from the French witch's kitchen of this
Jewish restaurant and pay a fortune for it...[the] reading
material in the train station is very limited. There are two
sorts of literature offered: obscenities and anti-Jewish hate
literature.

That terrible dining hall has vanished. The old neo-Gothic station was replaced in 1888 by a glorious Habsburg structure with a high dome, stained glass windows, sculptures of mythological figures, and a waiting hall modelled on an English gentleman's club. It was so badly damaged during the Second World War, the Soviets considered pulling it down. Fortunately, they didn't.

Ukraine's old train stations are a pleasure. Protected, cherished, their beautifully painted ceilings soar high, and seats are solid wood. Here, too, is all the excitement of constantly coming and going night trains. At a wooden bar smack in the middle of the elegant waiting hall, blowsy, sly-eyed women sell shots of very decent vodka (that I certainly enjoy) and picturesque travellers in cloth or woollen caps hold low but intense conversations. One slack-jawed hussar throwback with a proud moustache, fur cap, and high black boots, sleeps soundly, tumbled together with a wizened ancient in a knit cap. Everyone looks as though they've stepped out of a nineteenth-century Myasoyedov painting, and even I'm let into the fun when a woman beside me translates the bellowing of one tipsy character who refuses to give his son's name to the ticket seller: 'He's my son. Why do you need his name? Just put down he's my son on the ticket.' The equally unsteady but impassive son looks on wordlessly; he's used to this sort of thing.

If only someone would shut off the infernally howling junk music. If only someone would put an end to the video clips on the huge flickering screens, then I could escape the modern world. Even so, it still wouldn't much resemble that of Franzos':

> *Beware, you harmless traveller, if you venture into the entry hall of the station! Suddenly all around you are a knot of fighting, flattering, howling, whispering, shoving, tugging figures, kaftaned Jews with their peyes, so unbelievably dirty that you can hardly understand how they don't stick to each other as they push against one another. They are all here to help you...one mentions a wonderful hotel, the second, an elegant wagon, the third speaks of a visit to the king's tomb, the fourth of a tourist's visit to the salt mines, the fifth wants to change money, the sixth will give you a loan on your gold watch. And when you don't need any of this, you hear the whispering siren call of a young woman burning with desire to bring you into her salon.*

Finally, it's time for our train to depart, and it does so very slowly and discretely, then trundles along the rails in a leisurely, rather disinterested sort of way. For Ukrainian and Russian trains are not determined machines: they tarry, hesitate as if unsure of destinations, or lack the will to reach them. Often motionless, brooding sombrely in wind-blown obscure stations, on the inside they are soothing cocoons, warm and comfortable. At the end of each corridor, there is always a bubbling samovar; and the two gorgon-like creatures in charge of each wagon take you and your ticket in hand, make certain no one unwelcome boards, point out your bed-like surface with its comfortable mattress on a high shelf, bring you fresh bed linen and a soft pillow. This is easy luxury in the old way, even in the open third-class compartment, and fellow travellers are discrete.

***

*I*n Velvel's day, the three strongest Hasidic courts in the world—Sadagora, Wiznitz, and Bojan—were situated in Bukovina, a region that today straddles Ukraine and Romania. Competition between dynasties was rife and violent with murders, bans and counter-bans, excommunications, vitriolic pamphlets, and denunciations leading to deportation and imprisonment. Few modern Jews were on hand to fight their power.

Annexed by the Habsburg monarchy in 1775, Bukovina's Moldavian noble landowners had only a weak sense of national identity. They were rarely around anyway, preferring to frolic in fashionable European cities. Inhabited by Ruthenian and Romanian peasants with an exceptionally high illiteracy rate, this was a poor country of fallow fields, sad huts, and few roads.

Regimes, times, populations, the whole world has changed since then, but is the landscape so different? Outside the train window, early morning's pallid light shows the same empty fields, the absence of industry and culture that Franzos noted a century and a half ago. In scattered settlements, houses surrounded by heaps of rejected odds and ends slump into the snow, and only chickens peck with enthusiasm.

Soon enough, we are crossing the Prut River, heralded as a glorious event in old travel literature. It marked the arrival in Czernowitz, a model of civilization, a brilliant light caught in a barbaric hinterland. Today, too, civilization's by-products are apparent: filling the river are long trails of multi-coloured shredded plastic, and the twisted metal girders and smashed cement pillars of some thwarted construction dream.

Czernowitz's Imperial train station is still lovely, painted in pale blue and white, and outside is the old cobbled main road that climbs toward the town centre. Gone, thankfully, are the wretched, undernourished little horses that once dragged heavy cartloads of merchandise uphill and suffered merciless flogging. Not far from the station was the Jewish quarter with its many-spouted fountain providing artesian well water. That was destroyed in 1894, but another, the Turkish fountain, is still here, modernised by an ugly concrete construction meant, perhaps, to depict a pseudo archaeological ruin.

How did Velvel feel when he arrived in town? Did he know anyone? How long did he stay? Where? Here, in the poorer end of the city where Jewish clockmakers, goldsmiths, carpenters, tailors, and shoemakers worked? Where Yiddish was the spoken language, and there were many prayer houses; where men with *peyes* (long side curls), fur hats, black kaftans, and white socks scurried along the streets? Where women sold bread and pretzels from basements, howling children begged, and bargaining was strident in the used clothing shops? Here, too, were country folk seeking casual work, and they crowded around tavern doors while their crouching women in white scarves sold eggs and milk. Only those countrywomen are still around with their eggs and their bottles of milk, and they sit on the freezing pavement near a market of wooden sheds. These days, instead of thin scarves, they wear warm woollen hats.

Under a frozen pewter-grey sky, I tramp along the glacial streets, peeking over fences and into yards. Only a few of the low, old houses are left, for most of this area was destroyed by fire in 1867. Still, here is one shop with the name of a Jewish craftsman on its façade. I peer through the grimy windows, see only floors and tables covered by thick dust. The former Great Synagogue, a building smothered by a thick layer of cement, has become a builder's workshop. Two workers lounge outside sharing an almost empty vodka bottle. I ask them if they'll let me go inside. Their eyes are insolent. 'No, you can't take a look.'

Further along, I find a Jewish (state) school. Inside, I stop a few teachers, ask about Velvel Zbarzher. Does the name ring a bell? One says, in perfect English, that she'll question the others in the teacher's room. I wait in the middle of the usual hollering school chaos: the Jewish world is well and alive here.

The young woman returns. 'No one has heard of Velvel Zbarzher. One teacher thinks she's heard the name Meir Ehrenkranz, but she's not certain. No, sorry, she said she doesn't have the time to talk to you.'

For a bit of human warmth and a glimpse into daily life, I try to prolong the conversation. 'Do you enjoy living in Czernowitz?'

Her smile is tight, even condescending. 'It's way too small for me. I like being in New York or Los Angeles. Big cities where things happen, where there are good clubs. There's nothing interesting here.'

'It has a wonderful history. So many writers, artists, brilliant minds came from Czernowitz.'

She shrugs, indifferent, craving only American nightlife.

***

In the early 1800s, the city of Czernowitz, with its vivid mix of Ruthenians, Ukrainians, Hungarians, Romanians, Poles, Slovaks, Jews, Turks, and Roma, was firmly in the hands of the economically sound German-speaking middle class. A small community of German-speaking modern Jews eventually joined them, and soon the city's booming economic growth attracted other seekers of reform and assimilation. In 1843, with Austrian administrative support, power was wrested from the Hasidim.

It was here that Velvel cut off his long peyes, purchased shiny polished shoes, had a short coat made, and donned a white shirt—all the trappings of a modern man. As the expression went: Be a man in the street and a Jew in your own home, and Velvel later wrote in *Makel No'am:*

He did not disguise himself but dressed and looked like the Jew he was.

Traditional Jews, drab by religious injunction (or perhaps believing invisibility meant security)[52] wore grubby kaftans in the style—albeit without the colour or flamboyance—of the long dispensed-with Polish noble's Sarmatian dress. Women, enjoined to be equally drab, pushed limits with elaborate head coverings, beautifully embroidered aprons (worn to protect reproductive organs), and ostentatious jewellery.

> *...men and women wore clothing out of date elsewhere. Fur hats, shirts unbuttoned at the collar, throats wrapped in a cotton scarf in winter, pants, always, were tucked into once-white dirty socks and slippers or boots in winter. A true Hasid never walked slowly but always rushed as if in constant hurry. The women wore shroud-like gowns and caps and sometimes a veil. Wearing one's own hair was out of the question; this sort of loose woman would have simply been stoned. Even thread or silk wigs could not, God forbid, be worn on their shaved heads...A respectable person would not have dared to wear 'German clothing.' The education and worldly knowledge of these people can easily be surmised: They did not miss it and could not even have wished for another lifestyle.[53]*

To distance themselves from their shtetl brethren, the Maskilim assumed self-confident middle-class personalities, donned modern clothes, and adhered to new notions of hygiene and cleanliness, as did upwardly mobile non-Jews: good grooming and attention to fashion set them apart from the urban poor and rural dwellers. Most condemned the dirtiness of the kaftans worn by the religious, the filth of their living conditions, but hadn't non-Jewish ideologues always levelled this accusation at the community? To a certain extent, this criticism must have been unfounded.

---

52   If invisibility had once protected Jews, it only hindered their progress in the modern world.

53   Margoshes, *A World Apart.*

Jewish religious men were often more scrupulous in matters of hygiene than their neighbours, washing hands and face and rinsing the mouth before morning prayer, letting water flow over their hands before meals or reciting a blessing, and immersing themselves in water before Shabbat, Yom Kippur, Rosh Hashanah, or cleansing themselves of seminal impurities. Women were required to immerse themselves in the mikveh, the ritual bath, after menstruation. Clean clothes were another issue altogether.

Those living in rural areas, as well as townspeople without servants to tend to menial chores, rarely changed their clothes, often sleeping in them until they were stiff with sweat and soil before removing them and leaving them in a pile ready for the great wash that took place two or three times a year. Underclothes, meant to absorb perspiration, were replaced, at the very best, once a week, but most women of all religions usually wore no underpants. However, the traditional kaftans of wool couldn't be washed at all, and the Lemberg playwright Franz Kratter also described kaftaned Galician priests as unspeakably dirty.[54]

Washing clothes was a hard task, one allocated to women. It required lugging home quantities of water, a long soaking of clothes in a wooden tub covered by a coarse sheet on which lay the cleansing materials—wood ash, roots, nettles, crushed eggshells, even urine—over which boiling water was poured several times. After that, the heavy sodden garments were hauled to running water in a river or pond, then rubbed, beaten, rinsed, and wrung. It was hard work indeed, but there were modest compensations: new brides and the better off could display, in public, their fine linens or a talent for embroidery.

As for Velvel, braced by the new ideas, dandified and no longer resembling a pious village youth but a proud Maskil

---

54 Franz Kratter, 1758-1830, dramaturge and theatre director. His dramas were not only popular in Lemberg, but throughout the German-speaking lands because of his social awareness and his uncompromising portrayal of the living conditions and prevailing abuses in Galicia.

(dubbed a *Deutsch*, a 'German,' by the religious), he left Czernowitz and Galicia behind, aimed for the Romanian border. He couldn't have known that when he returned to this city many years later, it would be another world altogether.

Chapter IX:
Romania

When can the poet feel good
And live without worries?
Not in this world
Where he must borrow and lend.
Only good for him is the other world
There, he needs no money
And he can sing until he bursts

Velvel Zbarzher

*O*utside, there's a blizzard. At the Romanian border, customs officials and train mechanics stamp their feet, trying to keep warm. Inside this train carrying only a few passengers, life is pleasant, dreamy and snug, but we aren't advancing, merely jerking back and forth with a terrible grinding. To compensate for the difference between Ukrainian and Romanian track gauge, wagons are lifted off one set of bogies and placed on another. This discrepancy once slowed down the panzer units dependent on ammunition and oil and helped prevent Hitler's seizure of Moscow, but it's a costly process today. I'm one of the last travellers on the romantic-sounding Moscow-Sophia run. In two weeks, it will be cancelled, and no train will replace it.

After a final shudder of wheels and much thudding, we set off again, swaying through the soft white countryside, accompanied, since Czernowitz, by a narrow snow-covered Moldavian track. Forgotten, used only by farmers and shepherds today, a hundred and fifty years ago, despite its ruts, holes, and the frail horizontal poles bridging streams and quagmires, it might have been an important north-south way. Villages seem drowsy, empty. Swarms of starlings fill the air, fields maintain their long medieval swaths, and motionless shepherds are out on the frozen plain, timeless figures with crooks. Do they still follow the old custom of wintering where grasses pierce the snow? Apparently. Here and there are enclosures for their woolly creatures— odd-shaped reed-walled corrals. Close by are the modern shepherd's huts: no longer made of stalks and thatch, these tiny one-room boxes have walls of corrugated metal, plastic sheeting, any old salvaged, knocked-together material. Iron pipe chimneys sprout from roofs. Bored sheepdogs, taking a break from rounding up their silly charges, happily chase our passing train.

I transfer at stations with the crenulated roofs of small castles or Moorish palaces, journey further with grizzled men sporting extravagant moustaches and old-fashioned headgear. They hold their shoulders back proudly. Just remove those synthetic jackets and we could be in another era. School children of all ages travel for a stop or two before setting out on foot through the snow, hiking to some invisible homestead. One young man leaps agilely from the moving train, strides towards a hazy clump of houses and barns. I want to call out to him: 'Take me with you. Let me, a nosy intrusive person, peek into your life for a short time.'

Silence without media interference is too much to bear for a few travellers. A scratchy radio is snapped on—happily, the music is traditional Romanian, jumpy, nervous, and catchy. A few moustached men hum, sing along, slap their thighs, and whistle shrilly at all the right places. I encourage them with nods and grins.

**

Nestled between two rivers, the Danube and Prut, Romania snuggles against the Carpathians. The country's first Jews might have been early Black Sea traders, soldiers in the Roman legions, or purveyors to their armies. Who were the mysterious people described by Benjamin of Tudela in the twelfth century? Could they have been Khazar descendants?

> *The nation called Walachians live in those mountains. They are as swift as hinds, and they sweep down from the mountains to despoil and ravage the land of Greece. No man can go up and do battle with them, and no king can rule over them. They do not hold fast to the faith of the Nazarenes but give themselves Jewish names. Some people say that they are Jews, and, in fact, they call the Jews their brethren, and when they meet with them, though they rob them, they refrain from killing them as they kill the Greeks. They are altogether lawless.*[55]

Many Walachian Jews of Sephardic origin arrived with the fifteenth-century Ottoman conquest, and a small elite served as physicians, as diplomats influential with pashas and viziers. During the 1821 uprising, however, Jews were plundered and massacred, and the Greek monks in Moldavian monasteries sheltered the assassins. By mid-1800, the wealthiest Walachian Jews had assimilated into upper-middle-class society and intellectual circles.

Moldavian Jews were of quite another ilk. They had come from the German lands in the fourteenth century, and from Poland when escaping Bohdan Khmelnitsky's massacres in

---

55 Benjamin of Tudela, *Travels in the Middle Ages.*

the seventeenth. Nineteenth-century arrivals came with over-population in Galicia, and from Russia after the instauration of the twenty-five-year military draft. In earlier times, noble landowners, eager to profit from Jewish business acumen and international contacts, had encouraged them to establish market towns. But dependent on the inconstant benevolence of Albanian and Greek princes, Jews could, at any moment, be expelled from their homes, be forbidden residence in certain streets, villages, or whole districts. The 1640 Church Code banned all relationships between Jews and Christians; in 1771 and 1803, the Orthodox Church issued books of anti-Jewish incitement. There were forced baptisms, charges of blood libel, burnings, and pogroms.

Russia occupied Moldavia and Walachia in 1819, and conditions worsened. Russian occupation and Ottoman suzerainty also infuriated modern young Romanian intellectuals.[56] Educated in France, they nurtured dreams of an independent and united Romania. Their revolt of 1821 failed; their second, in 1848, brought temporary victory. A new provisional government extended political rights to all countrymen, encouraged the emancipation and assimilation of Jews, and the liberation of the Roma (Gypsy) slaves.[57] This liberal moment was, alas, brief. A few months later, Ottoman troops marched back into Bucharest.

Yet Jewish life did improve. Jews were permitted to own vineyards, serve in the army (up to the rank of non-commissioned officer), and enter institutions of higher

---

56 Some were Jewish. The painter Konstantin Daniel Rosenthal, born in Austro-Hungary, came to Bucharest in 1842, then associated with Walachian and Moldavian revolutionaries in Paris. When the revolution failed, he became itinerant. In 1851, while planning to return and rekindle the radical movement, he was arrested in Budapest. Refusing to denounce his co-conspirators, he was tortured to death.

57 The noble owners as well as the church possessed many Roma slaves, and they were compensated for their loss after emancipation. Although some boyars freed their slaves without demanding such compensation, others fought abolition. After the revolution was quelled by Turkish and Russian troops, slaves returned to their previous status.

learning. New synagogues could be erected (at a certain distance from nearby churches) and, although without civil rights, economic freedom was enjoyed: shop owners and moneylenders were fully visible on main streets, and there were many Jewish craftsmen—engravers, platers, tailors, shoemakers, watchmakers, hatters, typographers, and bookbinders.

The economy boomed and more entrepreneurs, craftsmen, fortune seekers, and intellectuals arrived. Those Jewish café comedians, the Broderzinger, showed up in the mid 1800s, so did Maskilim who, like Velvel, hoped for a useful life. But the dream of prosperity for all was illusory. Most Romanians were poor uneducated agricultural workers, and the social distance between them and the slave-owning landowners[58] with their fine horses and great houses, was unbridgeable.

...we were beginning to make arrangements for spending the night in the carriage, when a more respectable person accosted us [and] conducted us to a miserable hut, where a woman and a naked child, rolling themselves off a plank, placed it at our disposal. In a corner, two more children lay on the mud floor. The stove, a broad bench on three sides of the room, and a stick suspended from the ceiling, on which several articles of dress were hanging, constituted the only furniture. Three holes in the wall, covered with pieces of bladder, protected it partially against intruders. Undressing and wrapt in our cloaks, we lay down to sleep, with the two children in the corner, thankful for a sheltered spot in which to rest our weary limbs.

---

58 Until mid-nineteenth century, the Roma were slaves on many estates. Divided into groups—house slaves, field slaves, state slaves, and monastery slaves—they could be bought and sold in lots. Field slaves lived in mud and reed huts on the outskirts of estates; male house slaves were castrated to protect noblewomen, and female slaves were provided to male guests for entertainment. Flogged, whipped, mutilated, burned, sometimes forced to wear a three-cornered spiked iron collar, those Roma who managed to escape took refuge in the Carpathian Mountains.

The following morning we awoke to a sense of our miseries, and saw by daylight the full extent of the wretchedness by which we were surrounded. The screaming of the children had compelled us in the middle of the night to put them into the outer room, and they ceased to disturb us; but not so the insects by which we were almost devoured: an entomologist might have made a fair collection from the various species of our tormentors.[59]

A small Romanian intelligentsia did exist, but not much of a commercial or industrial bourgeoisie. Urban life was firmly in the hands of the country's Hungarians, Greeks, Germans, and Jews, and such foreign domination clashed painfully with Romania's new nationalist sentiment. The 'foreign' Jewish presence was a particularly nasty bugbear.

Moldavia's Jews numbered 125,000 by the mid-nineteenth century. Most spoke only Yiddish, were conservative, pious, and under the influence of Hasidism. Dwelling in overcrowded houses on the filthy back streets of self-imposed 'ghettos',[60] they were far removed from the country's political struggles. They nurtured no dreams of democracy or civil emancipation, and they had no respect for Romanian culture. With their long peyes and traditional garb, they were content with their 'foreign' status and indifferent to the anti-Semitic hatred they fuelled.

But, modernisation could neither be ignored nor prayed away. Wealthier, enlightened Jews were hiring Galician and Russian Maskilim as private tutors for their children; Haskalah writers, poets, and publishers were disseminating the new ideas; taboo-breaking Broderzinger were singing and playing to enthusiastic crowds in wine cellars and tea gardens. Still...how difficult to create a modern society! When, in 1847, a group of Maskilim dressed in European-style clothes, there

---

59   Elliot, *Travels in Austria, Russia and Turkey.*

60   The word ghetto was used by the Maskilim to describe the narrow, religious Jewish community, not the closed-off areas in which Jews were forced to live in earlier times.

was violent protest from the Hasidic community. A modern boy's school established in 1852 was boycotted and forced to close—a setback that was only temporary: under the Prime Minister Mihail Kogălniceanu[61] three Jewish secular schools for boys and girls were opened between 1865 and 1896.

Velvel arrived in Botoșani, a city judiciously placed at the bottom end of the Czernowitz-Leipzig-Brody trade road. He tried his hand at business, but it wasn't up his street, and he failed miserably. Did he lack the right mentality? The right contacts, the drive for material success, an aptitude for bargaining and wheedling? What else could he do? Write poems. His first, based on a Talmudic parable and written in Hebrew, appeared in 1848 in a Viennese annual.[62] Could he feed himself on obscure verse? Certainly not. Writers often paid to have their work published in the new Hebrew and Yiddish magazines,[63] and Velvel was forced to admit that, as far as poetry went: 'poor people have no money for such a thing although it gives them much pleasure, and the few rich who take pleasure in it won't pay.'

Like any starving Galizianer, he could teach Hebrew—hadn't God given him a gift for verse, a sense of justice? He was a modern man, a writer of poetry. He stood for progress. There would be no rote learning in his classes, just rationalist interpretation. Wasn't spreading the new ideas of political equality, reason, and fraternity one of the Haskalah's great goals? This would also be the perfect opportunity to emphasize the beauty of the Hebrew language. So Velvel the poet sought work as a Hebrew teacher.

---

61 Nonetheless, like many Romanian liberals, Kogălniceanu advocated anti-Semitic policies such as the expulsion of Jews from the countryside, and referred to the community with the insulting jidani. Accused, by his contemporaries, of a secret attachment to the Talmud, he later objected to the expulsion of Jewish scholar Moses Gaster, conferred citizenship on the Russian-born Marxist thinker Constantin Dobrogeanu-Gherea, and endorsed the Jewish scholar, linguist and Maskil, Lazar Seineanu.

62 *Kokebe Yizhak*

63 Velvel paid to have all of his own work printed.

Again, he was thwarted: 'Even the learned tongue God gave me to teach the bible to Israel's sons is no good to me in Moldavia.'

Work was hard to come by. What conventional Jewish school would be willing to hire an impractical Maskil, an idealist who saw himself as an apostle in a foreign land? A man who dressed in the modern way? Here, traditional Jews scorned the enlightened Galicians, dubbing them heretics or 'starving itinerant Poles.' Velvel lashed out, mocking such backwardness:

> *Trash comes here from Poland*
> *No-goodniks, loafers*
> *And lead from the right way*
> *Israel's holy people.*
> *With them comes a backwards written alphabet*
> *They don't learn Talmud*
> *For them, the Bible is better*
> *With commentaries*
> *From Moische[64] the devourer.*

The Hasidic community ruled education with an iron fist, and only traditional melamdim[65] could triumph as teachers. 'Lazy, backward loafers,' Velvel called them. 'Men with a petty shopkeeper's mentality. They use their tongues to brainwash pupils, to triumph over adversaries. They are greedy eaters, voracious drinkers, blind followers of powerful religious dynasties that hate foreign influence and all outsiders.' He again mocked them with satirical verses:

> *I don't like you*
> *You aren't part of my family...*

And these same 'despots in dirty clothes' (clean clothes were

---

64   The mocking Hasidic nickname for Moses Mendelssohn

65   The wealthier the family, the better the teacher. The status and salary of the poorest melamdim were very low.

reserved for the Sabbath), although imbued with religious learning, were deprived of all worldly knowledge:

> *One thing I realize now is that they knew very little themselves and were therefore incapable of accomplishing anything substantial with their students...My first melamed at age eight was a tall and broad man called Mordecai Abba... He barely maintained peace with his wife, who was a calm and quiet person. He would curse her and insult her in the worst possible way...The worst curses I ever heard in my life came from this rebbe...Every quarter or half-hour, he would select a different boy and seat him at his left hand (the ruler never left his paw). That poor boy! Aside from whacking students with his ruler, Mordechai Abba had a habit of pinching. And because one cannot pinch at a distance, he would unleash all of his wrath and fury upon the boy currently seated at his left. On more than one occasion, the boy would let out such big gasping sobs that it was difficult to quiet him down...[66]*

How could Velvel teach the beauty of Hebrew to fifteen students in one single lesson while fending off the attacks and accusations of both pupils and parents?

> *He works his legs off*
> *And has no money*
> *He's just another*
> *One of the writers,*
> *A miserable rogue.*

Eventually, the leaseholder of a wine bar just outside Botoşani hired him as a private tutor to his two boys. It was an agreeable situation. Velvel taught for only a few hours each day; the boys were intelligent, and he liked them; the house was tidy and pleasant; and he had his own room where he ate,

---

66 Margoshes, *A World Apart.*

slept, studied, and wrote poems. Life did lack adventure and passion, but this was a time of apprenticeship, one in which he sharpened wit and tongue, honed argument.

Like any poor Jewish scholar, Velvel was invited to dine with the family on the Sabbath and holy days. On one such a comfortable evening, confident and relaxed by much wine, Velvel dared sing a few of his own poems and saw, with great pleasure, how his words and melodies moved those around him. Laughing, crying, they cheered him on and clamoured for more. What a success! What a heady triumph, even though small and domestic.

He took to walking into Botoşani at night, going to inns and taverns, joining in the talk, but he didn't fit in. He was unconventional, scornful of fanaticism, and contemptuous of hypocrisy. His wit was too incisive, his ideas were too radical, and his loquacious brilliance played him tricks. Those around him considered him slightly mad. 'Go talk to the walls,' they jeered. Unable to conform, to squeeze himself into the mould of a socially acceptable character, he became a nineteenth-century archetype: a melancholic, rejected by society and as isolated as any romantic hero; a rationalist who, having discarded theological conventions and established norms, is trapped in a world of superstition.

Banishing any remaining provincial Galician mannerisms, he became an elegant figure in a bow tie, white shirt, vest, and short jacket. He perfected his German, read Schiller and Goethe. He defied those who believed that modern dress, foreign language, secular subjects, and individual thought were signs of Satan's intervention, or that the night's whistling, moaning, and creaking were devils afoot; who accused you of sorcery if you jotted down an address; who believed illness was the evil eye's doing and exorcism its cure; who, as protection against malevolent spirits, never stayed in a house without a *mezuzah*[67] on the doorpost and tightly shut

---

67 A parchment inscribed with Hebrew verses and contained in a decorated case.

doors and windows. Those who perverted sweet lullabies into terrified exhortations:

> *Go, my child, to cheder*
> *Learn the Torah always.*
> *Learning by tradition,*
> *Will protect you from the evil eye.* [68]

Those who never doubted that the pipe-smoking, whip-snapping Satan could spring from behind the oven at any moment in his brand-new disguise: as a Maskil, a *Deutsch*.

---

68 Rubin, *Voices of a People.*

Chapter X:
Botoşani

Singing for your supper is incredibly hard work.

Velvel Zbarzher

*T*he Suceava train station is another splendid palace, although its vast and graceful waiting hall is closed to the public these days. We travellers hunch together in the frigid wind tunnel corridor or stamp our frozen feet on the less crowded quay outside. A two-carriage train from some hinterland has just pulled in. Its doors open, and thirty or so passengers debark. Almost all are Roma women with tiny babies. The colours of the women's flowered scarves covering their long braids are faded; their flowing skirts are tired. Nine in the morning and, like any factory hand or office worker, they have 'punched in' and now set out separately to comb the city's streets and beg. They'll meet again at the station this evening, then catch the train home.

Botoşani, at the end of the line, is not the way I imagined it would be. Did I think I would see a main street of single-storey shops? That I would find the Jewish quarter, an inn, an old wine bar, a cellar where workers once gathered and

Velvel sat? Truly? Did I, once more, believe it would fit old descriptions?

> *The Jewish street...looked as strange as a piece of hieroglyphic writing set in the moonlight. Rows of small, poor houses, placed in monotonous, dull lines, like the laws of the Pentateuch, or colourful as the torn and worn clothes and stuff in the bag of the Jew.*[69]

The enthusiastic and friendly woman ticket seller in the station sends me hiking through the deep snow after I ask for the whereabouts of the synagogue—I have to start somewhere in my search for Velvel. I end up standing in front of a monastery: she'd been certain this is what I wanted. There's nothing else in this calm suburb, just some oldish houses, more new pretentious ones, a few Ceausescu-era blockhouse creations, and a line-up of abandoned, ruined factories, home to packs of sad, shivering and beautiful stray dogs.

I stop a woman on the street. 'Is there a synagogue near here?'

'In Botoşani? Certainly not. There never has been. In Oneşti, yes. Not here.'

Oneşti? Who's she kidding? That's at least a hundred and fifty kilometres away, and there were once plenty of synagogues in Botoşani. In 1930, there were still 728,000 Jews living in Romania: fifty-one per cent died in the Holocaust, and after mass immigration, largely to Israel, there are three and a half thousand in the country today. There must be more than one trace of the old community. So I trail around disconsolately in the snow for a while, find nothing, then retreat to the bus station (it's comforting to know there's a way out of here) and see a map on the wall. There's still a synagogue, all right, in quite another part of town, a trolley car ride away.

---

69 Eminescu, *Iconostas si fragmentarium*. Mihai Eminescu born in Botoşani in 1850 is considered one of Romania's great national poets. Reactionary, anti-Semitic, he opposed granting citizenship to Romania's Jews.

Roaring traffic, long avenues of glass and metal buildings, shabby high-rise housing, fast food boutiques (outside one kebab emporium two men glare at the busy hamburger outlet a few doors down. One mutters sourly: 'burgers, burgers...'). Here and there, a rare old house or graceful building has, by miracle or bureaucratic oversight, escaped destruction. But I'm unable to locate the synagogue: how does one navigate such sameness? I try asking passers-by for directions, but they must think I'm just another scrounger, a panhandler and, annoyed, they push past me.

I come across two men shouting at each other—at least they aren't moving around much and I can question them. They stop arguing. One nods when I mention the synagogue, wriggles his fingers, indicates I'm to follow. He, a sly and tricky-looking fellow, sets out at a murderous pace; I, slithering about on the ice and flapping my arms, am several meters behind. At one point, muttering to himself, looking about in confusion, he stops, calls someone on his cell phone. Then we're off again on our mad run, follow-the-leader through the urban ugliness and into a parking lot.

And here it is. The synagogue. Almost two hundred years old and squashed against a straggle of high-rise squalor. My crafty character peeks nervously over his shoulder, tells me a friend has a key but isn't around at the moment.

'He'll come later. Perhaps. At around three o'clock. You can wait if you want. He'll be here...maybe.' He shifts, uncomfortable, then with a backward wave, trots out of sight.

The 'perhaps' and 'maybe' are still hanging in the air. Three o'clock is hours away, and there's little chance I'll see the interior of this old building with its painted scenes of Jerusalem, its signs of the zodiac on the ceiling. Behind the synagogue's chain link fence, the snow is unbroken. With those smashed windows up near the roof, the interior will be chilly indeed. No one has been in there for quite a while.

Of the surrounding Jewish community, there is only one house left. Is the scar on its doorpost from a vanished mezuzah? What about the modern tavern across the road? It looks a bland place, far too featureless to be an historic inn. Followed by a diminutive but vicious ankle-nipping spotted cur, I circle the building. One part is rather old. Does its age, along with its position, mark it as having once been Jewish-owned? If, long ago, Velvel drank and whiled away the night in there, I'll never know. I return to the closed synagogue.

'If Velvel shows up, tell him I was looking for him,' I call out to no one.

But I doubt he'll be back.

***

*W*as it in a tavern that Velvel found his feet, or in some private house? Stories vary.[70] Some told how, in Botoşani's bars where craftsmen and workers met, Velvel would sit silently (had he given up the frustrating game of useless argument?) imbibing a considerable quantity of wine. Then, seemingly out of the blue, something quite magical would happen.

You can just picture it. We've all met such people once or twice in a lifetime, seen them in some public place—in a restaurant, bar, waiting room, or train compartment. Attention catchers, natural entertainers, sparkling improvisers, they never spout other peoples' chewed-over jokes. Word masters and idea twisters, at some point (perhaps remaining seated or standing, as if on a stage) they'll say something—nothing planned or definite, perhaps nothing astounding either— and some strange magic begins. Soon everyone in the joint is laughing, turning this way and that in their seats, sucked in, included in the patter, the puns, the joy, the natural outpouring, the snappy phrases you try to remember afterwards. That's how it must have been with Velvel. Only,

---

70   Half a century later, the writer David Yeshaya Silberbusch gave a fairytale version of Velvel's debut: it took place in a wealthy private home, he wrote: There, well oiled by good food and fine wine, Velvel sang to the other guests, and when he returned home, he found his pockets filled with golden ducats.

instead of just laughing, people wanted to copy him, write down what he said and keep it for posterity.

Velvel soon understood that this talent for words, when coupled with his wonderful singing voice, could be the perfect vehicle for spreading Haskalah ideas. So, with witty biting satire, he began poking at superstition, the ghetto lifestyle, the ignorance and outlandish practices of the Hasidic rebbes and their blind followers. His words appealed greatly to those gathered around him: the workers discriminated against in the religious world, and those who, less imbued with cant, sought a spokesman. Someone would introduce a subject—any would do—and with Velvel's tongue loosened by wine, the Yiddish songs would pour forth in endless succession.

***

Yiddish songs? The Yiddish language? That was a problem, all right. Singing in Yiddish was degrading. Velvel claimed it put him on the same level as a badkhn, that backwoods jester, that representative of the traditional world he'd fled. Yiddish tinged his words with whining Broderzinger entertainment. All the Maskilim agreed: Yiddish wasn't noble. It was only a cheap patois, not a language. It was the code babble of the lowest classes: the beggars, schnorrers, thieves, and smugglers. Its vulgar tones conjured up narrow shtetl streets, shameful characters, and culturally backward Hasidic cousins. To end anti-Semitism, Jews needed to integrate, use official, respectable languages: Polish, German, Russian, Romanian, and Hebrew. German was the main language of the 'new' Jew, but Velvel's loyalty still lay with Hebrew, the pearl of the Jewish people:

> *Oh you holy flower*
> *Always young and beautiful*
> *Only the ignorant*
> *Can't understand you.*
> *And when I'm lost*

When my soul is asleep
You hit me with your glow
And bring me new strength.

However, Hebrew hadn't gained much favour. How many people could understand and converse fluently in that language? Only men who'd attended cheder and the Talmudic schools, and their Hebrew was stiff, biblical. Even Velvel had to admit Hebrew wasn't yet a modern language to be used in front of an audience or in daily life. 'Hebrew is lonely and drowsing,' he said, 'but her heart beats, her lips move, her sound can still be heard.' He would never abandon her; she had a wonderful future: 'She will be loved again.'

Yet, Yiddish was a familiar chum. Sparkling, alive, it was the idiom of jokes, of haggling, gossip, and insult. It was the language of the cradle, the table, the workshop, and the street; it was the spoken and written language of Jewish women who, because their lives revolved around family and home, knew no Hebrew. Popular literature was written in Yiddish, as well as moralistic Hasidic tales and personalised prayers. Foreign novels had been translated into Yiddish to broaden the horizons of those who might never leave their shtetl; Joachim Heinrich Campe's travel stories and his adaptation of *Robinson Crusoe* provided information on natural phenomena and geography; *Slavery*, Isaac Meir Dick's 1868 adaptation of *Uncle Tom's Cabin*[71] was a particular success. Yiddish couldn't be abandoned. To educate the people, it had to be employed in tracts, newspapers, books, and plays denouncing injustice, ignorance, and poverty. What a paradox! Using Yiddish while persuading the masses to reject it.

Velvel continued to steep himself in German and Hebrew Haskalah literature, to refine his manners, and to behave with all the elegance of an enlightened man (although this last met with mitigated success, for some found him unpleasant and

---

71   In Dick's version of Harriet Beecher Stowe's book, the good master is
     Jewish, and the Negro slaves all convert to Judaism.

rough.) And in martyred self-sacrifice, he dressed his muse in two sets of clothing: the purest Hebrew and a vernacular Yiddish, not the day's fashionable Germanised Yiddish that was trying, so desperately, to show moral superiority.[72] And slowly, as the years passed, he, too, came to love the language he'd once scorned.[73]

***

*V*elvel's fame grew by word of mouth. By 1858, he had become a fully-fledged professional wandering minstrel, a troubadour, a bard, and although he never stooped to perform at weddings, he, mockingly, dubbed himself a badkhn. Ever faithful to his devoted public of workers and craftsmen in the lowest bars and inns, he'd down bottles of wine and extemporise on any proposed subject.

Although controversial and analytical, he never forgot that Jewish society had given him his social and intellectual values, his artistic standards. His ancient synagogal melodies were mixed with satirical laughter and the ghetto's supplications; his poetry, exposing all sides of each argument, was Talmudic pilpul;[74] and his humanistic God had an excellent sense of humour:

> *God sits on his chair*
> *Not far from paradise*
> *The many zaddikim come*
> *And want to speak with him*
> *What do you want, my children,*
> *What is it you don't understand?*
> *And each supplicant*

---

72 There were no set rules for Yiddish; linguists had not yet distinguished its distinct variations. Written phonetically, writers used the patterns of their native regions.

73 In his book, *Makal No'am*.

74 Hair-splitting casuistic argumentation used by Jewish scholars and much employed by the Maskil educator Joseph Perl.

States his request
With unbowed head
Each standing in place.
And God looks at them all
Smiles, but doesn't say a word.

***

I'm in a low bar soaking up mulled red wine. It's a seedy place, everyone sitting mutely at his or her table. I'm not the only woman present; an even more elderly lady is ensconced in the stairwell's shadow. High on the wall, a television is tuned to a station with traditional music, and Gypsy musicians hammer at cimbaloms or make fiddles weep. Up there, in a fantasy world of carved wooden houses and primeval forests, famous songsters warble traditional tunes, swaying mixed choruses trill, and dancers whirl. All wear traditional Romanian costumes. A handsome husband in a loose white shirt and black vest smiles adoringly at his exquisite full-skirted wife; an elderly couple, ever in love, are holding hands; here comes the jaunty son, axe slung over his shoulder, singing as he struts past blue-hazed mountains.

Where can I find that quaint and mythical Romania? Only in a television studio or at one of the country's uninhabited ethnological museums. Oddly enough, the music is not synchronised with the action: the singer's lips, the musicians' gestures, have nothing to do with what we're hearing. The sound is right, though, and from time to time, the drink-sodden men in the bar bestir themselves, whistle, and slap their thighs.

One man signals to me from a table across the room. He's evidently quite drunk, yet a handsome fellow, nonetheless, with his broad grey handlebar moustache and large head. I ignore his signalling, but he's quite determined to offer me a drink. I refuse with a smile, show that conversation is impossible—I know only a little Romanian. But he is charmed.

And straight away everyone perks up. The blowsy female

bartender is on my side; the men at neighbouring tables look cheerily at me, discuss me with one another, also offer me drinks. The atmosphere becomes decidedly merry, and all gather around my table to wait. For what? For my stories? Am I to be the traveller who regales the enthusiastic company with tales of foreign parts? With adventures of the high road? With a poem or two? A song?

I can't, even in my little way, emulate Velvel. What words can I use? Yiddish was the passepartout language in his day; you could travel all over Eastern Europe on its wings. But no longer. So I remain in my seat, smiling blandly. Stupidly and ineptly silent.

Chapter XI:
Inns

I went into the inn...My nose received the first greeting. As I arrived on the doorstep, that poor organ was assaulted by the sharp bitter odour of alcohol, tobacco and sweat all mixed together. After my nostrils showed their appreciation for this welcome by sneezing noisily as was their habit, it was the turn of my ears to be solicited. They were assailed by a mixture of high, shrill, deep, hoarse, bellowing voices that rolled in with deafening effect. Then after the nose and ears had had enough to keep them happy, my eyes got into action in the semi-dark...On the side, two drunks held onto each other and threw insults—probably because they loved each other. Near them, was a barefoot woman wearing a short dress and low cut embroidered blouse. She seemed very happy and hit them on their shoulders good-naturedly all the while telling them, laughingly, to come home. But the two drunks continued to be affectionate, and ended up by falling on the floor in one mass...The last figure to emerge from the fog was that of a lively woman, strong, with furry beauty marks on her face and her head covered by a scarf. It was the wife of the inn-keeper in person who busied herself amongst the barrels, handling the bottles,

glasses, carafes, crowns of bagels and boiled eggs, dried fish
and pieces of cooked liver. Her mouth never ceased moving,
her hands were never still, and she complained without
cease.

Mendele Moïcher Sforim, 1865

*L*et's stop for a minute, think about inns and low bars.
Examine Sol Liptzin's sentence one more time, the one
that started me out on Velvel's trail, sent me on this quest:

Zbarzher...might well have attained the pinnacle of fame...if
he had not squandered his talent in disreputable Rumanian
inns and Turkish coffeehouses.

Let's take the word, disreputable: disreputable how? Why?

All the inns are kept by Jews, and both these and the post-
houses are always situated in the public squares, which
occupy the centre of every town. The squares are also the
market places for horned cattle, and have never been cleansed
since their first formation: hence they are quagmires of filth,
the putrid effluvia from which are almost insufferable.[75]

In all the towns and villages through which I've passed, I've
sought those bygone murky places where sour cabbage
ponged in barrels, and the stench of alcohol mixed with sweat
and the smoke from clay pipes. I want to sit in an old shenk
with walls of glazed mud, occupy a rickety chair at a lame
table, watch the drink-sodden hack furniture to bits, and
smash crockery. I want to join those drinking endless glasses
of tea, schnapps, beer, or wine; I want to relish the innkeeper's
bagels, boiled eggs, dried fish, cooked liver, sour black bread,
herring, homemade buns, doughnuts, and cheese.

---

75   Shoberl, *Austria; containing a Description of the Manners, Customs, Character*
      and Costumes.

What I wouldn't give to be watching the lively show, rubbing elbows with peddlers, brigands, tattered cranks with paint box and crayons in hand, and itinerant poets. I want to see provocative women smacking their lips over glasses of acidic red wine, rascals with fingers as knotty as a hawk's claws, with eyes that are small, hard, and savage. I want to sit in Yekhezkel Kotik's[76] doubtful taverns where clients are ragged, mottled, ugly, talkative, mirthless, hook-nosed, solitary or ruminative. I want to hear loud discussions in disparate languages, the clatter of dice and dominoes. I'll wait for the blind musician, a gaunt hatless fellow with shaggy black locks, who will sing sorrowful tunes of yearning, play his fiddle, move, trance-like, from side to side. At two in the morning, he'll receive his collection, depart, and the grubby innkeeper will close the shutters. And in the morning, we will begin the day with dominoes and dice.

Now, tell me: how disreputable do such places sound? Wouldn't you like to see all that too? Have a peek?

Yes, some inns were wretched: the wretchedly poor kept them. Those on the open road were said to be the worst— little more than shoddy hovels with oiled paper or bladder windows, where walls were smudged black by the hands of the inebriated, and low ceilings were stained by tobacco. Where doors remained open to dispel the stench. In such places, guests slept on the floor, on tables, or on the barn's straw, curled together with dogs, cats, farm animals, and vermin. Those unlucky enough to find a bed claimed they stank abominably: far better to pull into the safety of the inn's yard and sleep in one's own coach:

This black Podolian earth, so black it looks blue from afar, and so sticky that once it gets a grip on a carriage or a human being it clings on like a leech and won't let go...Through three long, vast nights the moon rose up from behind the gigantic pines and lit my way, but there was nowhere I could have a wash,

---

76 Kotik, *Journey to a Nineteenth-Century Shtetl.*

*for to wash in those inns, on those clay floors, to step out of the
carriage on to those forecourts full of rubbish and antediluvian
mud, would have been dirtier than not washing at all.*[77]

But vermin, lice, and bedbugs were a fact of life everywhere,
and even Victor Hugo complained of their presence in French
country inns:

*Oh diabolic foul inn, hotel of fleas
Where skin, in the morning, is covered with red bites
Where the kitchen stinks
Where one sleeps uncomfortably
Where the travelling salesmen sing all night.*[78]

Besides, all those negative descriptions come down to us from
foreign travellers, and they were always apt to exaggerate,
sneer in a superior way:

*Happy...is the traveller, the dimensions of whose carriage
admit of his occupying it during the night what abominations
will he not escape!...From the centre of the roof of these
houses is always suspended a large brass chandelier, with
seven branches: this is the Sabbath lamp, which is regularly
lighted every Friday evening at sun-set, when all the fires
are carefully extinguished, and not re-kindled till the same
hour the next evening. Underneath it stands a long table
soiled with grease, occupying the middle of the apartment;
around it are ranged several wooden benches; with one
or two rotten chairs, and a cushion stuffed with hay...The
best food to be found in these inns is nearly as disgusting to
strangers as the lodging they afford.*[79]

Inns and taverns were the hub of life. They were islands of
capitalistic activity in a feudal environment; they were open

---

77 Krasinski, cited by Maczak, *Travel in Early Modern Europe.*

78 Cited by Burnand, *La Vie Quotidienne en France en 1830.*

79 Shoberl, *Austria: Manners, Customs, Character and Costumes.*

windows to the world. Here people met: Christians, Jews, the religious, and the renegades. Travellers brought tales of faraway places. Business deals were conducted here; gossip, that preferred human activity, was passed on; marriages were arranged, politics discussed, and friendships cemented. In such places, musicians, actors, and storytellers performed, and everyone mixed with the innkeepers—many were women, for men only lent a hand on Sundays, the busiest day—and told them their secrets.

An inn or shenk was home, was home away from home, was a place of escape. It was the link between peasant and Jew and the happy hunting ground of missionaries and prostitutes. After weddings or funerals, all came to the inn to celebrate or drown sorrows, and since Hasidism endorsed alcohol-induced joy, the most excessive drinkers could be rebbes.

Innkeepers sold knickknacks, rope, thread, and other supplies; some stored agricultural products, waited for prices to rise and advanced credit—although a too-successful innkeeper was blamed for local poverty and drunkenness.[80] Most inns were scrupulously clean, and wooden tables were scrubbed until they shone. Only anti-Semitic scorn made them tawdry:

When we crossed the threshold [of Avrum the Jew's inn] a stench made up of all the emanations on this earth pierced me through my brains: you would not have been competent to say whether it smelled of earth, of rotten eggs, of rancid fat, of salty fish, of un-tanned leather, of hot cheese, of brine cabbage...it smelled of none of these, and yet it smelled of all at once and more...I have nonetheless my nose to praise for having suffered with heroism this pestilential stench, without least of all smirching.[81]

---

80 Jewish innkeepers, propinacja, who had paid extortionate fees to the nobles, made inns profitable businesses. But they were not responsible for the peasant's tendency to resolve problems with alcohol: the nobles profited financially from high alcohol consumption and a befuddled peasantry.

81 Hogaş, *Pe Drumuri de Munti.*

***

I am in a modern inn where dinner and tooth-curdling wine are available. It is a place of flashing strobes, cement pillars, and orange miracle-material tablecloths, where ceramic bathroom tiles creep up the flesh-pink walls. For listening pleasure, four amplifiers hurl out the um-cha-cha of a sour man slapping at a synthesiser. The other clients, shrill young women and barking men, are seated at one long table. Is it an office or engagement party? An anniversary? One couple gets up to stiffly wriggle on the dance floor (in her exceedingly high, spike-heeled boots, the woman can do little else).

Then, without warning, the unsmiling musician snaps off the strobe lights, shuts down the synthesiser, and leaves the room. Expressionlessly, the howling revellers fetch their coats and disperse into the night. I sit in the unaccustomed silence, the only customer. Through an open doorway, the waitresses and a cook dawdle in front of a television. In some distant place, an invisible clock chimes beautifully.

I come back out into the night, walk through the snowy streets, leave the city behind me. I'm alone out here, and the only sound is that of ice creaking under my boots. Am I following in Velvel's footsteps? Could he have taken this same turning?

Look! Here's a building far along the main road. Long, low-lying, it is adorned with the elegant cornices of the nineteenth century and, at each end, bricked up depressions were once double doors wide enough to admit carriages. No doubt about it: this was a former inn. A shenk. The real thing! Perhaps this is where Velvel came, where men gathered to hear his stories.

There's an abrupt click, a hum, a buzz. Somewhere a switch has been pulled, and gaudy lights begin flashing from the roof edge. This building, gutted, has become a vulgar nightclub, a disco. The name on its fluorescent mauve sign sends out the brash affirmation of modernity: Las Vegas.

Chapter XII:
Fame

I heard a poor man complain all day,
Too heavy the load that on him lay.
'I cannot breathe, I am bent in two,
What does the Lord want me to do?'
But everyone who saw him said, 'Hey,
You must be crazy or your senses are astray.
You aren't bound, I see no ropes or chain,
And where's the heavy load, as you complain?'
'Listen then,' he said, 'I'll make it clear.
On my poor back I carry sixty years.
I carry loneliness and want upon my head,
And my great worry—how to make my bread
'And round my neck I bear the yoke
Of the laws of the land that stifle and choke.
A heavy lock upon my mouth weighs down my jaws.
I must not speak, though all things I hear.

Velvel Zbarzher

*I*n the late eighteenth century, flowers, birds, animals, insects, all of nature's beauty slipped into the human consciousness with Romanticism. This new appreciation of the natural world's underlying order and harmony was a reaction against the rational ideal, the nascent industrial capitalism and blatant self-interest that were bringing about deprivation in towns and cities, and despoliation of the countryside.

For a Jewish traditional world that prized study in dark rooms, any tribute to nature was dismissed as unworthy, even dangerous. Such contemplation would open the door to the secular world and the threat posed by art, music, drama, and literature. But, for the Maskilim, becoming modern meant adopting such 'Christian' ideas and fitting them into the Jewish identity. If religion no longer directed thought and action, the new Jew needed to think for himself, and an interest in natural phenomena was just another way of appreciating God's omnipotence.

Velvel's nature was a wild garden in which it was the small things that mattered—the soil, worms, and flowers. He mocked the ignorance of financially successful but narrow-minded religious businessmen, those obsessed with money and contemptuous of nature or poetry. Weren't poets richer? Possessions can be damaged or lost, but the poet's wealth can't be touched by fire or water. He might not be able to pay his rent, but he knows his worth, just like any simple herder who:

> *...lets his sheep graze*
> *And sings a song*
> *He sleeps sweetly*
> *And eats with appetite*

Yet even Velvel's herder mocks the poet's romanticism:

> *'Please help me understand*
> *What you're doing here.*
> *If you want to see animals*
> *There are far more of them in the city.'*

His poet sighs:

> *'Ah, if only I could tame my animals,*
> *As you do yours.*
> *But mine scream more loudly,*
> *Then do as they want.'*

***

*A*s Velvel's reputation grew, he travelled to Jassy (now Iaşi), Roman, Galatz, and Bacau, where new admirers crowded into the local 'low' bars to hear him. Soon, he was able to earn a considerable sum of money, but it seldom reached his pocket. Uncontrollable, good-hearted and generous, he shared what he had with the poor, with anyone with a good tale of woe, with barflies, sly hangers-on, and so-called best chums. He was rarely able to pay for his breakfast.

He was equally reckless with his words. Too drunk to note them down, his companions did the job for him, and he completed the poems the next day. Friends encouraged him to publish: 'If not published, these songs, these children of your soul, will die, be forgotten.' They also warned of those imitating him: 'You give your songs to ungrateful people, and they are sung and claimed by them too.' They were right. In one venue, when Velvel sang his words and melodies, the jeering crowd accused him of stealing another performer's work.[82]

As with any star, all wanted a rub of his glow. Many (apocryphal) stories about Velvel abounded—how someone

---

82 He eventually paid to publish five volumes of poems in both Hebrew and Yiddish. His first poem was published in *Kokhve Yitzhak* in Vienna in 1848. *Hazon le-mo'ed*, (The Time Has Not Yet Come) a satire on the Hasidim was published in Iaşi in 1855. *Makel No'am* (The Stick That Beats Lightly) Yiddish songs with a Hebrew translation, *Makel Hovlim* (The Stick that Hits) and Hebrew poems, *Sefati Yeshenah* (My language is sleeping) were published in Lemberg, Przemysl and Vienna between 1865 and 1878. In 1874, his Hebrew poem *Romanyah*, (This is a Book of the History of Romania for Eternal Shame,) appeared in *Ha-Shahar* and was dedicated to the Alliance Israélite.

had met him, heard him sing, talked to him, touched him, or enticed him with an offer of wine. The journalist H. S. Streitman told one such tale seventy years later:

I was five years old, and playing before the house when I noticed a stranger had entered the shop accompanied by two of our neighbours, Esrig and Kahane. My father, one of the leading scholars of the town, led the guests into my room, and he was very excited. Undoubtedly, something unusual was happening. A few moments later, the enigma was solved. Father, addressed the stranger, saying: 'Say something, Reb Velvel.'

Our guest was none other than Velvel Zbarzher, miraculous troubadour of those times, who, when offered wine and the goodwill of listeners, let loose his wonderful voice and inexhaustible verve. Father had taken care to prepare a great bottle of wine and Velvel Zbarzher began reciting verses, then singing. I was impressed by his appearance: he had a massive head, and although cleanly shaven, a few thick white hairs adorned his chin. That evening, Velvel Zbarzher told his famous joke:

'When I came to Moldavia,' he said, 'the first thing that struck me was that Jews went into and came out of certain businesses as if they were synagogues. Puzzled, I also entered into one of those shops. Great was my surprise when, for twelve copper coins, I was given a glass of wine which, in Poland, would have cost at least a florin. Well, I said, here's a way to save money. So I ordered another glass and then another. Each time I did, I won some more coins. After an hour of drinking, I had accumulated a great profit—more than ten gulden, and that, without having had even one florin in my pocket. Since then, I carry out these operations daily.'

After that night, the troubadour so loved by everyone, never came to our city, Piatra Neamţ, again. He was expelled from Romania shortly after.[83]

Can we trust Streitman? Could this story really be a childhood memory? Would a five-year-old understand such a complex joke? Even the date is incorrect: Velvel was expelled from Romania in 1874, and Streitman was born in 1873. Although still admired by some, Streitman was a curious and wavering character. Socialist, then virulently anti-communist, his political ambitions were hindered by anti-Semitism, yet he was friendly with those in anti-Semitic circles. He converted to Christianity, returned to Judaism, was appointed chairman of the Central Jewish Office created to carry out the Final Solution from February to December 1942.[84] He later became a revisionist Zionist. Trustworthy or not, he has given me a precious lead: Velvel was in Piatra Neamţ? That's where I'll go. I'll catch him yet.

***

*W*here did Velvel stay? Would he have lodged with friends, other Maskilim, or did he sleep in the back rooms of inns, hotels, or in rooming houses? How did he travel? With no rail lines, he must have taken simple wagons. Larger carriages—heavily laden vehicles—sank hopelessly into the mud on the notoriously bad roads that were impassable in winter and early spring. There were other

---

83   Streitman *Adam*, 1938, translation from Romanian by Irene Ehrenkranz Fishler. The article begins: 'during a conversation, our precious collaborator Mr. Streitman, described from memory the colourful figure of Velvel Zbarjer. We have recorded, with as great a fidelity as possible, Streitman's rich story.'

84   According to Michael Marrus in *The Nazi Holocaust*, Streitman limited his pro-Nazi actions to articles in the Jewish paper, *Gazeta Evreiasca*, and exhorting Jews to be loyal to the regime. He was replaced by the equally ambitious but more powerful Dr Nandor Ghingold, another Jew who had converted to Catholicism.

dangers, too: robbers, swarms of beggars, and impoverished soldiers all survived at a traveller's expense. There were few bridges, and rivers had to be crossed by small ferry or raft, and raftsman was often a Jewish occupation.

Perhaps the best way to proceed was by boat, and the Siret River flows southward from the Carpathians, passes through Roman, Bacau, and Galatz—all are towns in which Velvel sang. Could flat-bottomed sailing scows or pole-pushed punters once have navigated its waters, carrying goods, cattle, and passengers down to the Danube? These days, the broad Siret, far too shallow to be troubled by craft, slips, almost sluggishly, between sandy banks. I can only journey on by rail.

The train to Piatra Neamţ, another end-of-the-line city, is a rattling old thing. Fellow passengers, humble-looking peasants in dun coats, mite-chewed fur hats, or formless woollen caps, all chat endlessly and obnoxiously into their smartphones or check for e-mail. The bloated woman across from me, she who chooses literature as her entertainment, reads of Jennifer Lopez' latest antics in a lurid carmine, puce, and teal scandal sheet.

We pass more gutted factories and small villages with a few authentic houses, cherished and adorned. Most, however, have been modernised with PVC and cement. Here, too, are snow-covered expanses where lonely shepherds are in place: do they also possess smartphones and an Internet connection? Again, their dogs abandon duty to chase our machine. There are other dogs out there, too. Guard dogs are tethered to cruelly short chains: their life span is five paces wide. As for homeless beasts, free but unfed, they trot through the snow, hope for a treat, a meal, a friendly encounter with canine mates while avoiding kicks, thrown stones, bullets, poison, and speeding cars.

At the approach to Piatra Neamţ, large, elegant houses climb up the mountainside but the city centre is again discouraging: roaring cars, the ubiquitous advertising panels, cement and glass buildings, commercial centres. Yes, I should know better than to expect a quaint area of wooden houses and Transylvanian forests, but this urban sameness is soul wearing.

One building has a sign reading, Tourist Information, but it's merely a lure. Inside the small communist-era shopping mall, there's no further chitchat of tourism. I enter a bar, ugly and modern, with a hostile waitress and a large screen television showing soft pornographic video clips featuring huge-bottomed women in stretch elastic. Two men, dark and sinister-looking hoodlums of some sort, beautifully and expensively dressed, are hunched together at a table, having a *sotto voce* conversation. With my usual ghastly mixture of odd Romanian words, French and pidgin, I accost them: do they know where the synagogue is?

Astounded, they stare at me: who the hell am I? What do I really want? Then look at each other, amused. Tell me to take a seat. Order me a coffee. And, albeit disturbing-looking, they come up trumps. One begins making phone calls. 'To the city's Jewish leaders.'

I can hardly believe my ears. 'You know them?'

Both look scornful. 'It's our business to know who everyone is,' says the older man, the one with a deeply scarred cheek. (An old knife wound? A bullet hole?) He hands me his phone.

But the president of the Jewish community is impatient. To him, I'm just another tourist, a nobody. No, he can't see me today. He's busy. There's an important meeting. They're waiting for the arrival of a television crew. If I want to see the synagogue, I'll have to come back tomorrow. I'm not here tomorrow? Too bad. He breaks off the connection.

The two men look at me with pity. They, too, consider me a nobody, a loser: probably well-armed, they'd never accept such cavalier treatment or an unequivocal 'no'.

'This part of the world...' says the younger man and waves a dismissive hand. 'People in Piatra Neamţ all think they're superior. That makes them unfriendly. But they're fools. There's no work, and there's no money here either.'

'All those big houses on the outskirts?'

'Black market money.' He grins, proud to be part of that illegal microcosm.

'We do business with all of Europe,' says the other.

In the end, Scarface offers to drive me to the synagogue. Should I be wary? Should I hesitate before clambering into that man's large, black mafia Mercedes? Should I question his motives or think I'm taking a risk in this country where I know no one? Without hesitation, I make myself comfortable in the passenger seat. With my second-hand clothes, white hair, and wrinkles, I could be someone's low-income granny: definitely not white slavery material.

We slalom over black ice and deep snow for a while, then Scarface skids to a sideways halt on a hilly back road. 'Here's your synagogue. And that's the Jewish community office.' He points to a long, low house. 'Go in there.'

'The president said he couldn't see me.'

Scarface shakes his head dolefully. I'm quite a case. 'This is Romania,' he says with patience. 'Just knock on the door, then walk in.'

So I pass the synagogue (there are, in fact, two: the older, in wood, was built in 1776), and go inside the little house—shabby, wonderful—see that the main room is packed with people, a whole noisy unpretentious crowd in coats and boots, sitting on chairs, filling corners, gossiping, waiting for some event. The president I spoke to on the phone, the same man who refused to see me not thirty minutes earlier, is now utterly charming. He invites me into his office with great pomp and honour (so Scarface was right after all) and hands me the book he has written on the Jewish painter, Victor Brauner.

'Jews are very involved in culture in Romania. Not in politics. Sure, the journalists and the politicians make anti-Semitic comments, but in France, where you live, things are worse than in Romania, these days.'

He's never heard of Velvel, and he's never heard of the infamous Streitman either. 'Piatra Neamţ was a worker's town, not a rich community. There were many workers' cafés back then, but there's nothing left. The cafés are gone, the houses, the workshops, the Jewish area. The entire old city was destroyed in what we call Ceaushima, Ceausescu's urban renewal.'[85]

Outside the little office, a few low buildings remain, former shops and houses, but the rest is anonymous, modern, built to government directive. What did Velvel say about transitory fortune? His Shakespearean gravedigger merely sneers:

I earn my little bread
And make a bit of money
Living from death
That's the art.
With her hat, her womanly face,
She laughed at old men
Now the gravestone
Suits her better
She no longer laughs
Although her eye winks.
With his long well-tended hair
The stupid modern man
No longer an elegant courtier
Already stinks like the pest.

---

85   Coined by Romanians, Ceaushima (Ceausescu + Hiroshima) describes the urban destruction.

Chapter XIII:
Expulsion

Gold and silver is your Torah
Money is your God

Velvel Zbarzher

*B*acau's outskirts are like the grim city outskirts anywhere in the modern world: cheap housing, waste-filled rivers, the skeletons of rotting abandoned factories alongside new thrown-together industrial buildings where workers from China, Bangladesh, and the Philippines work long hours for pitiful wages. Refusing such conditions, Romanians abandon their villages, elderly parents, even children, to take up jobs in Spain, France, Germany, any western country.

Downtown, cars roar along broad avenues lined by functional architecture in concrete and glass, and gelid gusts swirl across the vast treeless squares. Pouting young people pass, telephone in hand, fashionably bored. In Bacau, there's still a functioning Jewish community with a synagogue and community centre. I'm able to find them, but on this snowy early evening, doors are locked tight and no one answers my knocking. Only when I'm about to leave does a man round the building. Is he from the Jewish community? Does he speak English? French?

He nods, raises his collar against the cold. 'A little French.'

Has he heard of Velvel Zbarzher, the singer? 'The nineteenth-century poet? He lived in Bacau on and off, sang in the taverns and inns.'

'No. Never heard of him.' The man moves off, impatient to be on his way, to escape the drilling wind. Then turns. 'There have been other famous Jews from Bacau. Marius Mircu, for example. He wrote about Romanian Jewish history and the deportations, but perhaps his work hasn't been translated.'

I head back to the train station; no point in looking for old taverns although there were fifty-five of them in the mid-1800. Aside from churches, there's nothing of the past. I end up in a café, one just like all the others, where brain-deadening video clips howl, and people on cell phones shout over the noise. Sitting at the table next to mine are four interesting-looking women—ostentatiously affluent Roma. Their golden earrings and many bracelets glitter, their long skirts sparkle with gold and silver, and their fringed and flowered scarves are soft and new. They sit gossiping, laughing, sharing a mug of beer.

I want to be let into their circle, understand what they're saying. The longing must be transparent, for they soon notice me, ask where I'm from, invite me to join them. But my language skills are inadequate for anything other than the dullest stab at conversation; never, will I understand the merry secrets behind their chatter.

Eventually, their sleek and elegant men arrive, and soon all sweep back out into the snowy night street, bound for the gaudy, pseudo-baroque palaces they call home. The fortunes of this wealthy elite have been earned by stripping the derelict factories of scrap metal.

*I*n Velvel's day, Bacau was a warren of unpaved back roads lined with small wooden houses and two straight main streets illuminated by candle-lit lanterns. An influx of peasants from impoverished villages as well as modern-thinking Galician Jewish craftsmen, tinsmiths, woodcarvers, and lace makers, contributed to a steady increase in population; and, as in all the growing urban centres throughout Europe and America, this posed problems. Water distribution depended upon water carriers, public fountains, standpipes, and wells, and the only privies were courtyard dung heaps. Garbage and faecal matter were dumped onto the streets where they mixed with the liquid oozing from nearby stables, horse droppings, the excrement of terrified animals being driven to slaughter, and rainwater, before seeping their sludgy way to open sewers and canals.[86] In the poorest houses, several families crowded into one or two fetid rooms that, by day, served as workshops for candle-making, leather-tanning, and the sorting of filthy rags. Lice and bedbugs thrived, and cholera pandemics swept through Europe. Adding to such daily misery, new official anti-Semitic measures were imposed upon the Jewish community.

In 1859, when Alexandru Ioan Cuza, a prominent figure in the 1848 Revolution, became Prince of Moldavia and Walachia, he declared himself willing to emancipate the Jews in exchange for financial compensation. But the Jewish Community failed to seize the opportunity, dithering over the sum to be paid, quarrelling over the necessity of obtaining political rights—the Orthodox claimed citizenship would only encourage modern thought and cause believers to stray from the righteous path.[87]

---

86 The same conditions prevailed in America's new pioneer towns.

87 Only in 1923, did a new Romanian constitution grant civil rights to all inhabitants.

Only a few years later, without rights and without protection, the persecution of the country's Jews began. Bacau's new anti-Semitic mayor drove some from their homes, beat and tortured others. Elsewhere, they were ejected from businesses, forbidden to peddle, run inns, or sell alcohol. Several charges of blood libel were levelled, and they resulted in pogroms in which the police assisted the perpetrators. One group, after proving Romanian birth, was forced across the Danube on a raft, and several drowned.

Velvel was unequivocal: 'Romania is a beggar's bowl of a country. It had needed Jewish linguists to develop its language,[88] to teach Romanians about trade and craft. And how are they rewarded? By being treated as foreigners, by being beaten to death, or being thrown into the Danube: Romania is worse than Russia.'

> *A man with understanding*
> *Has many problems.*
> *Without understanding*
> *He can be a baron in Walachia.*

Yet Moldavia's Jews were partly responsible for the hatred directed toward them, he said. The incoming Galician and Russian businessmen, teachers, traders, and workers made no effort to integrate into Romanian society. They only dreamt of returning to their homeland when they had made enough money. As for the religious, they fiercely defended a way of life no longer valid. Opposed to new learning, they founded no schools, but remained in their dark narrow streets, following religious law to the letter. Such men were not the Maccabee's[89] heroic descendants. Weak, lacking in courage and understanding, they passively accepted persecution

---

88 Some great Romanian Jewish linguists were Lazar Saineanu, Moses Gaster, Heimann H. Tiktin, Moses Schwarzfeld and Alexandru Graur.

89 Leaders of the rebel army that led the successful revolt against the Seleucid Empire in 167–160 BCE.

while nurturing a fairy tale vision of paradise to come:[90]

> *Wait till you see the beautiful expensive chapel*
> *Being built in the rebbe's house,*
> *Which the rebbe will get,*
> *When the Messiah comes.*
> *Not built of stone,*
> *And not of brick*
> *But of sweetmeats*
> *Dainty desserts and cakes;*
> *Brandies will feed the eternal light*
> *And the rostrum will be made from egg cakes*
> *The ground will be tiled with salted fish*
> *The walls smeared with fish sauce*
> *Oh sweet father*
> *Wine and brandy will pour from every corner*
> *And we Hasidim*
> *Will lick the walls.*

As for the Hasidic leaders, egoistic, heartless, they exploited their ignorant followers who showered them with gifts, scrabbled for their leftovers, and gave their last coins for exorcisms and amulets to ward off the evil eye: 'The only effort a rebbe makes is to be born into a wealthy dynasty, and he defends his privilege like a ferocious beast, like a wild ass in the desert':

> *Have they mercy*
> *For those in need?*
> *To orphans and widows*
> *Do they give a piece of bread?*
> *Those who like taking*
> *Have difficulty giving.*

---

90 After the 1905 pogroms in Russia, the poet Bialik attacked the passivity of
    Jewish men who hid while their wives were being raped, then only worried
    that Jewish law might forbid sexual relations with their unclean women.

Leaving the working of miracles to their gabbaim (sextons), the rebbes enjoyed life's juicy fruits, feasting gluttonously, purchasing castles—even entire towns—in Bukovina and Podolia. Accompanied by liveried lackeys, they drove about the countryside in fine carriages pulled by teams of glorious horses. And, said Velvel, how they mocked their gullible disciples:

The poor...
They have no happy faces
They have no strength
They care only about their exile
And look like beggars.
We have no worries
We live happily
Look like aristocrats
And very good Jews
Their wives are dirty
Their noblest
With their head coverings and scarves
Look like evil spirits.
But our women are very chic
They colour their lips
And look like ladies.

***

In 1868, a scandal at the Sadagora Hasidic court gave much delight to the Maskilim and added grist to Velvel's verbal mill. After Ysrael Friedman, a powerful Russian zaddik (spiritual leader) was accused of ordering the execution of two 'informers',[91] he decamped to Galicia, to the town of Sadagora just outside Czernowitz. There, he built a luxurious palace, maintained a court of cantors, choirs, and klezmorim,

---

91 Informers were community members who denounced to the Russian government those who ran unlicensed businesses, refused to pay tax, or avoided military service. Some were idealists hoping to fight corruption; others were corrupt.

and placed his son David upon a golden throne inscribed with the words 'David, King of Israel, lives and endures':

> *We climbed up the stairs, passed through a hall, and found ourselves in a large room in which the ladies of the house were gathered. They were the wife and the daughter of the zaddik, his daughter-in-law, and his niece. I thought I was in the harem of the Sultan of Constantinople. All these women were beautiful, or at least pretty. All looked at us, half surprised, half smiling, with their big, black velvet eyes. All were dressed in silk pyjamas and long kaftans of silk or velvet, which were filled and decorated with precious furs. You could see all the colours and types of fur, squirrel, ermine, marten and sable, yellow and pink silk, green, red and blue velvet. The women wore headbands with precious stones; the girl's plaits were interspersed with pearls.*[92]

However, Friedman's fourth son, Rebbe Beer (nicknamed Bernyu) was of quite another ilk: a studious loner who refused luxury and ostentation, he began keeping company with Maskilim and educated Christians. At age fifty-two, disillusioned with Hasidism, Bernyu abandoned his status as zaddik.

What a furore! The grandson of a great Hasidic apostle had gone over to the godless Maskilim? Fearful of damaging the dynasty's reputation, Bernyu's wife accused him of mental illness and, with the help of Bernyu's brothers, drugged and sequestered the mild rebel. This was too much for the Maskilim to tolerate. The Haskalah writer, publisher, and school director Moshe Orenstein[93] enlisted the help of

---

92 Sacher-Masoch, *Der Alte Pfarrer.*

93 Born in Galicia in 1839, Orenstein, son of an important gabbai at the Sadagora court, dropped religious customs after being exposed to Haskalah ideas. On Yom Kippur, the holiest day of the year with a twenty-five-hour fast, he appeared with a bun in his mouth. Branded an apikores-le'hachis, an apostate who deliberately provokes the community's ire, Orenstein was forced to leave home. He came to Romania, became an educator, and instilled Haskalah ideals in the younger generation of Jews.

the public prosecutor and, with a group of men, went to the house where Bernyu was being held prisoner and released him.

Now what to do with him? Bernyu had become so famous that a great crowd of meddlesome gawkers lurked in the streets, hoping to catch a glimpse of this shy man. Refuge was finally found in Czernowitz, in the home of the lawyer Dr Yehudah Leib Reitman,[94] and the house was put under police protection.

With child-like delight, Bernyu began experiencing heretofore forbidden pleasures: he desecrated the Sabbath, ate non-kosher food, cut his beard, dressed in the modern style, and attended the theatre. Reitman's ten-year-old daughter played piano for him, sang him German songs, taught him German words and how to write his name as Bernhard Friedmann. Enchanted, Bernyu called the child an angel.

But he was only a simple man, and although he did try reading the new literary works Orenstein brought him, Bernyu admitted he didn't understand much. With Orenstein's help, he published a letter in the Jewish press stating he would remain faithful to the Torah and continue to fear God, but his disgust with Hasidism's obscurantism and absurd ritual had resulted in his adoption of Haskalah values. It was time for Judaism to move forward!

Hasidic rivals of the Sadagora dynasty were delighted by Bernyu's defection, and there were violent street brawls with his former followers who ascribed the most implausible reasons for his apostasy: Bernyu was fighting with Satan to hasten the Messiah's coming; a Christian woman, with whom he'd had a love affair, demanded he convert. Others, equally determined to fault a female temptress, singled out Reitman's daughter. They heaped curses on the child's head, compared her singing to a dog's barking or the devil's noise. They appealed to God to make terrible blisters appear on her

---

94 Another former student of Joseph Perl.

fingers, ones that would force her to knock the piano's keys with her elbows.

When questioned, Bernyu only said he was tired of imprisonment within the dynasty, of his wife Sheindel's tyranny, of the gabbaim who had been spying on him for years and controlling everything he wrote.

For the Maskilim, Bernyu was a hero. But their triumph was short-lived. Terrified by thoughts of poverty and dependence upon others, Bernyu began fretting over his fortune, one that had been left in a safety box and was now in his wife's possession. After a mere few months of freedom, he returned to the court at Sadagora. Isolated by his family, he lived in unhappy solitude until his death, six years later.

How did he feel in that semi-imprisonment? Did he regret his return and his weakness? No one knew. Thirty-five years later, his relative, Aharon Matityahu Friedman, also abandoned Hasidism and became an editor and author. He wrote a play about Bernyu, a drama revealing the truth about those last years. But shortly after its completion, Friedman died in a typhus epidemic, and his pious family seized and burnt the controversial drama.

***

*V*lvel portrayed Bernyu as a man caught in the struggle between the truth and the lies of false prophets. Life as a Maskil, an outsider, was a lonely experience, and only the strong could survive it. Lacking that strength, Bernyu had returned to the fold: 'A holy life is comfortable. You can sin as you please, and the brotherhood will cover up for you. Praying, humming, jumping about isn't difficult. Drinking holy schnapps isn't hard work. It's easy to be a rebbe.'

In his poem, God's Bankruptcy, he portrays the various religious figures: the confident rebbe caressing peyes and beard; the *chazzan*[95] holding fat fingers around his throat to strengthen his singing voice; the *shamus*[96] wielding his big lantern; and, flashing their knives, are the ritual slaughterer, the shochet, and the circumciser, the *mohel*. All stand before God and demand to be rewarded with the three hundred and ten worlds, along with the heavens, earths, stars, and planets granted to the righteous.

And God looks at the holy faces
Of this crowd
Perhaps fifty thousand of them,
All with a request.
And he turns his back
And can hardly keep from laughing.
He has no idea
What to do with them.
'How can I pay you all?' asks he.
'Although I'm the great God.
How can I take so many worlds?
I'll come out of it bankrupt.'

So skilful was Velvel's mockery, even Hasidim sang his songs, although without understanding their barb. Those in power weren't duped. Offended by his jabs at their luxury, they denounced him to Romanian government officials so often and with such force, that Velvel's visa was not renewed. After twenty-five years in Romania, he was forced to leave the country.

---

95 Cantor, head singer
96 The beadle

Chapter XIV:
Brody

I, wretched coachman,
My toil is endless...
I play out my best role
And the wind blows away
I, a poor, impoverished watchman
Homeless in the night
Sleep breaks my bones
Am I made of iron?

Berl Broder

O, to have seen Brody in its heyday! A border city between two mighty empires—Imperial Russia and Austrian Galicia—Brody was an important commercial centre. It was also a hot spot, home to spies and smugglers, and bubbling with intrigue. In 1867, when the new Przemysl to Romania rail line passed through this city, the western world finally reached the eastern:

In the omnibus, you find Polish Jews, Bessarabian oxen traders, Russian grain merchants, Silesian businessmen.

*Perhaps here and there can also be found a girl like this pale,
blond shy one in her poor dark clothes... poor child: poverty
has forced her to seek her wretched livelihood as a governess
in some foreign land...The passengers are packed into the
train. Nowhere is space so rare as here...*[97]

In the early nineteenth century, Jews made up between
seventy and eighty per cent of Brody's population, and this
city had long been a stronghold of Jewish humanism. In 1815,
the Maskilim had opened a modern school in which German
was the language of instruction, and there were numerous
Haskalah publishing houses. Mendil Lefin, the father of
the Galician Haskalah, lived here; the influential reformer
Nachman Krochmal was born in Brody; and in 1816, after
being exiled as a heretic from Lemberg, the teacher Isaac
Erter became a doctor and spent his life here, helping the
poor and writing scathing parodies of Hasidism. Joseph
Perl, the founder of Tarnopol's modern school, had been
influenced by Brody's Maskilim, and it was he who appealed
to the Austrian Emperor to help 'wake my Nation from its
deep sleep,' and to close the traditional religious schools
that were no more than 'a place of refuge for vagabonds...
thieves.'

Just over the border in Russia, the nineteenth century's
industrial revolution had created a small class of wealthy
international traders and modern merchants: a great many
were Jewish. This elite enjoyed freedom of movement, and
they passed through Brody on their way to the Leipzig,
Frankfurt, and Breslau fairs. Local innkeepers, to attract their
custom, provided entertainment. Although the rabbinate
condemned all such amusements—Jews were to restrict

---

97 Franzos, *Aus Halb-Asien.*

themselves to songs of devotion and exaltation[98]—such worldly men were largely indifferent to rabbinic disapproval.

One apprentice baker from Brody, Yakova Dubinsky, had done his military service with the Austrian army in Vienna, and while there, had seen café cabaret theatre. He loved it. Why didn't Galician Jews have something as wonderful? Soon enough, he was donning sheepskins, blackening his face, and performing song and dance routines in Brody's inns and cafés.

The act caught on. Yiddish songs, emotional, introspective and humorous, filled a need. Innkeepers began banishing their old shows—magicians, acrobats, tragic moth-eaten trained bears and marmots—and replacing them with Yiddish singers, musicians with violins, and cimbaloms. But it was the folk poet, Berl Broder (formerly Margulis), who made such cabaret routines famous and assembled the first travelling troupe.

Born in 1815 in a nearby village, Margulis was employed in a Brody brush factory. Teaching himself to play the violin, he so amused fellow toilers with clever rhymes, songs, and imitations during working hours, they nicknamed him Berl der Vertizger (the rhymer, the word-player.) He later hit the road as a salesman and, in the roadside inns where he passed the nights, he drank heavily and kept up the show. How everyone howled at his grimacing, gesticulating shtetl characters, his whining shepherds, lonely night watchmen, draymen, cagey moneylenders, wanderers, cantors, and lamenting water carriers.

In 1857, Margulis gave up on brushes altogether, changed his name to Berl Broder and with two singers—a cantor, and a tailor who doubled as costumier—became a professional entertainer in Brody's Gasthaus Pinkus. His Yiddish songs all

---

98 In 1661, the Jewish Council of Vilna banned merry-making and curbed ostentatious wedding festivities. Public drinking, fire dances, and masquerades were forbidden, although the badkhonim were allowed to continue. The only theatrical performances allowed were biblical re-enactments during the Purim festival. Only later were comic elements—caricatures, songs, and dances in the mummer tradition—added.

began with, 'I am a lone and lonely toiler':

> *I am a lone and lonely toiler*
> *I carry loads all day, for I'm a porter*
> *I carry heavy bricks, I carry mortar*
> *Whose body aches as mine does and whose feet?*[99]

The press was scathing, but the act caught on. Broder was no Maskil, his songs were never meant to change the world, but the act was original. Soon, he was being copied by other secular taboo-breaking players, the Broderzinger (Brody singers—the name became generic) who smeared their faces with soot, donned wigs and comic costumes, and with the poems and melodies of bards like Elyokem Tsunzer, Yitskhok Yoyel Linetski, and, of course, Velvel Zbarzher, they sang and danced their one-act scenarios in wine gardens and inns throughout Eastern Europe.

After his expulsion, Velvel also came to Brody, but Berl Broder was long gone. They must have met earlier, in Romania, although Velvel never mentions the encounter. Both were big talkers, heavy drinkers, excessive, and gregarious, and they borrowed each other's words and routines. But if Velvel was still a star, for Broder, things were different. Once so admired and still imitated, he died alone, alcoholic and broke, in Romania in 1868.[100]

By mid-century, Brody was already in decline. Jingoist Polish nationalists were campaigning to replace Jewish merchants with Christian; there was an international financial crisis; suppliers of arms decamped to Romania during the Crimean War of 1853–56, and the Russo-Turkish War of 1877-78. The jolly Broderzinger followed them, eager to start the show in Romania's wine gardens. Even Velvel didn't tarry. He set out for the livelier coffeehouses of Lemberg where Hebrew and Yiddish intellectuals met, conversed, and debated.

---

99   Sandrow, *Vagabond Stars.*

100 Some claimed he died in Jassy, others in Ploieşti, or even Carlsbad.

***

*B*rody again made news in 1881 after Tsar Alexander II's assassination. Jews were falsely blamed for the murder, and pogroms broke out throughout the Russian Pale. New punitive anti-Jewish measures were applied, and Jews poured into Galicia. Brody, the main border crossing, saw thousands arrive daily, and the Alliance Israélite Universelle was besieged by desperate people begging for bread to feed their families, preferring suicide to repatriation:

> *The persecution of Russian Jews continues with violence, ruin and fires...thousands of families leave the country, seek refuge in Austrian territory, particularly in Brody and Lemberg, where the crowding of these unhappy people constitutes a real danger. According to recent information, there were some 6,000 refugees in Galicia and many were camping in the middle of the street since shelter was lacking; only a few days later, there were 7,000 and two thousand were without any resources. Their number increases daily, and it is believed that there are now 12,000...It is urgent to help these people, to provide them with bread and shelter, to send on to America those capable of earning a living, and to end a situation dangerous to the immigrants as well as to public health.[101]*

As many as possible—those without a trade, those thought dirty, or unsuitable—were pushed back over the border; others were sent on to Vienna, to the German cities, even to Turkey, although the Jewish community there protested it was financially unable to accept more. Five hundred men headed for Paris while their wives and children waited patiently in Brody. One arrogant French official at the AIU protested:

> *In no case will I consent to men leaving without their families, especially since such an attempt at rescue seems*

---

101 Bulletin de l'Alliance Israélite Universelle, 1882.

almost blasphemous. You know as well as I that Polish or Russian Jews are not in the least frightened by the idea of bigamy, and one shouldn't give them the opportunity to indulge in it.[102]

Some suggested separating children from their parents and redistributing them amongst other families, a plan rejected as economically unviable. Another problem was the great number of desperate Galicians posing as Russians and hoping to be sent west: there was no AIU statute to help Galicians.

***

I wander through Brody's streets. Could this have been the market where Jews traded? Where are the old inns and cafés, the wine bars? Where was the Gasthaus Pinkus? Where did Berl Broder and Velvel sing? In one of these buildings? Both must often have walked along this same road. Here is Golden Street or Ulica Zlota, now Vulytsia Zolota, where wealthier Jewish merchants once lived, but where did the refugees camp?

Beside a sad little park with dead grass, sleeping vegetation, unattractive plastic children's games, and much litter, is the Old Fortress Synagogue. There's nothing much left of its back wall, and waving grasses rim the ruined roof. As for the many *shtiblekh* (little Hasidic prayer houses) once surrounding the synagogue, they've vanished totally.

S. Ansky,[103] author, playwright, researcher of Jewish folklore, came to Brody during WWI and was witness to the

---

102 Ibid.

103 Ansky, *The Enemy at His Pleasure*. Ansky (Shloyme Zanvel ben Aaron Rappaport) was born in 1863. He rejected Orthodox Judaism when young and embraced socialism. Aged seventeen, he ran a commune for boys who, like himself, had fled the yeshiva's rigid education. Rejecting Yiddish as decadent, when pogroms changed his way of thinking, he took up Yiddish as the Jewish national language. At the outbreak of the First World War, he helped set up relief organizations for Jews trapped behind the front lines. He died in 1920.

rapes, humiliations, kidnappings, and massacres of Jews and ethnic Germans at the hands of Cossacks, peasants, and Russian soldiers (although many were Jewish).[104] The old accusation of blood libel justified the pogroms, and Poles, anxious to hide their membership in anti-Russian secret societies, accused Jews and Germans of treason and participated in the massacres. In 1942, there were still ten thousand Jews living in Brody, but most were shot by the Nazis. The rest died of starvation, or in labour and concentration camps.

Today, this seems an inauspicious town of sleepy streets and heaped rubbish. Largely destroyed during the Polish-Soviet War of 1920, destroyed again by WWII combat, the city was rebuilt with modern indifference. In the little museum on the main square, there is a display of guns, some pottery, a book in English about the Galician SS brigades, and a proud history of the Ukrainian Insurgent Army (UPA), and ultranationalist Organization of Ukrainian Nationalists (OUN). Both supposedly fought—but often collaborated with—the Nazi regime, helping in the liquidation of 50,000 Jews, and perpetrating the ethnic cleansing and horrifically brutal massacre of 100,000 Poles, mostly women and children.

A sad-eyed guardian comes over for a chat in Hungarian: her grandparents had been lucky. They had emigrated to Canada in 1947, escaping the Soviet arrest, murder, and deportation of over 500,000 Ukrainian civilians, many of them members of the UPA and their families.[105] But exile was heart-breaking, and they had returned to Ukraine during the communist regime. Her grandfather was immediately sent to the Siberian gulag. Everyone with their own interpretation of history; everyone with a tale of misery.

Another guardian, a stocky man, seeing I'm an amenable

---

104 Between 1874 and 1914, there were more Jews in the Russian army than non-Jews in proportion to the general population—almost 5 per cent of the military but only 4 per cent of the population (YIVO Encyclopaedia).

105 To bring to a halt the continuing guerrilla activities against the Soviet Union.

friendly person ever ready to listen, pulls me over to a painting of the Ukrainian hero, Bohdan Khmelnitsky, then waits for my admiring nod. In 1648, Khmelnitsky, a lesser noble, brought together serfs, Cossack and Tartar armies and, under the banner of an independent Ukraine, marched against the Polish Commonwealth. The Polish gentry, Catholic priests, and Jews, considered agents of the nobility, were hunted down, flayed, sawed asunder, burnt alive, and disembowelled. Thousands of Jews perished, or were forcibly baptised, or were carried off to the Crimean Tatar Khanate to replenish the slave market.

The Commonwealth never fully recovered from the onslaught, nor was an independent Ukraine ever created: it became a vassal state of Russia, and Khmelnitsky changed loyalties. Serfdom was reinstated, and Ukrainian culture was suppressed. Yet today, Khmelnitsky is considered a hero to both Russians and Ukrainians. How are we to reach a consensus, this man, proud descendent of a mass murderer, and I, a descendant of the murderer's victims?

I leave Brody, march past winter's blackened fields, and come to the former customs post far outside town. It's no longer a border crossing, and those once-great powers, Imperial Russia and Austrian Galicia, are long gone. This is just another part of the countryside, a place along a sleepy Ukrainian road. There's no drama, no emotion here now. I feel no ghosts floating on the frozen air.

So, quite alone, I strut between the two vanished empires. Twirl a few times, then dance a private little jig, one dedicated to the vagaries of history and the memory of all who passed— the hopeful, the desperate, those showmen with their trained bears and marmots, the sly con men, the America-bound, the beggars, traders, the pious, the free-thinkers, and all the escaping conscripts.

Chapter XV:
Lemberg

Come here, philosopher,
With your cat's brain
Come here to the rebbe's table
And learn something there
A steamboat, you invented
And you boast about it.
The rebbe spreads out his kerchief
And crosses the ocean!
An air balloon, you invented
And think you're clever.
The rebbe mocks, the rebbe laughs,
He can manage without it!

Velvel Zbarzher[106]

*H*ere is Lviv (formerly Lemberg) with its largely destroyed Jewish quarter. Velvel was always coming to this city, leaving, returning. How am I to find the once-famous Cafe Abatzya, not far from the Yiddish theatre, where

---

106 Rubin, *Voices of a People.*

he and other bards met? What about Yasha Hant's garden where klezmorim played all night, or coffeehouses such as Shoman's, home to writers, journalists, actors, and artists who:

...like pigeons who can only live in company, and who immediately begin pecking at one another as soon as they come across a grain of food.[107]

Once the royal city of Galicia-Volhynia, Lviv was renamed Lemberg when it became the capital of Austrian Galicia. This was an impoverished region, and Habsburg rulers were uninterested in its development: the province was to be exploited as a supplier of food, raw materials, and army conscripts. Nonetheless, conditions did improve for the Jewish community.

Under the 'enlightened' Emperor Joseph II (1741-1790) assimilation was encouraged, and Jews were able to expand their residential and economic rights. They could be apprenticed to Christian guild masters, attend some universities, have access to the liberal professions, and be drafted into the army. Jews were also ordered to adopt German surnames,[108] and to send their children to the newly created German-language schools. This last measure was a complete failure: the traditional community boycotted this ladder to a modern world, and the project had to be abandoned.

After 1800, a new Jewish society appeared in Lemberg, one composed of young intellectuals, the sons of wealthy merchants, moneylenders, and estate tax collectors. They were joined by those escaping shtetl life and, after 1827, by Russian

---

107 Ravitch, *Dos mayse-bukh fun mayn lebn, Zikhroynes.*

108 Time was short and names were selected hastily. Some were based on occupations—Schuster (shoemaker), Fiedler (fiddler)—or were descriptive—Klein (little), Schwarz (black). Those high on the social scale, preferred natural phenomena—Birnbaum (pear tree), Grunwald (green wood). Many were given the same name, and only nicknames identified them: one man, Schwartz, was dubbed, Without Underwear, possibly could afford none.

Jews fleeing military conscription. Since university education remained closed to most unconverted Jews, to sharpen wits, test the new ideas, and acquire worldly knowledge they met in the coffeehouses created by eighteenth-century Sephardic coffee traders who had been excluded from gentile clubs.[109]

Yet, most of Lemberg's Jews, particularly shopkeepers, were deeply pious, and, as usual, their reaction to modernity was violent. Religious life had to be maintained and change fought. Reviled as heretics, some Maskilim saw their careers ruined. When the chief rabbi, Jacob Orenstein, heard that young men in his flock were studying secular subjects, he excommunicated them. A few, like the liberal Hebrew teacher Isaac Erter, were obliged to leave the city in order to find work.

The arrival, in 1843, of Abraham Kohn, an educated and enlightened rabbi, only increased local resistance. His proposals for ritual reform created a rift so wide, he was stoned and insulted on the streets. Five years later, he was dead, poisoned by an Orthodox fanatic.

Still, Modernism couldn't be stopped. After 1870, Haskalah books were everywhere. School children found them in their father's libraries, discussed and exchanged them with school cronies. The day's heroes were the new young men who had, 'thrust themselves into the wide world,' who were reading Schiller, Lessing, Goethe, and Heine. But in smaller towns and villages, life stayed the same, as young Joseph Margoshes discovered:

> *I left Lemberg in a top hat but arrived in Tarnow in a satin Hasidic cap.*[110]

---

109 Coffee was a new commodity, and Jewish traders took up this commerce that was not forbidden to them.

110 Margoshes, *A World Apart*.

***

*P*oking my nose into corners, peering into windows, unashamedly slipping into courtyards, I try to find those coffeehouses where philosophers, teachers, and political activists argued. There were once hundreds of them. Some were elegant; others, smoky windowless one-room meeting places, were frequented by Russian Jewish exiles who, destitute and traumatised by pogroms, had little in common with sleek self-assured Galician bohemians.

Today's meeting places are the plethora of trendy locales and pseudo-historical theme bars that attract swarms of stylish young Ukrainians and international tourists, but there are other joints, too. Further from the beaten track, half-lit and home sweet home to steady drinkers, without even a half-curious glance these silent folk accept me as one of their own. What if I were to burst into song? What if, like Velvel, I could invent rhymes to stir their pickled hearts? The idea is laughable. In today's world, I'd probably be asked to leave.

No, I'll have to search elsewhere. Surely at the Center for Urban History someone can help me find the old Cafe Abatzya and the street where Velvel stayed in the home of his friend, a man named Oser Rohatiner. But my questions are of no interest to the fashionable young man and woman chatting by the coffee machine.

'You'll have to give us addresses, not names of cafés.'

'Have you ever heard of Velvel Zbarzher?'

'No.'

'What about his street, Ulica Lwia?'

'Street names have been changed from Polish to Ukrainian.'

'There are two people you can ask,' says the visibly impatient young man. Who am I anyway? Just some foreigner who has strolled in off the street. 'But one isn't here this week, and the other is in Los Angeles. You'll find him on Facebook.'

He and the young woman, plastic coffee cups in hand, want to get back to their amusing conversation.

On these roaring city streets, the vanished Jews are still very present. Here's a gouged doorpost where there had once been a mezuzah. Right next door, here's another. And on the buildings further down the street, and along the next, and after that. The scars are everywhere.

After the First World War, Poles and Ukrainians fought over Galicia, and Polish victory brought anti-Semitic policies. Yet the Jewish community flourished. The population of 110,000 doubled when refugees arrived from German-occupied Poland in 1939. Two years later, Germany captured the city. Ten thousand Jews escaped with the retreating Red Army, but those remaining were exterminated. Poles, mostly women, and children, were deported to Siberia or massacred by Ukrainian nationalists.

Under the Soviets, Lemberg/Lviv, once renowned for its multicultural diversity, ceased to be a melting pot. Those of German origin were repatriated, any remaining Poles were relocated to 'new' Poland,[111] and members of the Ukrainian elite were forced to leave. They were replaced by Russians, Soviet Ukrainians, Soviet Jews, Belarusians, and rural Ukrainians.

Today, predominantly Ukrainian with a significant Russian minority, this city, once called 'the little Paris of Galicia,' participates fully in the consumer dream. Instead of the old refinement, I find once-elegant dining rooms where shiny faux wood favours the 'rustique' look, and large-screen televisions shriek sports triumphs and video clip inanities. It's a far cry from Shmuel Yosef Agnon's nineteenth century Lemberg:

> *Tall buildings rise higher and higher and carriages move without horses, and bronze horses stand erect with bronze dignitaries astride them. And there are gardens planted in the city and stone figures spraying water from their*

---

111 Poland's borders were redrawn in accordance with the decisions made by the Allies, but large territories were ceded to the Soviet Union.

mouth, and big synagogues built on stone pillars...Isaac
found himself standing in a splendid temple with gilded
chandeliers suspended from the ceiling and lamps shining
from every single wall and electric lights turned on in the
daytime and marble tables gleaming, and people of stately
men wearing distinguished clothes sitting on plush chairs,
reading big newspapers. And above them, waiters dressed
like dignitaries and like lords on the King's birthday,
holding silver pitchers and porcelain cups that smelled of
coffee and all kinds of pastry.[112]

On the street, ice-covered cobblestones don't discourage
high spike heels, and self-absorbed people chat into cell
phones while imitating perfume models or film starlets.
Even the silicone weather-channel bimbo on the overhead
LED billboard postures lewdly while talking of lowering
temperatures and snowstorms. Indeed, my tired second-hand
Loden coat, my lumpy woollen socks, and my walking boots
receive strange looks; I'm as odd-looking to them as they are
to me.

I pass one bank after another, some are modern and
towering, others are shopfront affairs: how can so many
exist? Alongside cell phone dealers and luxury boutiques
are golden churches, perfectly restored and opulent, where
crouching old women beg. Wanting to assure me of her piety,
one jiggles her rosary, makes the sign of the cross, and smiles
like an icon Madonna. Only the Jewish beggars mentioned by
Margoshes are gone:

Around eighty beggars would show up [at the synagogue]
and many would take them home for the duration of the
shabbes.[113]

There is much splendid Austro-Hungarian architecture to

---

112 Agnon, *Only Yesterday.*

113 Margoshes, *A World Apart.*

be seen, beautifully proportioned buildings adorned with enamel, sculpture, and stained glass, but many are half-ruined with smashed plaster and shattered windows. Those glorious buildings can be saved, I think. Who am I kidding? Everywhere, signs advertise bank loans, leather sofas, modern apartment complexes, cars, and custom-fitted kitchens. Those are what people want: consumer products.

It's already late afternoon, and I still have to find Velvel. A resourceful young man in the town hall consults several books, manages to ferret out former street names, and I set off for a distant section of the city. Here, behind a street market, houses are even shabbier, and sidewalks are rubbish-strewn. Shadowy businesses of one unidentifiable sort or another—no signs, no names, blanked-out windows—occupy charmless courtyards and are guarded by shifty-eyed toughs. Ulica (now vulitsa) Lwia is still here, and I look for number 11 where, from the late 1860s until the late 1870s, Velvel sojourned.[114]

And, to my astonishment, here it is! Could this truly be where Velvel wrote his poems and songs? From where he sent and received letters?

Yes, it looks right. It feels right. Watched by a hostile beefy man sitting with his henchman in a new Mercedes, I take photos. Fatty starts the car, rolls up beside me. 'What are you doing?' he barks in Ukrainian. His teeth resemble a do-it-yourself cemetery.

I smile, pretend I understand nothing and wave my plastic camera. 'Tourist, tourist.'

'What do you want?'

'Tourist, tourist.'

I won't let him ruin my fun. The door of the building is open and, hoping he's too meaty to follow, I enter, climb up the old staircase. See the numbers 4/5 on a wooden door right in front of me. Yes, this is the exact address. This was

---

114 House numbers in this city only date from 1871: before that, personal names or architectural features were used.

Rohatiner's apartment. This was the doorway through which Velvel passed; these were the stairs he took. I go up and down, up and down, in his footsteps.

'Here I am, Velvel. Here I am. I've found you,' I shout triumphantly.

I haven't, of course. He isn't here. Up and down the stairway once again, along the corridor. Feeling like a ghoulish groupie, I tap timidly on the apartment door. What will I say when someone answers? All I want is a peek inside, a whiff of the past. Fortunately, no one is home.

Out in the dusky evening street, the fat man is waiting in his purring Mercedes. He follows me, an evil genie with bad intentions, and I only manage to lose him far below, in a complicated tangle of one-way streets and narrow alleys.

Chapter XVI:
Return to Zbarazh

There stands a maiden in the kitchen
And kneads the challah[115]
In comes the matchmaker, and chats with her
Imagine! You'll soon be a bride
She hadn't even washed her hands
The chuppah[116] was already there
And in a hurry
Mazel tov[117] in a happy hour
The mother screams, rips her hair
What have you done, you slut
The challah has over-risen
And you dream of the chuppah
'I have no fear,' she answers her
'Although you are rich.
My man will take care of me
Now, I'm a wife like you.'

---

115 Braided Sabbath bread
116 Wedding canopy
117 Congratulations

*V*elvel travelled to Russia, waited for the censor's permission to print his second book in Warsaw. While there, did he meet his counterpart and successor, wordsmith and 'people's bard,' badkhn Elyokem Tsunzer? I'll never know. Clearly, the two men, acquainted with each other's songs, borrowed freely from one another. In brilliant, hour-long rhymed speeches, Tsunzer, like Velvel, criticised injustice, poverty, backwardness, and the obsession with money:

> *From the mountain and the earth you come here*
> *And want to be man's pride*
> *You make him small, you make him big*
> *You make him cheap, you make him fine*
> *And wherever people go, whatever they say*
> *You are always in the middle of it.*

In Tsunzer's, *Song of the Bird*, a bird with a broken wing reflects, with melancholy, over its misfortune. Velvel's caged nightingale also sings of its sad fate:

> *I see the other birds flying*
> *I watch them with my eyes*
> *I want to fly after them*
> *Fly high as they do*
> *I want to relish*
> *The same fresh air they do*
> *But I'm locked up tight*
> *And sorrow is my lot.*

***

*A*ny exile nourishes a nostalgic view of home. Is that why Velvel returned to Zbarazh? When he did, it was on his terms, for celebrity was jogging along right beside him. No longer an errant son, a runaway, an apostate, he'd become the golden boy who'd made good. A legendary figure, famous and infamous, many oft repeated bon mots were attributed to his wit.

His father had died in 1853, and the town was much changed. The Haskalah had made great inroads, and Velvel found himself amid a cultivated crowd. Of course, the religious community wanted nothing to do with him. To them, Wolwel Moschkes (Moschke's Velvel, as they still called him) was a thorn in the eye, an embarrassment, a second Titus, a Temple defiler, a godless and shameful sinner (although the official rabbinic authority was pleased by Velvel's attacks on Hasidism.)

His brother, Meir, an enlightened Hebrew teacher, remained his closest friend; other family members, having heard rumours of his loose artist's life, scorned him—although they were eager enough to accept his money, no matter how earned. Generous, he neither begrudged nor punished them for their venality.

He was often seen in the streets, a stylish, polished man, strolling about, or on his way to visit friends. Without pretension, snobbery, or fussiness, but witty and possessing a great roaring laugh, he was one of those talkers who always stops passers-by for conversation. A lady-charmer, he had many admirers.

'Why not marry again?' friends asked.

'I'm too old for a virgin,' he'd answer. 'I'd have to leave a divorced woman, just like her previous husband did. And widows frighten me, for they're bound to outlive me.'

However, to his brother Meir, twice divorced and now remarried, he was less cynical. 'I like the wife you have now, and I'm looking for someone just like her. I've found three: one already has a husband, the second is dead, and you have the third.'

Some accused him of being a carouser, a man whose life turned around wine, women, and song. Wine, absolutely. Song, of course. But women? Where are all the compromising stories? Where are those fervid love poems? Only one has come down to us, and it never conjures up passion, merely fog, faint perfume, and yearning:

The voice of love with its sweet melody
I hear from every corner
And everyday it goes further away
And makes me sad
I would give all I own
In the blinking of an eye
Just for a corner of it
I would at least die in happiness
A man knows nothing of life
Although he lives well
He can exist for eighty years
Yet not live for a minute.

Surely, he was aware of his reputation as a skirt chaser—didn't that go along with the job? But, writing about himself in *Makel No'am* he stated:

He did everything he was supposed to: he dressed properly, went to the mikveh, did not look at girls or women, and minded what he said.'

We can believe him, too, for Velvel was an idealist, a romantic, although ideal love was a far cry from what he saw around him:

Romantic love in the ghetto? There's no room for such a thing. A ghetto youth is spoilt by his family. They surround him with comfort and riches. The women around him—his mother, sisters, aunts, and grandmothers—willingly satisfy his every desire. Then, long before romantic feelings can develop, he is married off. Unable to earn money, living in kest in his parents-in-law's house, studying, perfecting himself in religious casuistry, he remains a dependent child. Real love, with its turbulence and passion, is considered unnecessary, superfluous, and un-Jewish by such men. It remains unknown to them.

As for a young woman, her greatest worry was being left an old maid while her companions married and had children.

Insufficiently educated, with little to do until of marriageable age, she could let her fancy roam, be influenced by modern romance novels, and spin heady dreams of the ideal mate. But, those dreams ended abruptly with betrothal, a decision made by her parents and without her consent:

> *The bewigged women who carry out ritual duties and work in the markets have lost the bloom of youth. Dutiful providers, responsible mothers, and wives, they are devoted to religious and family values. Their husbands don't look at them with love. The Hasidim who dance, sing, and feed with their fellows, reserve all their love for the miracle-working rebbes. Their wives and their numerous children are left behind, and they have to fend for themselves.*

There was another problem: alcohol. Everyone knew that drink-sodden peasants beat their wives—there were many songs on this theme, even proverbs: 'The hungry Jew sings, while a hungry peasant beats his wife.' But alcohol and violence were very much part of the Jewish world. In his poem, *Der Shiker* (The Drunk), it was not only the husband who indulged:

> *My heart begins to tell me*
> *Something quite new*
> *I think I will beat my wife today*
> *And that is very nice*
> *A little bit of vodka*
> *At the head of my bed at home*
> *But she doesn't leave a drop of it*
> *She drinks the whole thing up.*[118]

***

*C*hatting with one and all, basking in the company of adoring friends (Landau, Kahana, Kroh, Minz,

---

118 Mlotek, *Pearls of Yiddish Song.*

Horowitz, Frohnglas, Barasch, and Goldberger), enriching wine-soaked evenings with poetic ridicule and song—'When you're young, do what your heart wants; when you're older, nothing matters anymore,'—were public displays of bravado. Melancholy was ever present, inserting itself between the mocking lines: 'When I'm old, please God, don't take my talent away.'

He continued to weave words that delighted his admirers, but he had wearied of the wandering life. He was plagued by small illnesses (his hadn't been an easy lifestyle.) Could he stay here in town forever? Settle? Zbarazh folk doubted it. They said: 'Wolwel Moschkes won't use up a whole vessel of salt in Galicia.'[119]

Then, he had a stroke of luck: one of his self-published books had come to the notice of Peretz Smolenskin, the Maskil publisher of a new radical journal, *Ha-Shahar* in Vienna. Although condemning Velvel's use of Yiddish, Smolenskin was appreciative of his work:

> *I am not happy with this poet because he has used the corrupted language of the Jews as his first choice, and Hebrew as his second, but I cannot deny that we see in this book the hand of a wonderful artist, not by his mastery of poetry, or by his language, but by his spirit...gracefulness, charm and humour are present in all his poems. There are several...which could have honoured even Goethe and Schiller...But, if the poet will listen to my advice, he should not continue to associate the Jewish with the Hebrew language. If he publishes only in Hebrew, he'll realize far greater success than he has had up until now, and he'll see his work appear in better shape, on better paper, with good typography and better orthography.[120]*

---

119 From Moses Fried who lived in Zbarazh at the time. The original expression was: Wölwel Moschkes wird hier kein Fässel Salz aufessen.

120 Translation from Hebrew by Irene Ehrenkranz Fishler.

Did such praise give Velvel new energy? Did he find hometown stability suffocating and the call of the road irresistible? His friends had been right. One day, Velvel upped and left Zbarazh—a sudden and unhappy decision, for his subsequent letters to Meir were gloomy. He had gone to Constantinople and was seriously ill; he'd lost all in one of the city's terrible fires (many were set by firemen to keep themselves employed.)[121] He deeply regretted his sudden departure from Zbarazh. 'It is my hope and longing that the day will come when God's mercy will bring me back to our town.'

But, instead of returning home, he turned around and headed for Vienna's magnetic glow.

***

I come back to Zbarazh with Irene, a French professor from Lviv. When very young, she lived in Zbarazh and, for her, this is a town of happy memories. She wants to show me her grandparent's house and a smaller building behind the main house. 'My grandfather built it in 1950 in the traditional way, with adobe bricks, right on the spot where an older building once stood. There's even a traditional oven of mud and straw with a cooking oven and hob: it's the real thing.'

Irene would like to keep the property for herself and her young son, but it belongs to her mother who wants to sell: 'Don't expect me to bury myself in a hole like Zbarazh.' That older woman is determined to have her way, telephoning eight times, demanding to know what we're doing, where we are. 'You have to go to the house as soon as you arrive in town. The buyer will be coming by in the afternoon. You have to let her in, show her around.'

Our train passes the shabby almost-empty hamlets with their pecking fowl and scrounging strays, the fallow fields

---

121 In Velvel's lifetime, there were major fires in Istanbul/Constantinople in 1826, 1833, 1856, 1865, and 1870. Other local conflagrations destroyed individual neighbourhoods.

covered with tumbling scrub. After Ukrainian independence, seven million rural residents were given plots of land for small-scale domestic farming; workers on the disbanded collective farms were given land shares, *pai*. Agriculture became a main source of income for many, but it attracted the large companies and powerful oligarchs who pressured the elderly, the inexperienced, and those with no financial resources, to lease them their *pais*. This has resulted in a modern re-feudalisation of agriculture, with soil degradation, rural impoverishment, and large-scale migration to the cities. More than six hundred and forty Ukrainian villages and hamlets have vanished in twenty years. Aren't the smashed and abandoned houses in Zbarazh testimony to this rural exile?

Irene is certain we'll find Velvel's house. I still have my cadastral map from the 1800s, and she can question everyone in Ukrainian. We leave the train in Tarnopol, take a bus, since the line to Zbarazh only runs late at night—but that's not a new story:

> *At Zolodievka the fun begins because that's where you have to change, to get onto the new train, which they did us such a favour by running out to Kasrilevke. But not so fast. First, there's the little matter of several hours' wait, exactly as announced in the schedule—provided, of course, you don't pull in after the Kasrilevke train has left. And at what time of night may you look forward to this treat? The very middle, thank you, when you're dead tired, and disgusted, without a friend in the world except sleep—and there's not a single place in the station where you can lay your head, not one. When the wise men of Kasrilevke quote the passage from the Holy Book, 'Tov shem meshemen tov,'[122] they know what they're doing. I'll translate it for you: We were better off without the train.[123]*

---

122 A Good Name is Better Than Good Oil

123 Sholem Aleichem, *On Account of a Hat*, cited by Tony Kushner in *Wandering Stars*.

In Zbarazh, we again pass the few remaining shops on what must once have been a busy street, go to the town's only eatery, an upstairs locale with Stalinist decor. It's almost warm inside the flesh-coloured room, and we're the only clients, but the television is on, and aliens in mufti caterwaul in their car-burning video clip world. In the kitchen, three unsurprisingly stout female cooks with many chins slump on sighing chairs, warding off boredom with gossip. Irene asks if they've heard of Velvel Zbarzher Ehrenkranz, the famous local poet. Of course, they haven't.

'And the Jewish cemetery has been dug up and moved to Brody,' says one.

'Why?' asks Irene.

'Who knows?'

We're served tepid watery borscht (the stretched, tasteless remains of a much heartier brew) and almost warm cheese blintzes, then return to bleak streets devoid of human presence.

It's cold out here, almost too cold for snow. On Sholem Aleichem Street is the synagogue/office complex behind the industrial barriers. The razor-fanged guard dogs are still here, too, ravenous, and baying. We pass the smashed abandoned houses of the lower town and, further up, where houses are in better shape, we turn right.

'Velvel's house must have been right around here... somewhere.' Irene stares at my cadastral map, and she seems as confused as I was on my first visit to this area. Streets have vanished entirely or changed direction. Houses, modernised, enlarged, and character-less, have altered their basic shape; little alleyways have been incorporated into gardens. We search for clues but find none. Could this be an old house? What about this one? Who knows? This has become a modest, well-kept neighbourhood of indefinable age. Irene questions two men walking past with their children. They've never heard the name Ehrenkranz.

One points to a pinkish building behind trees. 'I live over there. I bought it from a Jew years ago.' No, he doesn't remember the name of the former owner. 'Go question the woman in that corner house. She's old. Perhaps she knows something.'

Bundling herself into warm clothes, the 'old' (she's probably around my age) woman comes to her garden gate. 'Yes, a Jew lived in the pink house years ago. His name? Can't remember.'

What's the use of searching further? We won't learn anything. Followed by an eager, friendly little stray that hopes we'll take him on board, we head towards the house once belonging to Irene's grandparents. It's further up the hill, in the old peasant-end of town, where each dwelling has a small barn, and gelid pastureland scratches a gunmetal horizon.

This building Irene loves is modest, but I'm certain it's far older than she thinks. She unlocks the door and we enter. A row of potted green plants, ancient, knobby things that have outlasted their owners, are kept alive by the next-door neighbour. In three perfectly square rooms with high ceilings and nineteenth-century woodwork, only two or three pieces of forgotten furniture remain. High on one wall, are religious pictures; on the next, photos of dead relatives. Their eyes follow us.

Irene opens a drawer, pulls out an old album. She wants to show me a picture of her great-grandmother. 'Where do you think she came from? Look at her.' A long, humourless face, heavy braids. Not a Cossack, not a Mongol. A Cuman? A Gagauze?[124] Something exotic, an eastern foreignness that is also etched into Irene's handsome features. But she knows nothing about the mysterious great-grandmother: she's another unsolved ancestral mystery.

The album is slid back into its drawer. The people on the walls are still watching, but they're determined to keep their secrets. Hanging in the air is a faint sigh, a memory of long-gone days and happy moments. This house is a discouraged, ghostly place.

---

124 A predominantly Orthodox Christian Turkic ethnic group.

The potential buyer appears. Vulgar, noisy, resembling an over-stuffed laundry sack, she tsk-tsks through the rooms, is accompanied by her equally vulgar, equally noisy, overstuffed friend.

'Everything will have to go, windows ripped out, replaced with new ones in PVC. Those old (heavy, beautiful) wooden doors have to go too. So much work! It will cost so much.' The two women waddle back out to the street, tsk-tsking.

The still-hopeful spotted stray is waiting in the courtyard, just beside a narrow stairway leading down to an ancient-looking underground wine cellar. Irene and I cross the yard and enter a smaller building—the one rebuilt by her grandfather—standing alongside a barn and former vegetable patch. Inside is the oven made by him a traditional, homemade object, uneven, beautifully functional, and just like the legendary Jewish oyfen or pripitchik. Beside it is a low window and, alongside, his old treadle sewing machine. At one point in its history, it had stitched together uniforms for the Russian military; and, in deepest night, those of the Ukrainian Insurgent Army.

'This was such a lively place,' says Irene. 'My friends came, and we played in the courtyard while my grandfather tended to his animals in the barn. Here's something that might interest you: when my grandparents rebuilt this part of the house in 1950, they had to dig down for the foundations, and when they did, they found all sorts of things—glasses and plates, different objects—Jewish objects. Everything had been buried in the ground. Once, long ago, this was a Jewish tavern, although my grandparents said there was nothing much left by the time they got the plot. But each summer, when we dug the garden for vegetables, we'd find more Jewish things.'

Vanished Jews. A Jewish shenk? Is that what the main house was with its square rooms and high ceilings? Plainly, the deep, old wine cellar in the courtyard dates from that earlier time. When was this part of the shenk destroyed? Had the Jewish owners buried their plates, glasses, and valuables before being marched to the killing grounds beside the railway station? Before being shot down in the nearby forest and thrown into mass graves?

Irene knows nothing more.

Have I, in some terrible way, found Velvel again? Surely, he would have come here, to this hometown shenk, had a drink or two. Sung a poem. There are no signs of anything. The houses, the courtyard, the cellar, the garden, all remain silent in winter afternoon's waning light. No one is left to tell us anything. Like the Jews, the stories are gone.

Irene locks the doors. I want more than I can ever have: a rocky jolting time-trip back a century and a half—just a few speeding minutes—into a vanished world. Enough time to feel, see, hear, smell. Meet Velvel. Even more fantastic, I want to stop history, warn all of imminent and terrible doom.

The next-door neighbour, surly, sour, steps into the dusk. 'Zbarazh.' He spits. 'There's nothing here. Nothing. Nothing you can do in such a place. Just drink.'

Chapter XVII:
Vienna

One morning when he awoke, shrill hateful noises filled his ear, like the bellowing of wild beasts; he looked around and his revered goddess of liberalism lay without life, on the ground.

Dr Joseph S. Bloch

'*A*fter I came to Vienna, I was very low,' Velvel wrote. Had he hoped to settle? Be recognised? Earn good money? If so, things didn't go the way he'd expected. Eastern Europe's Yiddish entertainment had never been adopted in Vienna. In this city, professional entertainers—singers, bards, caricaturists, acrobats, and magicians—performed their acts in variety theatres or wine bars (*Heurigen*). The first authentic cabaret, the Nachtlicht, opened in 1906, thirty years after he left.

Vienna's assimilated Jews had no love of Jewish tradition, and they despised Yiddish. There were no Yiddish newspapers; there was no Yiddish literature. When a Yiddish play by the Galician Moses Horowitz was performed, the angry audience, claiming the Polish-Jewish jargon was incomprehensible, left the theatre.

Depressed, ill, Velvel stayed in bed for days on end, only rousing himself to go sing to Romanian and Galician workers in Edelhoffer's Tavern. Such taverns (*Wirtshäuser*) were nesting places for newly-arrived provincials. Here, they made contact with other incomers, fought loneliness, tried to adjust to life in a city that, despite the oft-vaunted Viennese charm, has never been known for its chumminess.

Edelhoffer's Tavern has vanished—where was it? What was it like? Surely, not like this Wirtshäus where I now find myself, where a smug violinist plays cheesy tunes to simpering diners.

'You see,' says Heinrich, a shiny florid man at the next table. 'Taverns haven't changed in a hundred years.' He wants me to love Vienna, his birthplace, as much as he does.

I sip my Grüner Veltliner wine. 'I'm looking for a place where workers met, heard singers and folk poets.'

'Then you should go to a *Heuriger*, a wine bar. Schrammel[125] musicians used to play folk songs and dance music in those.' Heinrich glances nervously at his spike-haired son slumped supine in a chair and plugged into a phone. 'Not the sort of place young people appreciate.'

They aren't what I'm seeking either. Despite their quaint trappings—rustic interiors, a woven crown of conifer twigs above the door— city Heurigen have become licensed restaurants where professional performers produce the songs tourists request.

Pleasantly tipsy and singing softly but atrociously (why worry in a city where people ignore me?) I continue through the night, heading for Leopoldstadt in the centre, nourishing the pale memory of a long-ago romance and a lover's third-generation anger at the loss of aristocratic title, privilege, status, and property after WWI defeat and the end of the Empire. His once-illustrious family had been projected into this more tawdry area, provoking his puzzling belief in

---

125 In 1878, the violinists, brothers Johann and Josef Schrammel, formed an
     ensemble with guitarist Anton Strohmayer and clarinettist Georg Dänzer
     and became famous playing in Viennese taverns.

violent revolution and communism's Bright Future.

After 1848, residence restrictions in the Habsburg lands were lifted, and peasants, agricultural workers, Jews,[126] all rolled into Vienna from Bohemia, Moravia, Hungary, Bukovina, and Galicia. To accommodate the influx and make way for new housing, surrounding towns were annexed, ancient city walls destroyed, and centuries-old, architecturally irreplaceable wooden houses were pulled down.

Many Jews took up residence on these side streets and back alleys, once part of the Unter Werd ghetto, now close to their port of arrival, the Nordbahnhof train station. But here and further outside the central district, living conditions could be worse than in towns and villages left behind. In the new cheap housing, kitchens were entered directly from outside corridors, and there were no taps, bathrooms, or toilets. Sometimes ten to fifteen people crowded into one-room apartments, and those unable to afford accommodation rented beds by the day or the night. Prostitution was rife; children with rickets were a common sight; Jewish beggars crowded slum streets. It was quite a different scenario from the idealised coffeehouse society tourists fantasise about today.

In that other world, the wealthy inhabited new luxurious apartments with lofty ceilings, marble fireplaces, and elaborate mouldings. Idealists dreamt that all classes, freshly schooled, would mingle in the newly constructed opera house, theatres, concert halls, and be refined by high culture's offerings. Nourishing such aspirations, façades were embellished with allegorical figures, vines, and flowers.[127]

The many coffeehouses—large, elegant and famous, or those smaller, simpler, and local—were the living rooms of middle-class men (apartments were used merely as

---

126 By 1870, the Jewish population numbered 40,200 and at the end of the century, it had risen to 185,000. During the Holocaust, 60,000 Viennese Jews died in the death camps.

127 Many of those buildings are still here, but modelled stucco has too often wasted away. Renovation, when carried out, has been done cheaply, stripping the façades entirely, or covering them with cement.

bedrooms). In these public places, German was spoken, billiards and games of tarot were played, newspapers read, and discussions were urbane and fervent. Jews who could afford to do so also frequented these establishments, and freed from religious constraint and shtetl life, they adopted middle-class values, ideas, and a sense of social superiority. Dedicating themselves to secular learning with the same passion once reserved for Talmudic study, they soon, out of proportion to their number, became great consumers of culture and its creators: journalists, publishers, playwrights, novelists, poets, critics, theatre directors, painters, classical musicians, and university professors.[128]

Middle-class women generally avoided coffeehouses. Adhering to the Germanic idea of respectable female domesticity, they stayed home, raised their children, and used theatres, fine shops, the opera house, and private venues as places in which to display the wealth and status of their successful husbands.[129] Coffeehouse society was also shunned by Jews wishing to deny their heritage or to further their careers by marrying gentiles: Vienna had the highest conversion rate in Europe.

This unique culture with its original characters, wit-sharpening conversations and passionate exchange of ideas, disappeared with Hitler and the murder of Vienna's Jews:

> *The Jewishness of Vienna's cultural elite gave the capital of the Habsburg Monarchy a cultural and intellectual importance for that time which it had never known before and certainly no longer possesses.[130]*

Considered old-fashioned by the younger generation, many coffeehouses closed in the 1980s, and even today, there is a

---

128 They were professors only in the sciences, considered a secondary field. Positions in the humanities remained closed to Jews.

129 Until 1856, women were banned from coffeehouses

130 Beller, *Vienna and the Jews.*

preference for Italian espresso bars, American multinational chain establishments, and background music. To attract custom and pay high rents, coffeehouses have equipped themselves with Internet connections, designer food, designer decoration, and designer furniture. Most customers are tourists, and they're discussing travel plans and shopping triumphs, not philosophy or insurrection.

I once—was it only seventeen years ago?—knew another tavern, perhaps similar to Velvel's (although a posted sign forbade spitting and singing). Far off the tourist track, a dingy drinking den of high yellowed ceilings and wood-panelled walls, it was home to those down on their luck—most slept at the homeless shelter across the way. The barmaid was always surly (a recognised Viennese talent), but regulars were welcoming and chatty.

I search for it now but see it has vanished. The homeless shelter is also gone. Where is everyone? The lively man who could recite all of Dante's *Inferno* by heart and always bought me a red rose; the 'professor' whose knowledge of German literature was endless; Leo, the failed actor who, when sufficiently well-oiled, played all the best roles for the assembled company; the cheery philosopher who, unable to sleep in a closed room, wandered the city, peddling hats to night-birds. 'Although I know many important people through my work,' he said, 'I'm only a poor sod. But then, aren't we all?'

***

*T*he publisher Peretz Smolenskin had known a childhood of extreme poverty: his father died while fleeing false accusations of fraud; his brother, snatched by *khapers*,[131] was inducted into the Russian Imperial Army and never seen again. He became an itinerant preacher and choir singer, but

---

131 Khapers or catchers were those appointed by communal leaders, the kahal, to seize conscription candidates for the Tsar's army, usually the poorest in the community, or outsiders, or the children of Maskilim. Tsar Nicholas I had instituted the 25-year draft to remove children from Jewish influence.

after discovering the Haskalah in Odessa, Smolenskin began studying music, languages, and writing stories. When Russian censorship blocked his words, he came to Vienna and created the most revolutionary Hebrew paper of its time, *Ha-Shahar* (The Dawn).[132]

Publishing the work of the foremost Maskilim (and much of his own), *Ha-Shahar* circulated throughout Eastern Europe. Many of his readers were Yeshiva students who, when discovered reading this radical publication, were expelled or punished. Not a few starry-eyed fans arrived in Vienna and hoped Smolenskin would ease their way into the new society. He did help those he could but was dismayed by others who, naïve and insufficiently educated, were corrupted by the city's bright glister. Such men, part of the new pseudo-Haskalah, filled their aimless lives with debauchery, card playing, and drinking.

Velvel, too, showed up on Smolenskin's doorstep. He wanted to give up singing, to earn money as a writer. His newest poem, *Romanyah*, had been published in *Ha-Shahar*, and he must have thought success was just around the corner. Earlier, Moshe Orenstein had sent Velvel's book *Makel No'am* to Albert Kohn at the Alliance Israélite in Paris, and Kohn had responded:

...in his own handwriting, and, with a thousand thanks, gave me four Napoleons from his pocket and assured me my work would be presented at the Alliance.

Wonderful news indeed! The French Alliance was known for helping Jewish intellectuals. Even Smolenskin received subsidies for *Ha-Shahar*, which, despite its success, never managed to earn money.

Confident, Velvel paid to have several hundred examples of *Romanyah* printed, dedicated the work to the Alliance

---

132 *Ha-Shahar* continued to be published until Smolenskin's death from tuberculosis in 1883.

Israélite, and sent a copy to Kohn. Surely this new poem denouncing Romania's official anti-Semitism and comparing Moldavia and Walachia to Sodom and Gomorrah would create a tumult:

> *This is the book of Romania's history, the story of a shameful nation, of its corrupt people who stubbornly and stupidly destroy law and order with no fear of God in their hearts, and with no human love. The sun shines gloomily on this degenerate people who merely play at being a nation, who use theft and murder for no other reason than a childish desire to be bad.*

Then Velvel began the writer's frustrating wait for praise, recognition, and financial aid. Waited...and heard nothing. Waited some more. Still nothing. No support arrived; there was no letter from Kohn, no admiration, and no criticism. Velvel suffered, raged, wrote to Paris again, appealed to well-placed friends and begged them to contact Kohn, ask him why he was treating the poet Ehrenkranz so badly. If they did so, no answer reached Velvel. The copy of *Romanyah* was incorporated into the Paris Alliance library—it's still there today, I've held it in my hands, turned its yellowed friable pages. So, what could have happened?

Had Kohn, depressed after failing to help Morocco's coerced and humiliated Jews, already withdrawn from public life and abandoned his great library? Perhaps the Alliance, just then setting up schools and distributing aid in Romania, allied itself with Bucharest's wealthy Sephardic Jews. Such men, loyal to the Romanian government and friendly with those in high positions, would never react favourably to Velvel's politically incorrect attack.

Distressed, drinking heavily, Velvel dreamt of returning to Romania but had no money to do so. Although still condemning his use of Yiddish, Smolenskin tried to alleviate his friend's poverty by arranging for a pension from a wealthy Viennese family. When they discovered Velvel spent his time in the lowest taverns, that he frequented beggars, workers, and those living in the promiscuity of tenement cellars, that he squandered all he earned, and that he still sang in embarrassing Yiddish, the subsidy fell through.

Perhaps to illustrate Velvel's lowly status (and elevate his own) Dr Saloman Rubin, a Hebrew writer, claimed (in what is most likely another apocryphal story) that Velvel's desire to dedicate one poem to Emperor Franz Josef, created a scandal: how dare a nobody, a barfly, a drunk, address the Kaiser?[133] And Velvel was encouraged to leave this city.

Who would have imagined that, after 1900, Yiddish would gain respect as the language of secular Jewish culture? That, even in Vienna, there would be a Yiddish press, and Yiddish theatre would be popular. That Eastern Europe's brilliant writers—Sholem Yankev Abramovich (Mendele Moykher-Sforim),[134] Shalom Naumovich Rabinovich (Sholem Aleichem), Jacob Dinezon, I. L. Peretz—would prove Yiddish was no religious relic, no patois, and no jargon, but a wonderfully picturesque language, as modern and valid as any European tongue.[135]

***

*A*fter 1880, anti-Semitism spread throughout Europe, resulting in the Dreyfus affair in France, expulsions from German universities, charges of blood libel, and more

---

133 Franz Joseph, dubbed by anti-Semites the 'Judenkaiser,' had annulled restrictions on Jewish occupations and ownership of real estate in 1860, granted Jews full citizenship in 1867, and ennobled twenty. When Pope Pius IX detained a six-year-old Jewish boy, Edgardo Mortara, after a servant claimed to have secretly baptised him, Franz Josef appealed to the Pope to return the child to his parents. The Pope refused.

134 1835-1917 The founder of modern Yiddish prose.

135 Although the snobbish still dubbed it 'jargon' in 1917 when writing about Velvel in the *Mittagblatt des Neuen Wiener Journals*. According to Yudel in, *Never Say Die*, the Yiddish Dictionary contains 200,000 words, and the Russian dictionary only 125,000. Thirteen million people spoke Yiddish before WWII.

pogroms throughout Romania, Hungary, and Russia. Once taunted as inassimilable, Jews were now accused of being too assimilated, and their conformity was proof of duplicity and infiltration.

In Vienna where the term anti-Semitism was first coined,[136] hatred came mainly from the lower middle classes. Under-educated (too much learning was a bad thing; education was reserved for priests), these former country folk had been shunted into the city's factories along with the craftsmen whose skills had been sacrificed to industrialisation, the shopkeepers whose businesses had failed when department stores opened. All steeped themselves in nationalist nostalgia, Hungarian, Czech, Austrian, Croat, or Serb. They resented the success, intelligence, and educational advantages of Jewish 'capitalists.'

In 1885, Viennese liberalism ended with the election of the Christian Social Party. Jews found themselves isolated, excluded from cycling and walking clubs. Many took up their Jewish identity once more, building grandiose synagogues in Austro-Hungary's important cities: Vienna, Budapest, Bratislava, Oradea, Szolnok, Debrecen, Tarnopol, and Czernowitz. They created Jewish student associations and clubs.

Peretz Smolenskin, aware that assimilation had been an illusion, lost faith in the Haskalah, and in those modern Jews who flattered and did business with their anti-Semitic enemies and the powerful Hasidim. He warned that rising anti-Semitism and recent pogroms were not temporary anomalies, but harbingers of horror to come. It was time for a new solution: the creation of a Jewish homeland.[137]

You wish to be like other peoples. So do I. I pray you, be like them. Search and find knowledge, avoid and forsake superstition; above all, be not ashamed of the rock whence

---

136 By the right-wing writer Wilhelm Marr in 1880

137 Smolenshin, Mosheh Leib Lilienbaum and Eliezer Perlemann became the founders of a pre-Zionist nationalist movement: Hibbat Zion.

you were hewn. Yes, be like the other peoples, proud of your literature, jealous of your self-respect, hopeful, even as all persecuted peoples are hopeful, of the speedy arrival of the day when we, too, shall re-inhabit the land, which once was and still is our own.[138]

But the majority of Vienna's Jews didn't share Smolenskin's views. They felt safe, invulnerable, more Austrian than the Austrians. Their ancestors had weathered centuries of persecution, torture, massacre, burnings, and banishment, but things were different now. Kaiser Franz Joseph was on their side. Jews had status and strength. Progress meant reason would triumph. Why be frightened by a few modern anti-Semites? All would work out for the best.

---

138 First published in *Ha-Shahar*, cited by Abram Leon Sachar in, *A History of the Jews*

Chapter XVIII:
Itinerancy

Only drinking and eating
Passionate discussions until I burst, that's my plan
The way to forget everything
Is a glass of wine.

Velvel Zbarzher

*V*elvel shuttled restlessly between Lemberg and Drohobych, Brody, Boryslav, and Sambir, then travelled to Russia, to the port of Odessa,[139] where the French, Germans, Armenians, Poles, Greeks, Italians, Moldavians, and Spaniards schmoozed with squat fezzed Turks and turbaned Persians with henna-stained fingernails. Lawless and corrupt, home to smugglers, forgers, tomb robbers, and counterfeiters, this city offered the excited crowds brandings, floggings, executions, and whole streets of brothels:

They come freely and simply, as to a restaurant or a depot;
they sit, smoke drink, convulsively pretend to be merry

---

139 Now Ukrainian Odesa

they dance, executing abominable movements of the body imitative of the act of sexual love. At times attentively and long, at times with gross haste, they choose any woman they like and know beforehand that they will never meet refusal. Impatiently they pay their money in advance, and on the public bed, not yet grown cold after the body of their predecessor, aimlessly commit the very greatest and most beautiful of all universal mysteries—the mystery of the conception of new life.[140]

Velvel visited his friend the Hebrew poet Eliahu Mordecai Werbel—they admired each other's writing. Twenty years older than Velvel, born in Tarnopol and educated at Joseph Perl's school, it might well have been Werbel who had given young Velvel that copy of Moses Mendelssohn's *Bi'ur*, the book that started his secret study in Zbarazh so many years before.

Velvel also met Werbel's daughter, Perele, and her new husband, Avrom Goldfaden, a perfect example of the modern Odessa Jew. An author, Goldfaden had published several Yiddish poems, and, in his student days, had created a few catchy Yiddish songs that people still hummed. He'd also written two plays although, in the early 1870s, there was no Yiddish theatrical tradition and no audience. There were also no theatres in which to perform Yiddish plays and no Yiddish actors.[141] It would be up to Goldfaden to change things.

Back in 1661, the Jewish Council of Vilna had banned public merry-making, fire dances, plays and masquerades.[142] Only in the eighteenth century did the German Maskilim Aaron Halle-Wolfson and Yitshak Euchel write satirical comedies about enlightened intellectuals confronting superstitious Jews. Never performed, their works were read in

---

140 Kuprin, *Yama: the Pit.*

141 It's possible but unverified that, briefly, from 1868 to 1870, a group of Broderzinger performed Yiddish plays in a Warsaw theatre.

142 Biblical re-enactments were permitted during the Purim festivities.

literary salons. In the early 1800s, Solomon Ettinger, Maskil poet and one of the most influential nineteenth-century Yiddish writers, also wrote several Yiddish plays but, refusing the Russian censor's cuts, he never saw his work published. In 1861, five years after his death, his most famous play, *Serkele*, the story of a scheming and brutal woman, was performed in Zhitomir's teacher's seminary: the leading female role was played by Avrom Goldfaden.

At this first meeting in Odessa, Goldfaden sang a few of Velvel's songs. To his utter amazement, Velvel then sang a song of Goldfaden's, one that had recently been published in the liberal Yiddish periodical, *Kol Mevaser*.[143]

Soon, a deep friendship developed between the two men, and they were to meet many times over the years. Each time they did, Velvel sang Goldfaden's latest creations. As Goldfaden later said, it was as if Velvel was keeping an eye on him, that he considered him the heir to his soul.

***

*W*ith economic decline in Brody and Tarnopol, several hundred enlightened Galician families came to Odessa, settled, and in 1826, founded the first Jewish public school for girls and boys. Other intellectuals, writers, artists, and musicians showed up, delighting in a freedom unavailable elsewhere in the Pale. In the 1840s, a choir and modern singing was introduced into the Brodskaïa Synagogue, and in May 1860, the first Jewish magazine in Russian, *Rassvyet*, was published here. By 1867, Odessa was Russia's main Haskalah centre, home to the largest branch of the Society for the Promotion of (Haskalah) Culture outside of Saint Petersburg.

Although a small religious community did exist, most Jews spoke Russian and showed little interest in Torah

---

143 *Kol Mevaser* was considered the most important early Yiddish periodical. It standardised Yiddish vocabulary and spelling, called for educational reform as well as the wider use of Russian and a positive attitude towards military service in the Russian army.

learning. For the pious, Odessa was a shameful pocket of sin:

> *My father made a hit with everybody...and the rabbi of the town couldn't satiate himself with my father's knowledge. Nevertheless, a tiny flaw was found. It didn't please him that my father lived so near to Odessa; he was too worldly and wore a newly pressed shirt and tie. And another thing, when it was time for leave-taking, everyone went outside and my mother, the bride, also went outside. So my father said to her: 'Sarah, dearest, better go inside, it's cold, you could, God forbid, catch a cold.' Well, now the town had what to talk about! What does it mean that a groom could take such a liberty and talk so intimately to a bride before the wedding? This type of conduct smells too much of Odessa![144]*

In this port, hundreds of ships arrived daily with cargoes of rum, peppers, oranges, wines, coffee, tobacco, silks, nuts, olives, cocaine; and when they sailed off, their holds were heavy with Russian grain. Although there was poverty, there was also great wealth, and fine houses were built, theatres, an opera house. There was also a ready audience for anything innovative.

In 1878, a pop-eyed buck-toothed actor with a saucer-wide mouth left Romania and returned home to Odessa. Yisroel Rosenberg was a penniless swindler, also an unqualified practising lawyer fond of snazzy clothes and fine dining in expensive locales. Managing to finagle a little money, he scraped together an eclectic crew—a few badkhonim, synagogue choir singers, cantors, women running from arranged marriages—and began presenting plagiarised versions of Avrom Goldfaden's plays in local taverns.[145] Russian Yiddish theatre was born.

---

144 Levin, Ontario Jewish Archives.

145 After 1881, tsarist authorities began restricting Yiddish theatre. Many companies left for America but Rosenberg refused. He ended up begging on the streets and died shortly after.

***

*T*he first pogrom in Odessa took place in 1821 and was perpetrated by the Greek community. The next, in 1859, was again carried out by ethnic Greeks, the economic rivals of Jewish merchants. But in the later pogroms of 1871, 1881, and 1886, Russians joined the Greeks. With the futility of Jewish integration made evident, Odessa became a centre for the early Zionist movement.

***

*V*elvel returned to Galicia, stayed for a while in Tarnopol, sang somewhere in this city. Where exactly? I have no names and no addresses. Where was the cheder he had attended in his youth? Is anything left of Jewish life in this once-important centre where Joseph Perl's school had created generations of intellectuals?

The area between train and bus station with its market vendor's stands, its army of crouching country women selling milk, cream, a few winter vegetables, and its illegal hawkers beside their cars heaped high with smuggled-in goods, does resemble some chaotic Middle Eastern souk, albeit without Jews. In 1939, Tarnopol's community numbered thirteen thousand; there are a few hundred left today but, aside from the cemetery across the river, there are no Jewish landmarks.

The centre is elegant with golden churches, the theatre, and monumental buildings, but on the main plaza's graceful sweep, a giant digital LED billboard, as high and wide as any two-story house, flickers images of expensive cars roaring over third world sierras, and laughing families comparing smartphone applications. Where is the great, fortified synagogue built after the Khmelnitsky massacre and once considered Galicia's most beautiful?

'It was torn down years ago,' a man on the street replies. He looks apologetic, even embarrassed. 'It was a ruin by then.'

Escaping from the cold, I choose a ritzy hotel dining room where heavy curtains surround the windows as in some grand chateau. There are original paintings on the wall and, on each table, real carnations dip their toes into glass vases. The sophistication is only superficial, for the Ukrainian hit parade, interspersed with ear-splitting commercials, blasts through multiple loudspeakers and slams against the walls. Two English-speaking men at a neighbouring table stare curiously at me for a while, decide I'm reasonably appealing, then invite me to join them. I accept with alacrity, for company and easy conversation are always a welcome relief. What am I drinking, they ask? A soda? Fruit juice? Coffee?

'Wine.'

One, an American, is visibly displeased at my choice (not that disapproval has ever stopped me). The other, a friendly Swede, looks as though he'd be happy to order the same only...

The American questions me: What am I doing here? Who am I working for? I'm on the trail of a poet? What sort of poet? A Jewish poet? Does this mean I'm also on a mission? He is. He's in Ukraine, spreading the word, the true doctrine, inviting people to repent, change their lives through faith in Jesus Christ and to live in agreement with God's will. His mission, motivated by love, is to provide for the needy out in Ukraine's villages.

The Swede watches me covertly. He'd much rather change the subject, go for something with flirtatious overtones, but as the American's business colleague, he can't waltz me in the desired direction.

The American continues preaching until he notices I'm not coming up with any Biblical responses.

'How are you helping the needy in the Ukrainian villages?' I ask.

'Our church runs a small factory where the mentally handicapped make furniture that we sell in America and Sweden. Handmade furniture. It's a very desirable product and brings in a nice profit for our church.' He smiles. Expecting admiration?

'Do you pay your Ukrainian workers minimum wage?' It's only an idle question, one made to show I'm listening.

But his smile is gone. He leans across the table, aggressive. 'Let me tell you something. No one cares about the handicapped here in the Ukraine. They leave them to die. Without us, they'd starve. We feed them, clothe them, and house them. They need people like us, people willing to show Christ's love through action. Jesus wants us to love others, not sentimentally, but through work performed out of kindness, and powered by tangible love.'

His words hurtle through the dining room, for Ukrainian pop music's yelp has inexplicably expired. Now, the brocade curtain on the back wall rises, revealing a huge screen. And the strident hysteria of a re-transmitted football match effectively precludes the sermon.

***

*I*n the 1870s, Jewish intellectual life was blossoming in Galicia. The religious monopoly had been broken, and those opposing change had been left behind. The new Austrian constitution of 1867 granted freedom of religion and conscience, and guaranteed full civic equality. The first direct parliamentary elections for seats in the Austrian parliament were held in 1873, and four Jews were elected from East Galicia. In 1874, Jewish mayors were elected in ten Galician cities, and in forty-five others, Jews were the majority on municipal councils.

As well mannered as any Austrian bourgeois, educated Galician Jews spoke Polish, German, Russian, French, and participated in high culture. There were literary salons in all the major cities, and Jews were journalists, editors, publicists, poets, novelists, and teachers. Modern scholars dedicated themselves to critical analyses of religious texts; rabbis with broad, secular knowledge were being sought. But disillusion had also set in: the older generation of Maskilim pointed warning fingers at the modern men of the pseudo-Haskalah, their lack of ideals, their break with Jewish culture.

Velvel, although finding no favour with those middle-class Polish-speaking Jews, was still loved by the tailors, sewers, and cutters who warbled his melodies in their factories, and by the coachmen who made his Yiddish words their own. Such men, unhampered by new social codes and 'worldly' behaviour, were not ashamed to weep when he sang to them in their own language. With such people around him, Velvel could always be certain of earning money and garnering applause. But singing in Yiddish to the humble in 'low' bars meant the door to a higher status public remained firmly closed. Those up there on society's peak never even knew his name.

Chapter XIX:
Return to Czernowitz

Says the tailor, he wants no songs
Not everyone needs them
Give me money, good brother,
And I'll sew you clothes
What will I do with songs?
They're not letters that I can understand,
Give me money, I'll sew you boots,
If you don't want to go barefoot

Velvel Zbarzher

*T*he fubsy Austrian in the breakfast room is desperate to talk about himself, his childhood, his role as an artist: 'I'm a sculptor, a photographer, and a painter of abstract expressionism, hyperrealism, impressionism, everything.' He works hard at making himself sound interesting. He's also determined to teach me, an ignorant foreigner, a thing or two about geography, history, philosophy, literature. There's no stopping the flow. He tells me where to go—to the Jewish museum, the theatre, the synagogue, the Turkish fountain—talks of his own love story with Czernowitz: 'This is still such a beautiful city; the Ukrainians have a nice feel for things.'

This glorious outpost of the vanished empire has fired his imagination. But an empire isn't what interests him, he insists, just the Jews who lived here. He's been diligently tracking them down.

'People like Celan, Ausländer. Franzos went to school here in Czernowitz—there's a commemoration plaque on the building. Velvel Zbarzher? Never heard of him. Moshe Orenstein? He died here in 1906? Never heard of him either. But there was Burg. And Reich. And, of course, Itsik Manger. Manger was born here, did you know that? So was Aharon Applefeld. I once wrote to Applefeld in Israel, but he never answered my letter. I wonder why.'

'You must be one of many who did that.'

'Perhaps.' Evidently the idea doesn't displease him. 'There are quite a few Austrians who come to this city and look for the Jewish past. I've met three other photographers this week.'

Obsessed by Bukovina's famous but vanished Jews, he knows their works and all their former addresses. His hired driver ('I pay him very well indeed,') takes him to cemeteries, back streets, and outlying villages with ruined synagogues where he takes photos. He's a groupie of sorts. A groupie of the dead. Is he Jewish? Does he have Jewish antecedents?

'Most definitely not. But I'm charting life just as Marcel Proust (another Jew) did.' He smiles with pompous satisfaction: 'I even feel...well...that I'm a modern Proust.'

***

There are only a few of us out in the Sunday morning streets, but a loudspeaker high on a lamp post pumps out commercials and disco music for our benefit. As late as 1904, here on the Ringplatz, Jewish moneylenders sat at little tables offering their services to farmers and, most frequently, to indebted garrison officers burdened by a night's gambling.

Across the road, is the literary café with its commemorative plaque:

> *In Czernowitz, Sundays began with Schubert and ended in duels. Czernowitz, halfway between Kiev and Bucharest, Krakow and Odessa, was the unofficial capital of Europe, where butcher's daughters sang coloraturas, and coachmen argued about Karl Kraus, where sidewalks were swept with bouquets of roses, and there were more bookshops than bakeries. Czernowitz was a perpetual intellectual argument, and every morning a new theory was invented only to be discarded by evening. Here, dogs were named after Olympian gods and the chickens scratched verses of Hölderlin into the soil. Czernowitz was a pleasure boat that crossed from east to west with Ukrainian crew, German officers, and Jewish passengers all under the Austrian flag.[146]*

The empty streets give the impression of an occupied city, one taken over by those who, lacking the refinement of earlier times, have bedecked it with gaudy signs and commercial slogans instead. The beauty is still here, though. Just look behind the plastic panels and under the graffiti.

Czernowitz had changed much since Velvel's first passage in the 1840s. By the 1870s, thanks to the relative liberality of the Habsburg Empire, the economically sound German-speaking middle class, and those Jews educated in gymnasia and German-Jewish schools, this city had become 'Little Vienna', the glory of Eastern Europe. Here, learned conferences were given. There were libraries, theatres, exquisite buildings, and beautiful hotels: the Palace Hotel, Hotel Bristol, Hotel Gotlieb, Hotel Paris, and Hotel Lemberg. In Jewish-owned cafes—Café de l'Europe, Café Hapsburg, and Kaiser Café—men gambled, smoked, debated, and read newspapers, and in 1874, Franz List gave a concert in the ballroom of the Hôtel de Moldavie. On that same hotel's upper floor:

> *...a rather frightening mixture of an inn and a bar...in the*

---

146 Heinzen, *The Rheinischen Merkur.*

tobacco smoke-filled atmosphere [are] Ruthenian and Walachian farmers, those who trade the profits earned in the yearly market for mind-altering drink, under-officers from the barracks who play billiards and, in all possible languages, swear and spit, Russian businessmen from Akkerman and Odessa who, in their wolf furs, drink tea and count their greasy banknotes, Jews who offer their services to everyone and for any reason, and finally Gypsies, lured here by the yearly market.[147]

Oh, to have seen all that! But the Hôtel de Moldavie went out of business in 1892, and the building was torn down.

Still standing is another building, quite as famous: the hotel, Zum Schwarzen Adler. Once a stopping place for well-heeled guests and people of importance, it was here, that Velvel and Avrom Goldfaden met up again. Velvel was in Czernowitz visiting his brother Meir, then teaching in this city; having left Odessa, Goldfaden was hoping to publish a Yiddish-language daily, *Dos Bukoviner Israelitishe Folksblatt.* Unable to pay the registration fee, he counted on the local enlightened 'Deutsch' Jews to contribute generously. He was particularly encouraging to young writers,[148] especially those who, like twenty-two-year-old David Yeshaya Silberbusch, had been raised in a Hasidic environment and were new to the Haskalah.[149]

One Sunday morning in the spring of 1876, Silberbusch

---

147 Eckardt, *Die Grenzboten.*

148 Another, Mark Warshawsky, was an unsuccessful Kiev lawyer. Encouraged by Goldfaden, Warshawsky began creating songs about the daily life of Jews in the Russian Pale and singing them to friends, but he didn't take his work seriously and never wrote down his compositions. Near the end of his life, Sholem Aleichem persuaded Warshawsky to dictate them to him. Today, *Oyfn Pripetshik* and *A Brif fun Amerike* are still well known.

149 While living in his father-in-law's home Silberbusch was given the opportunity to study German with a children's tutor. Later, after reading European and Haskalah literature, he began editing for Smolenskin in Vienna. He became a prolific author and, in 1934, moved to Palestine where he was warmly received as one of the last Maskilim.

came to see Goldfaden in Zum Schwarzen Adler, where, despite a lack of funds, he was relishing life in an expensive room (he never did fail to offer himself luxury, and later, while actors in his troupe went hungry, Goldfaden stayed in splendid hotels.)

> *He had a large sitting room, with an alcove for bed and washbasin. The doorway was hung with blue velvet drapes. A thick carpet covered the floor. There were [sic]a sofa, a polished dark-wood table with leather-upholstered chairs around it. In a corner, near a window, stood a piano and a writing desk.*
>
> *When I arrived at about eleven o'clock, he had, I think, been sitting at the desk. He was wearing a grey dressing gown with blue stripes at the collar, and embroidered velvet slippers. On his nose, highly polished, gold-framed glasses... what impressed me were the golden frames and the expensive lifestyle of a Jewish author.*
>
> *The elegance cost me. In keeping with the Hasidic custom of paying the rebbe for his advice, I had prepared three Austrian guilders to pay in advance for a half-year's subscription to his paper, Izraelitisches Folksblatt, which he was planning to publish in Czernowitz. I knew this was the way to soften the heart of an editor. But three guldens seemed too paltry for an editor with gold-framed spectacles, who treaded a thick carpet in embroidered velvet slippers.[150]*

After making it clear Silberbusch wouldn't be paid for any articles published in the new paper, Goldfaden invited him to return later that afternoon and talk about his literary ambitions. He arrived at four, saw that Goldfaden was no longer alone: his two guests were the Hebrew writer and school director Moshe Orenstein, and folk singer Velvel Zbarzher Ehrenkranz.

---

150 Silberbusch, *Mi-Pinkas zikhronotai.*

Silberbusch was awed by such famous men. He didn't know Orenstein's writings, but knew he'd helped obtain Bernyu's release during the Sadagora scandal. Velvel, however, was very near his heart. Silberbusch knew all his Hebrew and Yiddish poems as well as his melodies. And now, here he was, in the same room as the great man himself: 'in the flesh, not tall, but with a round, shaved face, small tearful eyes and a steady fine smile.'[151]

They all sat around the table talking calmly until, quite suddenly Velvel did something that, in Silberbusch's eyes, was very odd: leaping to his feet, he began singing to the bubbling samovar:

> *Why are you sitting there*
> *And boiling all the time?*
> *Tell me, I don't understand it...*

Shocked by the unconventional outburst, Silberbusch and Orenstein looked at each other—they had no idea the verse had been written by Goldfaden. But roaring with laughter, Goldfaden went to the open piano, began playing and singing the next stanzas.

> *You don't know the things*
> *I see and hear,*
> *Things that make me angry.*
> *The polite host serves tea to his guest,*
> *But I know how he hates him*
> *And wishes he would choke.*
> *A man comes to visit.*
> *The hosts laugh, mock, offend him*
> *They don't care if his heart bleeds.*
> *A wife fights with her husband*
> *He talks sweetly, she throws the glass at him.*
> *How can one bear such things?*[152]

---

151 Silberbusch, *Mi-Pinkas zikhronotai*, translation Irene Ehrenkranz Fishler.
152 Ibid.

When Goldfaden finished his song, Velvel ran over, hugged and kissed him. Orenstein smiled. He was used to Velvel and knew how to calm him down. Softly, he began reciting one of his exquisite Hebrew poems, a satire on the Rebbe Bernyu recently published in Smolenskin's Ha-Shahar. Velvel listened to Orenstein's performance with pleasure. Then standing, waving his right hand over his forehead, he began reciting his own satire about the Rebbe.

All in the room were amused...except young Silberbusch. Still much influenced by his childhood environment—he had just spent Purim at that Sadagora rebbe's palace—he was miserably uncomfortable when the Hasidim were attacked by outsiders.

That evening, Silberbusch followed Velvel and Goldfaden down into the cellar-restaurant on the corner of the Postgasse. Velvel had promised his fans he would bring along a friend—a young important Odessa folk poet. When they arrived, everyone stared: Velvel was as well-dressed as ever, and his gold watch on its golden chain sat nicely in his vest pocket, but Goldfaden, tall, with styled hair, and golden glasses, looked like a real aristocrat.

On this particular evening, Velvel took his admirers by surprise. As usual, a row of wine bottles waited on the table, glasses were filled, and everyone drank. Only Velvel's glass remained untouched. The new guest, Goldfaden, ordered black coffee, and Velvel did the same. Then he began singing, occasionally stopping to sip his coffee. It was most unusual.

His followers later said that Velvel had never performed more brilliantly. His cynical wit always provoked laughter, but on this occasion, he left his audience in a meditative mood. Goldfaden, more impressed than anyone, penned, in tribute, the first few lines of a new poem:

Velvel
Sweet hope and soul
Satire and wit

He is the people's soul
He is their ideal
A folk poet must never be proud
He must go where his people are
In cellars he must rehearse
His literature with them alone.[153]

***

Goldfaden flopped in his attempt to publish his newspaper. He left Czernowitz to try his luck in Romania. There, in Jassy he met Broderzinger Israel Grodner, a flexible performer deft at playing different characters and singing Goldfaden's songs. Goldfaden was impressed: most Broderzinger were content to sing in cellars and back kitchens, but Grodner demanded a theatrical setting, a stage, numbered benches, and printed announcements of future performances. He was a professional, the first real Yiddish actor.

Goldfaden and Grodner decided to join forces. Unable to rent a theatre in Jassy they travelled on to Botoşani, Galatz, Braila and Bucharest, took on board hopeful actors, starstruck shopkeepers, servants, singers, badkhonim, musicians, apprentices[154] and—a very radical departure—employing women for the female roles. They were joined by Goldfaden's two brothers, Tobias and Judah ('To get money out of Judah would be like bringing a man down from Mars'),[155] and by 1876, the first official Yiddish theatre troupe numbered forty.

Early Yiddish theatre met with great opposition from the Orthodox community, from the Romanian bureaucracy, and from writers who refused to create plays. In Goldfaden's productions, characters were caricatures, and songs were a mixture of Polish, Ukrainian, and Hasidic chants. Although

---

153 The poem was only completed thirty years later, in New York.

154 Yisroel Rosenberg, an actor in this first troupe, was the man who used Goldfaden's plays to start Russian Yiddish theatre in Odessa two years later.

155 Kessler, *Memoirs of the Yiddish Stage.*

each play did have a plot, there was no formal script, and actors relied on improvisation. But the craftsmen, labourers, and well-off businessmen in the audience were delighted. As David Kessler later wrote:

> *If the Yiddish theatre was amateurish, then the non-Jewish (and I mean the Romanian) was a thousand times more so. And the Romanians knew it…80% of our audience was non-Jewish.*[156]

***

The stately Zum Schwarzen Adler, built in 1863, once welcomed the city's most illustrious visitors. It is no longer a hotel; since its closure in 1999, it has become a school of economics. I want to slip inside, sneak through corridors, but the new white plastic door is locked tight. On the corner of the Postgasse, another door—it once opened into Zum Schwarzen Adler's renowned Grand Restaurant, Bar, and Cafe—is also closed: this part of the building has been taken over by a bank.

I peer through the modern display windows hoping for the hint of a decorous past—lofty ceilings, the grandeur of marble and oak—but find only suffocating plasterboard covered by banking slogans and posters showing laughing families acquiring computers, houses, cars, and going cheerfully into debt. Little doubt, that cellar restaurant where Velvel performed is now the bank's basement.

Things have changed so much. Even Velvel, a mere phantom on this frosty street, vanishes totally in today's pop rackety restaurants, bars, and cafés. Equally impossible to find Dr Reitman's house where Bernyu began his new life and admired the piano-playing daughter. The gardens where popular Jewish theatre once took place (were these performances by Broderzinger?) are frozen expanses under the falling snow. Here was the elegant Jewish theatre; here is

---

156 Kessler, *Memoirs of the Yiddish Stage.*

the once-glorious synagogue, minus its proud cupola.

In 1941, the German army poured petrol near the synagogue's arc, burnt the sixty-three Torah scrolls, then bombed the building. The last rabbi, Jacob Mark, was brought to Gestapo headquarters in Zum Schwarzen Adler. After being locked into the cellar for forty-eight hours, he was forced onto the Adler's roof to watch the synagogue's dome burn before he was murdered.

The building resisted total destruction. No longer a synagogue, it has been converted into a movie theatre. Painted bright blue, the outside walls are covered by gaudy posters of cinema's celluloid ladies and movie-star toughs with machine guns. Less than a third of Czernowitz's Jewish community of over 50,000 survived World War Two. The Soviet murder of the kulaks, the Ukrainian, Russian, and Romanian intelligentsia, the ethnic cleansing and deportation of Gagauzes, Germans, Poles, and remaining Jews destroyed Bukovina's multiculturalism. Today, Ukrainians are the city's dominant group.

***

'*I*'ll have taken around one thousand five hundred photos by the time I leave,' says the Austrian fuddy-duddy. Again, he lists the Jewish cemeteries and villages he's visited, the houses of writers he has photographed for posterity. Two days ago, he was in Sadagora.

'Of course, everything's already been photographed by hundreds of other people. You can see all their photos online.' He is unabashed at being a copycat. 'After breakfast, two of us are going to the house of Josef Burg, the Yiddish poet.'

He stops, shakes his head with the confused regret of a man whose father and grandfather helped smash a civilization to smithereens. 'This was all part of Austria once. What culture! What talent. The Holocaust, terrible, terrible. Well, I'm off. My driver will be here at nine. He has to work hard, but I pay him well.'

***

I also go to Sadagora, but not on a pilgrimage. The synagogue and palace became a factory in Soviet times and, today, the Hasidim are restoring what's left. Both places were mentioned in S. Ansky's report of Jewish destruction: [157]

> *In the largest room, the walls were lined with cots, on which sick Romanian soldiers, newly arrived from the front, were sitting or lying. Dark, haggard, gloomy shadows in wet, muddy tattered overcoats, half barefoot, squeezed together, they trembled with fever, moaned...Amidst dense steam and a suffocating stench, a few dozen naked soldiers were shuffling about, sick and emaciated...the senior physician... said to me: 'How do you like our heroes, our brave allies? Ha! They thought that waging war is as simple as playing in a Romanian band.'*
>
> *...I entered the large and very lofty synagogue...peered around. Torn, naked, filthy walls, with a few traditional pictures left here and there: lions and leopards, musical instruments. An expensive but broken chandelier hung from the ceiling.*
>
> *Then my eyes alighted on the eastern wall—and what I saw made me tremble. The rich ornamentation of the Holy Ark with the Tablets of the Law above it was untouched. But at the centre, on the Holy Ark, a Christian icon had been inserted. Desecration.*

---

157 Ansky, *The Enemy at His Pleasure.*

On foot, I cross the River Prut and take the straggling, potholed main road lined by trees violently hacked off mid-height. New villas sit side-by-side with a few wretched huts, and in the yard of one, an ancient crone, bent double and dressed in rusty black tatters, fetches water from a pump. She is snagged into an earlier century.

Finally, here is Sadagora, sitting in the Carpathian's shadow. It seems a mild enough town where the old buildings seen on postcards have been replaced by modern supermarkets. At the town's edge, just where fields start, is a new suburb. And here is another castle—not of some charismatic zaddik, Polish or Ukrainian aristocrat. This brand-new construction belongs to a wealthy modern consumer, and like any respectable castle, possesses a (fake) crenelated roof, two concrete towers, (fake) old stonework, and an iron gate so grandiose, it harkens back to some forbidding medieval abode. Only lacking are a moat, a drawbridge, and a gaggle of itchy-fingered archers with steady bows. But, approaching, I see it is only a barbarian's bastion: the yard is filled with plastic, rubbish, discarded toys, rotting clothing, and a rusted car wreck.

***

*T*his morning, the door to the former Zum Schwarzen Adler Hotel is open. I enter, and although the receptionist in her little cubical is a bulldoggish and surly leftover from Soviet days, I will not be deterred. Like the Viennese rubbernecker, I, too, want to poke my nose into once-magical places; I want my stock of photos.

Seeing communication with me is hopeless, the mean-lipped termagant enlists the help of Julia, a philology professor who speaks excellent English and German. I explain my mission and am led, pronto, to the administration office to meet the director and other staff members. Magically, my status has changed from loathsome voyeur to honoured guest, although the names Velvel Zbarzher and Avrom Goldfaden mean nothing to anyone. Where am I from? Am I not afraid to travel alone in Ukraine? Do I like Czernowitz? It's such a beautiful city, and they're all proud to live here.

'When I travel anywhere else, I'm always happy to return,' says the director. 'This city is so international. We even have two Russian students in our school.'

Julia leads me down long hallways with their original wooden doors (although the ceilings have been covered by some grisly modern miracle-material), then into classrooms, once the hotel's bedrooms. 'Back then, a wall divided these into two parts.' Just as Silberbusch described: alcoves for beds and washbasins.

But aside from the waxed wooden floors, there is nothing of the past. Where could a piano have stood? A sofa, leather-upholstered chairs, the polished dark-wood table, a samovar? Can I imagine heavy blue velvet drapes covering a vanished doorway? A thick carpet on the floor?

'Come, I'll take you into the library,' says Julia. 'I think it was once part of the restaurant's dining room or bar, and it probably hasn't changed much over the years.'

A painting of the Austro-Hungarian eagle hangs on one wall, just as it must have done a hundred and fifty years ago. A wooden counter, perhaps once a bar, runs along on wall. Could Orenstein, Velvel, and Goldfaden have dined here, sat at one of these many tables? Could this have been a meeting place for vanished Ruthenian and Walachian farmers, Austrian officers, Russian businessmen in wolf furs, Jews, and Gypsies? There's no way of knowing.

When Julia returns to her classroom, I sit. Wait. Wish for cigar and pipe smoke, the clink of glasses, the brouhaha of twenty different tongues, the ribald laughter, the beasty odour of rough fur coats and greasy skin. But the air in this dark room is perfectly still. Nothing, other than imagination, will bring back the past.

I'm just another groupie, running after Velvel and his crowd a century and a half too late. Chasing spectres. In the end, it's the era I'm in love with: a glorified past, unreal, untouchable. A colourful inaccessible panorama.

Chapter XX:
Malkele

If you talk a lot, you talk of yourself.
Yiddish proverb

'*A* dear and precious man—I have already told you he once gave me ninety-five francs for my work—invited me to Buhuşi for Purim,' Velvel wrote to Orenstein. He was in Romania again and in high spirits, but the return wasn't as pleasant as he'd imagined. On the Shabbes evening, just after the Kiddush, Velvel's host informed him he had read his book, *Romanyah*, and it had made him very angry.

'Why are you attacking in such a hard way?'

Velvel must have been astonished, but he was never one to back down. 'On the contrary,' he said, 'my attack was far too weak. You are patriots of murderers. I wish to be their murderer.'

His host immediately changed tone: 'I'm not defending injustice. I merely wanted to warn you that you're in great danger here.' Opening a law-book, he pointed to a paragraph stating that Velvel could receive twenty years imprisonment for his scathing verses.

'I was immediately beset by fear. All my limbs began to

quiver,' Velvel wrote. His host was a member of *B'nai-Zion* or *Infratzirea Zion*, the Brotherhood of Zion (*Fraternitatea Zion*), or *Noua Fraternitate*, (the New Fraternity).[158] Comprised of wealthy radical patriots from the Sephardic community[159] who called each other 'brother' and maintained strong links with the Alliance Israélite Universelle, they contributed much money to Romanian cultural institutions and promoted collaboration with non-Jewish intellectuals.

Were these men dangerous to Velvel? He thought so, but his reactions were always extreme. Immediately, he contacted a lawyer friend who laughed at his fears: 'First, there's freedom of the press in Romania. Second, this is an old law. Third, you can always claim that you're not the author of *Romanyah*, and that the charge is false.'

To be on the safe side, Velvel wrote to Vienna (probably to Smolenskin) asking for a letter confirming he was not the author. Then, calmly certain he was out of danger, went on to Galatz for the Pesach celebration.

'I borrowed eight ducats, prepared an exquisite Pesach, just the way I like it,' Velvel wrote to Orenstein. 'But, disaster! On the second day, a friend came to see me, a trustworthy man who loves me. He told me he'd been invited to the Buhuşi rebbe's table, and while he was there, people talked about my *Romanyah*. And one man, a stranger, shouted: "I was in a coffeehouse and heard that the Zionists are doing everything they can to hand Zbarzher over to the authorities."'

Again, Velvel panicked. 'I couldn't stop trembling. My holiday was ruined. People in Galatz tried to comfort me. They said that perhaps my friend was untrustworthy. But I know those members of B'nai-Zion. They are many and have

---

158 The Fraternitatea Zion was founded in Bucharest with the help of the Jewish American consul-general Benjamin Peixotto. A former B'nai B'rith president, Peixotto was sent to Romania to combat anti-Semitism. This organization had nothing to do with the (later) Zionist movement.

159 By the eighteenth century, several Sephardic businessmen were running successful banking institutions. The Jewish-owned Marmorosch-Blank Bank, founded in 1874, remained Romania's largest bank until 1880.

much money; I am only one man, and I'm poor. I thought about things carefully, then immediately after Pesach, together with my wife, I left for Tulcea.'

***

*D*id you catch that? So, now we know: there's a woman in the picture. A wife, no less! And she's the beautiful Malke. Rumour said that Velvel had met her many years earlier, in the 1850s, in Bucharest. How? Where? Can we imagine a dusky evening in some cushy home where, by a kerosene lamp's gentle light, Velvel sang, flirted, charmed? Or was it Malkele who made the first move?

What do we know about her? She, Malkele (or Malciu) had children and had been married. Most likely, she is the married woman Velvel mentioned to his brother in Zbarazh in 1869. She was, perhaps, the muse for his yearning poem. Had he loved her for all the long years, waiting on the off chance that, one day, she'd be free? She had supported her family as a seamstress in Bucharest, had gone to Constantinople and opened a coffeehouse near the Galata Tower. Surely, she was an unusual person in her own right, an independent woman, a toughie, an original, and the femme fatale who had lured him from Zbarazh to Constantinople. She's just the sort of woman I'm rooting for. Yet, aside from this one 1875 reference to his wife, Velvel never mentions her again. Was she with him when he travelled? Perhaps his friends disapproved of the match.

Weissberg claims Velvel married this Jewish-Polish woman 'out of pure love,' that she was a 'well-known Lady of the Camellias' in the Constantinople German-speaking community. The more prudish Silberbusch (he would always insist that Velvel's conventional first marriage had been a love match) was far less flattering about this independent woman, this 'seductress':

In his poetry [Wolf Ehrenkranz] often reached the highest level. Yet, he remained a big helpless child. Malkale from

Bucharest was an enthusiast of his Yiddish songs. She was his greatest devotee. She seduced him, and they married in his later days.[160]

***

*V*elvel and Malkele tarried in Ottoman Tulcea, today a modern Romanian resort. Back then, it was a quaint hilly town with dusty roads, low-lying red-tiled houses, and a garrison of fez-wearing Turkish soldiers in baggy trousers. It was a snug port—the Danube Delta wetlands are not far distant—and back then, the Black Sea knew an inconceivable (by today's standards) abundance of marine life with porpoises, dolphins, hordes of anchovy, river spawning salmon and sturgeon, turbot, sprat, goby, ray, grey mullet, and whiting—all so tame, they could be caught with bare hands:

> *All was bustle on a small scale. Fishermen were every now and then bringing in the trophies of their success. In one quarter, under a canopy of dried leaves, the only shelter from sun and rain except the miserable huts already described, might be seen the houseless host of travellers sitting on a board, which served likewise for a table, regaling themselves with slices of tonny or sturgeon fried on a skewer and eggs cooked in wood ashes; while, a little further off, a party of boatmen, squatting on the ground, sent round the black bread and acid wine with all the glee of health and appetite, nothing disturbed by the numerous dogs and pigs, each of the latter with a triangle round his neck, which surrounded them with beseeching cries.*[161]

---

160 Silberbusch, *Mi-Pinkas zikhronotai*, translation Irene Ehrenkranz Fishler.
161 Boileau, *The Great Empires of Austria, Russia and Turkey.*

Safely outside of Romanian territory and with nothing more to fear, Velvel declared he would hit out at all his detractors:

> *From Turkey, my new country of residence, I will take revenge on the infamous patriots of murderers who torture and torment their brothers. Now they'll be the ones who tremble. First, I'll print a manifesto in Hebrew and Yiddish warning people not to adhere to this organization, telling those already in it, that they should leave. I'll write a newspaper article in Moldovian, claim the Zionists gave me the money to publish Romanyah. I'll fulfil the precept of Deuteronomy 19, 19: "Then shall ye do unto him as he had thought to have done unto his brother; so shalt thou put the evil away from among you." And because I can no longer step onto Romanian earth, because I'm afraid, I will go to Russia.*

What happened in the end? Did he write those vitriolic poems and that accusatory article? Did he go to Russia? No. What vengeance did he wreak? None.

Velvel soon realised that the members of *B'nai-Zion* had no intention of harming him. On the contrary, when he and Malke returned to Romania, they were his strong supporters. Eating and drinking with them, his sound and fury evaporated. Had marriage and newfound security tamed him? Was he softened by the lucre and ease of Bucharest's middle class? How can I condemn him? Perhaps he was simply tired out.

'I wanted to leave on Sunday but our friend Akiva Khashmal came and invited me to sing, and I have earned some ducats. After that, Auerbach invited me and, again, I earned some nice ducats. Now I am invited after the Sabbath to a society-friend. As long as I can earn money here, why leave Bucharest?'

But he did leave. Had he ceased to be a novelty in an affluent world that always craved new diversions? Perhaps the cushy salons and required good behaviour eventually wore at his soul, for his comfortable road companions had always been candid provocation and poverty.

So, with Malke, he moved back, or—according to the ever-denigrating Silberbusch—was lured back to Turkey:

In the years 1879-1880, after the Russian–Turkish war, she tempted him to Constantinople. There, she was the bread earner, and he sat in a separate room, composing poems and dreaming.[162]

---

162 Silberbusch, *Mi-Pinkas zikhronotai*, translation Irene Ehrenkranz Fishler.

Chapter XXI:
Constantinople

No Jews live in the city, for they have been placed behind an inlet of the sea. An arm of the sea of Marmora shuts them in on the one side, and they are unable to go out except by way of the sea, when they want to do business with the inhabitants. In the Jewish quarter are about 2,000 Rabbanite Jews and about 500 Karaïtes, and a fence divides them...No Jew there is allowed to ride on horseback. The one exception is R. Solomon Hamitsri, who is the king's physician, and through whom the Jews enjoy considerable alleviation of their oppression. For their condition is very low, and there is much hatred against them, which is fostered by the tanners, who throw out their dirty water in the streets before the doors of the Jewish houses and defile the Jews' quarter (the Ghetto). So the Greeks hate the Jews, good and bad alike, and subject them to great oppression, and beat them in the streets, and in every way treat them with rigour. Yet the Jews are rich and good, kindly and charitable, and bear their lot with cheerfulness.

Benjamin of Tudela, 12th century

*L*ook at old photos of Constantinople, what do you see? Along the Bosporus, there are a few fishermen, and streets lined by wooden houses seem calm. Absent are fashion-conscious Turks shouting into cell phones, troupes of tourists shepherded by guides, hordes from high-rise cruise ships, honking cars, and ear-ripping motorbikes.

In wealthy Jewish, Christian or Muslim families, the male head is dressed like any Turkic pasha; his heavily-costumed women are doe-eyed, pulpy, and protected. They must have been as ingenuous as the girls of thirteen with whom I sat on an Anatolian rooftop many years ago. There, under a gentle spring sun, they happily sewed their trousseaux, for they would all be married off within the year. 'Do you have cows in Europe?' they asked me. 'Do you have flowers and trees?' Not permitted to attend school or read books, pure happiness meant a wedding, a husband, and the position of wife. Like the promises made to those young girls, photographic Ottoman tranquillity was superficial:

We met a man leading a long train of negresses, whose merry faces and gay chattering consorted ill with their name and condition; for they were slaves, returning unsold after the day's market, as no one had bidden for them. It was difficult to conjecture whether their hilarity arose from satisfaction at not having passed from the hands of a dealer into those of a new master, or from a conviction that they would prove more saleable the ensuing day...Most of the foreigners brought here for sale are from childhood taught to regard their condition in Turkey as one leading to promotion and happiness: the few years they have passed in Georgia, Circassia, or Africa, have generally been so miserable, that they look forward to a master's, as to a father's, house, and are thankful when they exchange their first keepers for the probable contingency of a better home.

The market, where during certain hours the captives are submitted to inspection, is a square, in which the more valuable, that is, more beautiful, among the women have separate apartments; while the Egyptians are generally huddled together in an open veranda. When a purchaser arrives, an examination of the captives is permitted; but the whole transaction of transfer is said to be conducted with more propriety and consideration by Turks than by Christians.[163]

Once called the 'Vienna of the Balkans,' Constantinople was a cosmopolitan mix of Greeks, Turks, Armenians, and Jews, but by the nineteenth century, the Ottoman Empire was rotting. Degenerate Sultans had too long idled in harems and become the pawns of female intrigue; the once-fearsome Janissaries and Sipahis were lacking in military efficiency; the lazy and unremittingly corrupt administration, composed of adventurers, Christian renegades and former slaves, was cut off from the populace—a considerable handicap in this century with its new promises of democracy.

To reverse the decline, Sultan Mahmud II attempted to disband the Janissaries in 1826, but almost 135,000 of them revolted—a problem he only resolved by their massacre, imprisonment, exile, and replacement. To bring the country up to European standards with modern schools, roads and railways, new measures known as the *Tanzimat* (the Reorganization) replaced religious law with secular and guaranteed the protection of all the sultan's subjects.

Ottoman decay was reflected in the depressed condition of Constantinople's Jewish community. After 1492, the original Greek-speaking Romaniotes, resident since Byzantine days, had been outnumbered by incoming Ladino-speaking Sephardic Jews displaced by the Inquisition in Spain and Portugal.[164] They were followed by Yiddish-speaking Eastern European Ashkenazi Jews fleeing blood libels and massacres. Modern Jews arrived after the Russo-Turkish war.

---

163 Boileau, *The Great Empires of Austria, Russia and Turkey.*

164 Derived from Old Spanish and spoken throughout the former Ottoman Empire by Sephardic minorities, like Yiddish, Ladino is enriched with Hebrew vocabulary and written with Hebrew letters.

Unlike Christians who dreamt of restoring Christian supremacy in the country, Turkish Jews had been content with Ottoman rule. There were Jewish artisans and guilds, and the wealthiest were powerful international traders, bankers, moneylenders, suppliers to the unruly, corrupt Janissary infantry units and Sipahi cavalry, and influential with pashas and sultans. However, by the nineteenth century, the community was no longer flourishing. Bogged down by Jewish religious fanaticism, decimated by cholera epidemics and catastrophic fires, it was being squeezed out of commerce by Armenian and Greek middlemen:

> *Jews in Turkey are objects of pity, whether we regard their physical, moral, or civil condition; they cherish the disease engendered by dirt, because they believe it purifies the blood; they cling to ignorance, because they interpret each effort to instruct into an attempt to Christianize them and they submit, because without resource, to a double portion of every indignity which a capricious government is pleased to inflict on its helpless dissenting dependents.*
>
> *They are trampled on even by the persecuted Greeks; and are actually obliged, during the week preceding Easter, to confine themselves to their houses, lest they should suffer violence from those whose feelings are more than ordinarily exasperated against the murderers of their Lord at the time when they commemorate his crucifixion.*[165]

When Sir Moses Montefiore came to this city in 1840, he found schoolboys reading the Talmud and translating it into Ladino. This greatly displeased him. With reforms such as the Tanzimat, Jewish life in Ottoman lands could be bettered, but modernisation was necessary. Children had to learn Turkish and prepare for change.

Montefiore and Adolphe Crémieux attempted to create modern schools, but community leaders opposed the new

---

165 Boileau, *The Great Empires of Austria, Russia and Turkey.*

institutions, banishing any who challenged their power. In 1860, a modern school was only allowed to open after four rabbis were appointed to censor books and purge them of 'unacceptable' information. Instructors were persecuted, and parents were threatened with excommunication. So great was the religious community's power, that few Jews entered the city's Military Medical School despite the installation of a kosher/halal kitchen. Once the leaders in Ottoman medicine, Jewish doctors were being replaced by Armenians and Greeks, and the penury in medical personnel delayed the creation of new hospital facilities. Baron de Hirsch, the financier of the Turkish railways, observed:

> *During my many long stays in Turkey, I have been painfully struck by the ignorance and misery of the great many Jews who inhabit this empire. There is progress everywhere in Turkey, but the Jews hardly profit from it because of their poverty and lack of enlightenment.*[166]

Officials from the Alliance Israélite[167] were shocked to discover that Jewish children seeking a modern education could only find it in the Christian missionary schools where they were being converted. Hoping to provide a European-style education and a modern approach to religion, a Jewish school was set up in 1875, a girl's school in 1878, as were trade and agricultural schools throughout the empire. So effective were these institutions, they were attended by many Muslim Turks who later came to prominence.

> *Outside the wall is a modern establishment for the instruction of native youths in French, which may be regarded as an innovation fraught with important consequences. The law has hitherto rigidly prohibited Turks*

---

166 Bulletin de l'Alliance Israélite Universelle

167 Peretz Smolenskin headed one delegation, but he wasn't an effective administrator and accomplished nothing.

*from learning any language spoken by infidels, and has
thus compelled them to seek interpreters among their Greek
subjects, whose interests are often directly opposed to the
success of the diplomatic negotiations they are called upon
to conduct; but in a few years, the Porte will be enabled
to carry on her external relations through the medium
of Turkish agents whose personal ties bind them to the
state.*[168]

***

Although Silberbusch claims that Velvel no longer sang while living in Constantinople, his biographer, Dr Moses Fried suggests he did. If so, who would his audience have been? Probably not supple Turks in fezzes and baggy trousers, and not members of the conservative Ottoman Jewish community. Perhaps expatriate Galicians and Romanians craved the old notes of home, but could a Yiddish poet earn money? Velvel and Malke were impoverished, so there were no wealthy patrons on hand: in this city, the marriage of a Haskalah songster to a seamstress-cum-coffeehouse-owner kept gentility's doors shut tight.

What about the many poems Silberbusch claimed Velvel wrote in this period? No one has seen them. Against what would he have protested? Like Smolenskin and the other Maskilim, he must have been aware of anti-Semitism's new virulence.

In May 1883, Velvel's lungs became infected, and he was treated by a Dr Schwarz. 'I never learnt much in life,' Velvel told him. 'I never even read all through the Tanach.[169] But the Hebrew language lives inside me.'

His condition continued to degenerate and he died on the second of June 1883, at the age of fifty-seven. Malke paid

---

168 Boileau, *The Great Empires of Austria, Russia and Turkey.*

169 Canon of the Hebrew Bible

for his burial costs and gravestone:[170]

Here lies the poet Benjamin Wolf, son of Moses Ehrenkranz
You have brought honour to the Hebrew language
Your heart-rending songs have conquered many hearts
You have reached the poor and lit up their darkness
By the whip of your tongue, many hypocrites were chastised
Lovely plants are all your writings
Future generations will honour you

***

*D*isconsolate and glum because my quest is ending, I search half-heartedly for Malke's coffeehouse on the chaotic tourist-jammed streets near the Galata Tower. While female vocalists warble over echo chamber whine, people line up at ATMs, nimble-fingered youths filter in amongst the unwary, and glib-tongued hucksters peddle modern cell phones alongside blue amulets that give protection from the evil eye. Ubiquitous are the odours of grilling meat, frying fish, fast food grease, sweet honey, perfume, and bad drains.

What exactly am I looking for? Some rustic thrown-together affair with chipped plaster and sagging floors, the replica of some homey Eastern European shenk? Or was her coffeehouse exotic and oriental, with arches soaring high and broad windows? Today, such places resemble modern cafeterias and, by 1900, even Malke's was long gone. It had become Lichtenstein's Apothecary, and that business no longer exists either. Perhaps it's still around, as a modern pharmacy, and there are many of those, slotted between shops selling sports shoes, baseball caps, sunglasses, bicycles, and souvenirs. Occasionally, in the distance, I glimpse the dun-blue polluted Bosporus.

I veer onto narrower streets where the windows of ageless buildings are barred, and walls are defaced by doodles. Now

---

170 Leib Kneper, a long time Constantinople resident, claimed he composed the inscription.

look at this rosy-coloured building on my right, yet another pharmacy, the *Ege Eczanesi*. What if it's the right one? An old building, it has fine moulding and tiny panels of stained glass. On the floor above, is a pleasing cantilevered oriel window.

I enter, try to be discrete, but fool no one. The man and two women behind the counter immediately identify me as a foreigner, and once I begin asking questions, they also consider me eccentric. Could this pharmacy once have been a coffeehouse? Was it once called Lichtenstein's Apothecary? That door in the far wall, does it lead to a back room?

I receive no answers. A hundred and thirty-seven years have passed, and these people in front of me are in their forties. They don't know the building's history. They aren't even curious. Why should this surprise me? Who reads Velvel's poems now? Who thinks about Malke? What happened to her? After her brief appearance, she has vanished from history. Did she stay in Constantinople? Did she find other lovers? Do her descendants know about her once-famous love story with Velvel?

Even the Haskalah has been forgotten by all but scholars and historians, although modern Jewish life with all its choices is the result of that battle. What would Velvel have said? Perhaps just this:

Under the little hill
Where bones and skin rot
Are those once beautiful
Perhaps more beautiful than you.
Now they are food for worms.
Children, the world is only a dream
Man is born to die.

Chapter XXII:
After

Tell me, oh wind
You hover over the world,
Where can a poor man find,
A resting place a home?
Where injustice has ceased,
And brutalities ended,
Where the righteous never complain,
Where no eye has ever cried,
Where the just have never suffered
And all live at peace.
The wind stays silent, stills its course,
Sighs and goes away: 'No, no.
There is no such place, there is none.'

*D*espite his last years in relative obscurity, after his death Velvel became a legendary figure. Brochures were written about him, and one local noble likened him to a god-like figure, a Homer. In 1905, Ivan Franko, Ukrainian poet, socialist, and political activist, published a translation of Velvel's Messiah poems, and until the Second World War, men in factories and workshops in Europe and America were singing his songs. In the 1920s, the itinerant poet, Itsik Manger, adopted Velvel Zbarzher's persona—that of a hard-drinking, marginal troubadour—and, in 1937, he wrote his own love poem to Malkele the Beautiful:

> *I see you by your sewing machine*
> *A waking dream*
> *And a golden stripe shines*
> *In your black hair*[171]

Events, half-true or completely imaginary, were attached to Velvel's story. One fanciful article in the 1908 Bukowinaer Post[172] claimed that, in 1876, together with Goldfaden, he had hidden in an attic in Botoşani to avoid conscription into the Romanian army, that they had gone on the stage together to sing duets. Chaim Jedidjah Pollak[173] alleged that Malke possessed a bundle of Velvel's writings that were not to be read until fifty years after his death. And in the 1920s, David Yeshaya Silberbusch, who admired Velvel but was shocked by his excesses and displeased by his romance with Malke, penned a new version of his first marriage based, he claimed, on a story told half a century earlier by Issac Thorn, an elderly Maskil.

Deeply in love with his wife Chavale, (Silberbusch won't call her Chawcia) Velvel spends his days strolling through deep forests and writing her poems. One day, he meets a group of young men arriving from Russia with the new Haskalah literature, and hidden in the vegetation, he begins reading these works. When rumours of his heresy begin to circulate, Chawcia's parents demand she divorce her renegade husband. She refuses but gives Velvel her dowry money to go to Romania. Velvel writes to her for a few months, then stops. Her epistles to him are returned unread, and she dies of a broken heart.

---

171 Manger, *Velvl Zbarzher Shraybt Briv tsu Malkele der Sheyner.*

172 Abraham Goldfaden Obituary, January 14, 1908, *Bukowinaer Post.*

173 Pollack began life as a Hasid, became a Maskil, then converted to Christianity.

By attributing to Velvel the stories of Yitskhok Yoyel Linetski and Avrom Ber Gotlober who were forced to divorce when their 'heresy' was discovered, Silberbusch turns Chawcia and Velvel into star-crossed lovers. Her grass widow fate takes on a delicate hue; and he, the devoted husband, is obliged to abandon his post.

If this rosy fairytale did find favour with some, it denies too much: Moschke Shochet's attempt, through the arranged marriage, to tie his rebellious son to home and duty; Velvel's flight from Zbarazh shortly after the wedding; the community's fruitless search for his whereabouts. Why would the Haskalah have been brought from Russia when it began in Galicia? Feasibly, Velvel might have felt guilty: According to Thorn (via Silberbusch):

> ...one summer evening Velvel arrived unexpectedly at my place [in Botoşani]. He came into my room a distraught, broken man, his face as white as the wall. He mumbled in a few words about the bad news: 'something broke in my heart. The thin thread that binds me to my past has been cut by a mysterious, violent hand. I've had enough of this life as a melamed. I sat shiva for only one hour, then I came to town. I'm alone. I don't know what will happen to me now. I'm tormented by the thought that I'm not blameless for her young death.' I tried to comfort him. But his look was hard, as if saying 'don't say stupid things to me.'
>
> Unfortunately I was in a hurry. I had a very urgent business on the market. I put all the food I had on the table, a glass and a bottle of wine and told him to help himself, I would soon be back. After a short hour, when I returned, he was sitting at the table. The food was untouched and he'd sipped only half a glass of wine. But his face was smooth and calm.
>
> 'I have just operated on myself,' he said with a bitter smile. 'I have drowned my pain in the big ocean of eternal Weltschmerz.' He seemed transported, his cheeks were aflame...he sang his poem, In the Graveyard, and only

after did he drink with me, one glass, then another, and another. [174]

Had Chawcia been his great love, wrote Dr Moses Fried, Velvel would never have treated her so cavalierly.[175] And Dr Meir Weissberg, agreed that, as lovely as she might have been, Velvel could never have remained in a traditional marriage.

Fried and Weissberg were both right, for Velvel gives us the true story in his introduction to *Makel No'am*, and no later fanciful anecdote can override it:

> *He married but his wife was not his beloved. She didn't like touching him and he had no sons. His wife's sister came and scolded the wife for disrespecting such a fine man who could write and who was well thought-of and well spoken-of.*

Nascent bard, dreamer, Velvel refused frustration, family ties, and docile acceptance. Hightailing it out of Zbarazh, he headed into his uncertain future, perhaps not fearlessly, but without renunciation. And near the end of his life, he did find love...in beautiful Malkele's soft arms.

***

*I*n 1887, Velvel's old friend Avrom Goldfaden also left the Old Country. He went to New York but had difficulty adapting. When his new play flopped—it was declared not up to New York standards—he founded a newspaper and acting school. Both failed.

Back in Europe again, he drifted through Paris, Lemberg, Bucharest, Czernowitz, and London, earning a little money as a poet, journalist, and creating new plays. Rarely paid the royalties owing him, often hungry and ill, Goldfaden returned to New York.

---

174 Silberbusch, *Skizzen.*

175 Dr Moses Fried was born in Zbarazh and had known Velvel there.

Still elegant in top hat and golden pince-nez, much like Velvel, Goldfaden began seeking his audience in wine-bar cellars. And remembering that gone-by magical evening on the Postgasse in Czernowitz, when life had seemed rich with promise, and Velvel had sung with brilliance, Goldfaden completed the poem he'd begun thirty years earlier:

I wish I could ask
The Ba'alat Ov, the magic power, [176]
Who drew Samuel the prophet
From the earth
To again work
Its secret magic.
And, for me, call from the grave
A great important person.
Sweet hope and consolation,
Satire and joyful moral.
He was the peoples' soul,
He was their ideal.
Yes, witch, command the spirits,
Let them do their witches dance
And bring back for me the master:
Velvel Zbarjer Ehrenkranz. [177]

---

176 Ba'alat-ov, the Biblical female necromancer.

177 Goldfaden, *Dorhaflaga*, (The Generation of the Tower of Babel,) translation by Irene Ehrenkranz Fishler.

Part Three:
THE RUSSIAN PALE

Chapter XXIII:
Dubno

One of his friends advised him to make the acquaintance of the poet Gotlober, who, at that time, was teaching in one of the local Jewish schools. The old man who was giving him that counsel added: 'Go to see him some evening when no one will notice you, and make his acquaintance. He is an apostate who shaves his beard, and he does not enjoy the confidence of our community. Nor do we permit young men to cultivate an acquaintance with him; but you are a learned man, and you will know how to meet the statements of that heretic. He is a fine Hebrew scholar, and it might do you good to meet him. Remember the words of Rabbi Meier: 'Eat the wholesome fruit, and cast away the rind.' I'll tell the beadle to show you the way to the apostate.'

Sholem Yankev Abramovich meets Avrom Ber Gotlober[178]

'Svinich, the town where I was born, now that was some place, all right,' said Harry, my paternal grandfather. 'Everything you did, everywhere you went, there was always

---

178 Wiener, The *History of Yiddish Literature in the Nineteenth Century.*

somebody watching, somebody who saw evil. But what do you expect? There were no good teachers and no good schools. Russian, the language of the country, we didn't learn at all, because people who did were considered free-thinkers. If you associated with them, they'd spoil your religious sensibilities.'

Harry was born in the same year Velvel died—1883. His generation should have profited from the Haskalah that had reached the city of Lutsk, only thirty kilometres away. But it didn't touch backwaters like Svinich. There, life remained as conventional as it had been a hundred years before.

What did such towns and villages look like? What remains? Of course there will be no Jews to question, but why not prolong my journey into the past? Cross that defunct border, enter the Russian Pale and see how life differed from that in Galicia. The memory of my grandmother's painted landscape is still with me. I'll step into its gilded frame, find those very fields, penetrate the little copse and see what's in there.

***

*V*ia the Hungarian border, I travel into Ukraine by train. In Brody, I board a minibus heading for Dubno, pass sleeping fields and vegetation frozen into translucent spikes. Here, again, is the scrabble of trees replacing uniformed guards, wooden huts, and striped barriers. And, finally, I'm bumping along the roads of the vanished Russian Empire.

Life here depended on the whim of each tsar. In 1772, to exploit Jewish economic usefulness in the newly conquered Polish Lithuanian Commonwealth, Empress Catherine II (Catherine the Great) established the Pale of Settlement, a vast area of fifteen provinces.[179] The only Jews permitted to settle outside its borders were agriculturalists, the ennobled, those with a university education, members of affluent merchant guilds, certain craftsmen, military personnel, the Mountain Jews of Persian origin, Georgian Jews of Babylonian origin, Crimean Jewish Krymchaks, and Bukharan Jews who trace their ancestry to the Lost Tribes.

In 1804, under Alexander I, a new constitution granted freedom of religion, opened some universities, elementary, and secondary schools to Jews, allowed them to own or rent land, and reside in agricultural settlements. To destroy the feudal relationship between innkeepers and Polish aristocrats, Jewish participation in the liquor trade had to end. Expelled from the villages where their ancestors had lived for centuries, Jews were resettled in towns and cities.

The most hated policy was Tsar Nicholas I's 1827 instauration of a twenty-five-year term of service in the Russian military.[180] Once considered below contempt as warriors, conscription was now seen as a way of ending the Jewish medieval way of life, providing the education and skills necessary in a modern society, and promoting assimilation. [181] Community leaders, who were responsible for selecting candidates, manipulated lists, bribed Russian officials with money raised from the wealthy and the Hasidic rebbes,

---

179 Ukrainians, Poles, and Byelorussians, not Russians, were the dominant ethnic group in the Pale.

180 This was applied to all, including serfs. Russian conscription was consistent with that of other European monarchies, although the term of duty was much longer. It was an improvement over the 18th century's life-long term. In 1855, it was reduced to 12 years plus 3 years of reserve duty, then reduced again

181 Craftsmen, clerics, shop superintendents, factory mechanics, guild merchants, and those on agricultural settlements were exempted.

exempted those able to pay one thousand roubles for a substitute, and preyed upon orphans, the poor, the offspring of dissenters, free thinkers, and the Maskilim. Protests were suppressed with violence, even murder.[182]

Before each recruitment drive, youths hid in remote forests and ravines, but when quotas fell short, Jewish children as young as nine and ten were taken; so were the sons of Polish political prisoners, and Polish children kidnapped on the streets after the 1831 uprising. Malnourished, marched long distances in the cold, many perished:

The children were lined up in proper formation. It was one of the most gruesome sights I had ever encountered; The 12- and 13-year-old lads were still holding up, somehow; but the little ones, those of eight and ten years...No dark brush could create such horror on canvas...Pale, exhausted, they stood frightened, wearing clumsy army overcoats with stand-up collars eyeing pitifully and helplessly the garrison soldiers who continued to line them up rudely. White lips, blue rings under the eyes—symptomatic of fever and illness; Unfortunate children without any care or tenderness; assailed by the gusts from the Arctic Sea, they dropped dead.[183]

Recruits eighteen and over joined the regiments; those younger were placed in military-run schools where, despite starvation and forced baptism (it is estimated that more than 40,000 were converted) they received instruction in Russian, mathematics, geography, crafts, and were trained to become auditors, artillerists, engineers, military surgeons, or cartographers.[184] Those with musical talent received the finest

---

182 After Ysrael Friedman, the powerful Russian zaddik, was accused of ordering the execution of two 'informers', he took refuge in Sadagora, just outside Czernowitz. See the kidnapping of Bernyu.

183 Herzen, *My Past and Thoughts*, cited in Dubnov, *History of the Jews*.

184 Baptised Jews could rise to high-ranking positions in the Imperial Army and Navy.

schooling and inclusion in military bands; many moved on to careers in classical music. Even Klezmer music changed: military instruments—cornets, keyed trumpets, trombones, the poyk (a bass drum with a cymbal or slab of metal on top), clarinets, and flutes—replaced the softer-sounding cimbaloms and violins.

Haskalah ideas and literature were brought to the Pale by Jewish merchants travelling to Galicia via Brody, or down the Dnieper River to enlightened Odessa. When Yitshak Ber-Levinsohn,[185] the father of the Russian Haskalah, returned from Galicia in 1820, he wrote a satire of Hasidism and urged Jews to study science, literature, languages, and history, to become craftsmen and farmers. In 1827, Avrom Ber Gotlober left Russia to avoid military service, and discovered the Haskalah through Joseph Perl in Brody and Tarnopol. He became a poet, translator, publisher, and writer of satires:

Then the musician would start playing mournful and elegiac tunes to rouse women into tears (though they are easily roused on their own; each one of them brings along the affliction of her heart, this one lacks her daily bread, the other suffers the ordeals of raising children, and yet another always sees before her eyes her husband's fist, hitting her without mercy. In short, each of them comes ready for a good cry) and the badkhn would rise, he who at that moment is a preacher and a moralizer, and call out in a loud voice: "Hush!" and the women immediately would raise their voices with redoubled vigour and force...And as soon as he would finish preaching, the klezmer would start playing dance tunes, and the women's mood would revert from weighty grief to joy, and they would prance and cavort with vigour around the bride even before wiping the tears off

---

185 He had gone to Brody to be treated for an illness. After meeting Isaac Erter and other enlightened men, he went to study in Tarnopol. Returning to Russia, he was so persecuted by the Hasidim in his native Kremenitz, he was forced to leave town.

their faces; at times their noses would still be running from
all their sobbing.[186]

As one of the Haskalah's most important spokesmen and a
teacher in Zhitomir's academy, Gotlober also inspired men
like Sholem Yankev Abramovich (Mendele Moïcher Sforim),
Shalom Naumovich Rabinovich (Sholom Aleichem), Yitskhok
Yoyel Linetski, and Avrom Goldfaden.

Velvel Zbarzher's Russian counterparts were the folk
poets Elyokem Tsunzer and Mikhl Gordon,[187] and both
attacked Hasidic backwardness in their songs. Gordon was
considered so dangerous that the Hasidim denounced him
to the Russian authorities on a false charge of conspiracy.
Arrested, temporarily expelled, he continued to mock
their obscurantism, drunkenness, and primitive behaviour,
as in the song where a pious wife laments her enlightened
husband's vanished beard:

Did the beard do you any harm?
Did it cost you one single kopek? Did it ask to be fed?
Did it mix with your business?
Help! Help! The beard is gone![188]

Tsunzer, a professional badkhn who could improvise for
over an hour without stopping, decried social injustice,
poverty, Jewish backwardness and insularity until, troubled
by pogroms and fluctuating policies, he became a fervent
Zionist. Jews had to become agriculturalists, he said. They
had to train their sights on Zion where they could:

...sow and reap merrily,
Free in God's world

---

186 Gottlober, *Zichronotmi-yemene'uray*, cited in Stern, *From Jester to Gesture*.

187 Gordon had been a secret Maskil, living in his father-in-law's house. When
his wife died, he married into an enlightened family.

188 Gordon, *Di bord un dertsu andere sheyne yidishe lider.*

***

*W*ith the Habsburg Empire's modern schools as an example, Russian Maskilim called upon the government to create institutions that would produce a productive population, enlightened rabbis, and new intellectuals. In 1840, Sergey Uvarov, Minister of Education under Nicholas I, established a commission to discuss educational reform, and the German Maskil Max Lilienthal was called in to found schools and employ teachers. But, here too, traditional Jews fought change tooth and nail. Even those more open-minded protested: what good were modern schools without civil rights?

In 1844, when schools for boys and girls, and the liberal seminaries of Zhitomir and Vilna opened, most refused to send their children. Only orphans, those without means, and those whose parents embraced Haskalah ideas profited from the new opportunities.

***

*T*his minibus in which we're travelling (a rusty skeleton with skinny wheels and a roaring motor) fills with folk carrying tied-up sacks and bundles. Many are elderly, and with no free places available, they brace themselves as best they can as we slam into yet another metal-ripping pothole or heave heavenward on banked ice.

One weathered biddy isn't far from where I'm seated on a narrow, tattered slab. Beside me, is a young zombie in headphones. I stare pointedly at him, wondering if he'll offer his seat. He ignores me. Perhaps public transportation is synonymous with suffering, but as no one else makes a move, I stand, give the woman my place. She refuses, I insist, and she accepts with a grateful nod. For a brief second, the zombie is disconcerted. Then, resentfully, he also stands, gives me his spot. Instead, I offer it to an elderly man. This is too much for another man seated two rows behind who takes my arm quite firmly and steers me onto his own seat. And, suddenly, people are popping up all over and offering places. It's done expressionlessly, there are no smiles, no words, but it's a revolution, all right.

Night has come on by the time I arrive in Dubno. It's too late to look for the Jewish heart of town where Avrom Ber Gotlober might have lived—but I've seen a hotel. When I approach, I notice that the forecourt is ominously empty, although the reception area is lit by a dim, warty-looking plastic lamp. Since it's the only hotel around, and the glass door isn't locked, I enter. Two square-shaped women emerge from a back room and announce the hotel is, indeed, closed.

Dismayed, I stand there. Now what? Must I wander through the streets all night? Perhaps the women feel sorry for me. They whisper to each other, look at me with sly smiles. If I promise to stay one night only, they'll let me have a room. There will be no receipt and I must leave very early in the morning. Will I agree to this? Of course, I will. They state their price then, cackling, divide and pocket the wad of cash I hand over.

In a deep early morning fog, I prowl through town, looking for the former Jewish community that, by the end of the nineteenth century, comprised fifty per cent of Dubno's population. There are many buildings from the old days to see, but most are disregarded and ruined, and their yards are filled with trash and scrap. These neglected houses could so easily be gussied up. It would only take a few nails, a bit of mud and straw rolled together in the old traditional way—renovation done with no money—and the result would be exquisite, would create a showcase of a burg. But right smack on the main street, a three-story-high LED billboard displays a large white 'international' style house in cement, with PVC windows embellished by 'Olde Worlde' gold plastic strips: if you can't participate in the consumer dream, spurn what you do have.

Here are the ruins of the Polish castle: two thousand Jews, refused sanctuary within its walls during Khmelnitsky's onslaught, were massacred. Where is the synagogue? Perhaps it has been torn down or converted out of recognition. Take this cemented-over supermarket with its adjoining red brick edifice. Up at its top, are high arched windows. This must have been a fabulous building, something important, something worth seeing, yet new openings have been pierced through the brick façade, right beside those older ones: why take the time to render something hideous?

After a sagging arcade, I arrive in a courtyard and here I am, in the old Jewish shtetl. Nothing could be more obvious. This is the way I've pictured it. Just look at the houses, the alleyways! This is truly a voyage into the past. Here's how things looked when Sholem Yankev Abramovich came to meet Avrom Ber Gotlober, that 'apostate who shaves his beard'. Through which archway did he pass? Somewhere near where I'm standing? Is this where Gotlober's circle of Maskilim met when he lived here (a wanderer, he was forever shifting between Dubno, Zhitomir, Vienna, Lemberg, and Odessa)? If so, in which house? I follow the twisting lanes of this shtetl where only the Jews are missing.

Then I see it, still soaring over the rooftops: the synagogue. Circumventing more rotting houses, I reach what's left of it: huge, shattered, bombed-out as if the destruction happened only yesterday. Yet it retains a proud, waiting dignity.

'Shalom,' I say.

The resident pigeons coo.

Chapter XXIV:
Lutsk

I heard from my friends that Kalman was a kind of cursed Jew who had sold his soul to the devil, and now his only job was to commit all kinds of sins, day and night, in order to vex God, so that the Messiah could not come to release the Jews from the Exile. I remember how cheder boys ran after him and called out the letters of the German alphabet with a certain melody: 'kay, el, em, en, oh, pee, ar, es!' Yet Kalman just went on his way, smiling to himself, as though he enjoyed it.

Jacob Dinezon[189]

*B*road peasant women in shapeless coats leave the icy minibus, trundle up dirt lanes toward invisible villages only hinted at by the church spires peeking over hilltops. Unlike Galicia where soils were poor, here, in the 'breadbasket of Europe,' wheat, barley, rye, oats, sunflowers, and beets grew fat in the rich black earth.

---

189 Jacob Dinezon, *Memories and Scenes,*

By 1860, the enlightened urban Jews were using Russian in daily life, reading Russian literature, and identifying with Russia. They still hadn't been emancipated, but residence in the formerly forbidden cities outside the Pale was permitted to some, and those able to enter universities and technical colleges were becoming judges, academics, lawyers, doctors, and military surgeons. A small wealthy class of Jewish merchants and financiers were building railways, developing mines, and investing in Russian national enterprises; books and literary journals in Hebrew, Russian, and Yiddish were being published; and the Society for the Promotion of Culture was assisting a new class of (poorly-paid) literary men. Middle-class women, educated at girls' schools, gymnasia, and universities, were playing musical instruments, frequenting the theatre, the ballet, and dressing in Paris fashions.

Both men and women wished to study medicine, become doctors and nurses, and if the quota system denied them admission, they studied elsewhere in Europe: many joined the medical staff in Parisian hospitals. Although there were those who did abandon Judaism entirely, most helped promote modernisation, for the Golden Age had apparently arrived. It was glittery fool's gold.

When expulsion or economic necessity forced Jews and former peasants to abandon their villages, they opened shops in the cities, or found work in the textile industry, in sweatshops, steel mills, factories, food plants, or on the railways. Living in crowded slums, working seventeen-hour shifts, workers weren't hard to radicalise. Many new insurgents were former Yeshiva students who firmly believed revolution alone would save the masses from the evils of capitalism and end discrimination. To disseminate radical propaganda, they translated Marxist writings into Yiddish.

Tsar Alexander II grew disillusioned with his liberal reforms and his generosity toward the Jews: their bubbling political movements were threatening his empire. An emerging urban proletariat and new middle class, influenced by the Orthodox Church's medieval image of Jewry, equally resented Jewish success. Weren't Jews Christ-killers? Weren't Jewish bankers buying up land or whole towns and living at the expense of the true Russian people? Weren't they exploiting the peasants and plotting to take over the country? Wasn't the Haskalah a conspiracy linked to the Alliance Israélite? In 1881, Jews were blamed for the tsar's assassination, although only one woman, Gesya Gelfman (or Helfman) was Jewish (she had run away from home to avoid an arranged marriage), and pogroms swept across the Pale:[190]

> *Long Live Alexander III*
> *Who loves us as his children*
> *We have to save him*
> *And assassinate the Jews.*[191]

New measures barred Jews from acquiring land outside the cities and limited to ten per cent their attendance in state schools: several yeshivas and schools like Zhitomir were closed. After the reverses of the 1904-1905 Russo-Japanese War[192] pogroms flared in two hundred villages.

> *In all of Russia, whenever Gentiles took the notion, they could rob and pillage, beat and kill Jews without restraint. They could burn businesses. Suddenly, on a Thursday night, hooligans attacked the three towns near us... They began by first burning the stores, breaking windows, burning houses and beating whoever they wished and looting Jewish goods.*

---

190 The assassination was carried out by left-wing terrorist organisation *Narodnaya Volya* (The People's Will). Gesya Gelfman, the mistress of one assassin, hid dynamite in her attic. Tortured in prison, her death sentence was commuted because she was pregnant—the father was Nicolai Kolodkevitch, a radical from an aristocratic family. Gelfman died of peritonitis after giving birth, the baby died soon after. Kolodkevitch died in prison three years later. When the other members of Narodnaya Volya were released, they instigated a reign of terror.

191 Bulletin de l'Alliance Israélite Universelle, 1882

192 The first modern military victory of an Asian power over a European nation, thus considered humiliating.

The police didn't show up in the streets...Many fled to us. The whole day, Friday, people were arriving, men women and children. The mud was deep and there was rain as well...All night, we saw great red flames... This type of thing happened in many towns at the same time.[193]

Nurturing the dream of a new life without fear or hatred, between 1881 and 1900, three-quarters of a million Jews left Eastern Europe. By 1914, another one million six hundred thousand immigrated, mostly from Russia and Galicia.

***

*I*n Lutsk, I look for Nathan, my maternal grandfather, and his brother, Lev. Where to begin the search? A dirt lane just behind the town leads down to the river set in its bucolic little hollow. Choked with branches, plastic, and rubbish, stinking of effluent, it still bubbles on merrily, a hooch-sodden derelict singing of lost love and lost chances. The trail takes me past abandoned buildings, once mills, and wanders towards a bridge, the ruined Polish castle, and a former Jewish quarter.

This town's Jewish population grew after 1804 after the expulsions from surrounding villages, and by mid-century, there was a modern community of brewers, doctors, dentists, haberdashers, printers, traders, craftsmen, and shopkeepers. An upper class of merchants and manufacturers built the graceful buildings in the centre. There is still a Jewish community here today.

Born in 1881, Nathan must have lived down in the poorest section of town, once a tumble of wooden houses, alleys, and narrow courtyards clumped between the castle and the synagogue. The old houses, yards, and alleys have vanished—the area is now one of respectable domesticity—but the synagogue perched beside a roaring intersection is easy to

---

193 Levin, Ontario Jewish Archives.

find. In this frontier region, once vulnerable to Tatar attack, Jews were required to construct fortress-like prayer houses: this one was part of the city's defence wall, although that wall is long gone. Today, the building is a sports hall. I stand on the street and watch men with blue totes enter.[194]

Orphans, scruffy urchins, Nathan and Lev survived by collecting scrap. They lurked in bars, waiting to catch empty bottles before drunks smashed them to bits, then turned them in for coins. Poverty meant they were lucky enough to be educated in Lutsk's modern school, first opened in the 1830s by a tiny circle of Maskilim.

Nathan became an intellectual and a creator of the new abstract art, but by 1905, he, too, had lost faith in Russian promise. Packing up his brushes, he headed, via Denmark, for America, where he fell in love with Miriam.[195] Like other immigrants, he discovered life in the New World was very different from that in the Old, and New York was very unlike the city of his fancies. The father of two, Nathan no longer had time for redefining shape, form, and colour, and an artist's studio was abandoned for a car repair workshop.

I knew Nathan as a weedy man in a rug-smelling Bronx apartment. To the tune of a clattering IRT just outside the window, he told stories: of a crony who, hidden under the putrefying catch in a fishing boat, defected from Siberia; of too-clever friends who had disappeared without trace; of forgotten artists, and all-night debates around an iron stove; of twisting lanes, sighing fruit trees, rocks that grew, and spirits that lurked.

Nathan's brother Lev was another kettle of fish altogether. With monocle, elegant walking stick and fashionable clothes,

---

194 According to Jewish Heritage Europe, (April 19, 2021), the synagogue's ownership has now been transferred to the local Habad (the Orthodox Jewish Hasidic Dynasty).

195 My maternal grandmother claimed to have been a well-off miller's daughter who left home on a whim. Who was she really? She changed her life story, her forename—Minnie, Miriam, Mary—maiden name—Tennenbaum, Tennen, Tucker—hair colour—blond, flame orange, black—and birthplace—Rivne, Lutsk—with slippery ease.

he became a professional dandy, one that adoring ladies kept in cravats, clean shirt collars, and smart vests. A small-time impostor, he claimed to be a dispossessed Russian aristocrat in Paris, and a French count when in New York. Itinerant, ever shifting between continents (and mistresses) his existence conjures up sensual evenings in over-heated rooms with chandeliers, marble fireplaces, and unlaced corsets. There must have been a flipside to that lifestyle, too: bad times in cold boarding houses, bedbugs, doubt, and the stink of desperation. He vanished in 1940s Paris: wrong place, wrong time.

Lev, Nathan, the revolutionaries, the businessmen, teachers, and doctors, were the Pale's modern urban Jews. But, only a few kilometres away, things were very different.

Chapter XXV:
Harry's Story

You think serfdom is gone for good, never to return? Come look at our village, and you'll see for yourself. Of course, officials and gendarmes no longer ride around with whips; there's no longer an oak log in the landlord's yard, where 'communal flogging' took place every Saturday, but look at the people and talk to them! They are as dark as the earth itself; their houses are bedraggled and old, skewed off to the side.

Ivan Franko[196]

*M*y paternal grandfather Harry, a full-bellied braggart, never hesitated to tell his story to all comers.[197] Born in a shenk in the village of Svyniukhy (Svinich, in Yiddish), my great grandmother ran the bar and oil press, and her sister was in charge of a brewery in the buildings out at the back. The business had been in family hands for generations,

---

196 Franko, *Woods and Pastures*, from *Faces of Hardship*.

197 Taped by his son, Dr Mike Culiner in 1976. The tape and its transcription are in the Ontario Jewish Archives.

and the rules were 'business as usual,' and 'just adapt.' It was existence at a cliff's pinch-edge; it meant ignoring political landslides.

'My mother was always very busy with the inn,' said Harry. 'She worked hard and didn't have many friends, just the miller's wife, and a woman who negotiated for horsehair to use in stuffing chairs. My father? All he did was take us to cheder. My mother's family accepted him, an educated boy, when he was sixteen years old, and they thought they'd make a famous rabbi out of him, but all he ever did was study. He knew very little about life.

'The shenk was on a crossroads just above the river, and it was a big place—I don't know how many horses and wagons you could put inside. The peasants would come into town with their sacks of seeds. There were two inns, ours, and another place across the street, and both were in the same business. When we were kids, my brothers and I would go out into the road and pull the peasants into our place. The inn across the street had a boy and a girl, and they did the same thing as we did: drum up business, pull the peasants in.

'The peasants had linseed, poppy, sesame, sunflower, three or four different kinds of seeds, and the inn was very busy. They had to wait while their seeds were being pressed, so they'd put straw down in the hall, lie there during the night. What did we get out of it? We got the compressed grain after the oil had been taken out. Then, each spring, people came to us from Galicia and bought the grain. They used it to fatten cows. We did a lot of business with Galicia—we were right near the border. Everyone knew us, and we knew practically every peasant living there, too.

'When I was two years old, I slept in bed with mama. Later—I must have been three or four—I slept on the oyfen. In the old country, when you wanted to make a house warm, you put straw in the oyfen and it warmed the house. When I was five or six, they made a room up near the roof of the inn, put in a bed, and my brothers and I, all four of us, slept in that one bed. Once, when I was just an innocent boy of about eight or ten, the peasants who were staying overnight waiting for their oil to be pressed, came up to our bed. One girl grabs me, starts to kiss me and play with me. Then, she says to the other girl, "No, he's too young." I was a kid. What did I know?

'At the bottom of the shenk, was the river. People used to come to our place from Austria (Galicia) with great big barrels to buy fish, and they stayed at our inn. They were always on the road, they knew everybody, and they'd spent the night, talking, bringing news of relatives and places that were far away—other towns, the whole world. Some had been to the Black Sea; some had been to America. My father even got the address of my uncle who'd gone to live in New York from one of them. I used to listen to the stories and already, when I was just a young boy, I had my heart set on leaving Svinich.

'When I was around fourteen or fifteen years old, I started to revolt. I'd sneak into the barns at night, steal the hair from horse's tails, and sell it to make some money. I cut my peyes shorter than I was supposed to, and when my father came in—it was a Friday night and he hadn't seen me at shul—he took a look at me and said, 'Get out.' I had to go to the house of an uncle, a blacksmith, not far away from us, and live there for a while. Then I bought a stylish cotton shirt and, for my father, that was another bad thing. He was no fanatic, but living in that town, in that family, he couldn't think anything else. My mother couldn't go against my father: if Baruch Areya said something was wrong, then it was.

'My mother came from a very fine family and, at home, that meant a lot. When you came from a fine family, you'd never think to marry a shoemaker or carpenter's daughter, even if she was the most beautiful girl in town. We had a rabbi, every town did, and my older brother liked the rabbi's girl. She loved him, too, but you never married the girl you loved.

'I had a cousin, Frima. I was very much in love with her, and she was the most beautiful girl you've ever seen. She loved me too, I know she did, but in a town like that, I couldn't even tell Frima I liked her. I used to sit on the bench in front of the inn and, on Saturdays, a group of five or six girls would walk by, go to a sort of warehouse where villagers stored things just in case anything happened. One of the girls was Frima. I'd look at her and almost fall into the ditch, she was so beautiful.

'Afterwards, I started going to see her in the evenings, at sunset. She'd be sitting on the veranda in front of her house, and we'd talk. Right in front of everybody. Just talking. That's all. Suddenly people started saying her family was running a bordello. Why? Because I came to talk to her? What was the big deal?

'One night, the house her family lived in was struck by lightning. It burned down completely, and her family had to come live with us. But not Frima. They sent her to other relatives in another town and married her to someone else. Why? Because we'd fallen in love with each other. Everyone said that the Almighty had sent that lightning and burnt down the house because of the way Frima and I behaved. That's the kind of town it was. Full of gossips with nasty minds. Full of superstition. That's what life was like in the Old Country. Just like that. Don't let anyone tell you different.

'When I was twenty-one, four months before I had to go into the army, they found a bride for me. I went to her town, got married, stayed for a week or two, then went back home to take off weight: two friends and I tried to lose weight so they wouldn't take us in the army. We didn't eat; we stayed up all night long. It was the Russo-Japanese war and we didn't want to go to the Russian army. And what happened? They took me anyway. So, I went to a man my father knew, a Hasid, and he punctured my eardrum, but sthey still wanted me to be a soldier. My friend Zalman, he cut off his big toe, but they took him too.

'I spent four, five months in the army camp near Warsaw, most of the time in the hospital because the ear got infected. Then, one day, I just walked out. Nobody was paying any attention to me. I went to see some Hasidim who belonged to the same rebbe as my father and said, I'm Baruch Areya's son. They took away my uniform, gave me civilian clothes and put me on a train. They didn't look for you for eight days when you disappeared from the army, so there was no problem. I went to see a Ukrainian I knew—he used to come to the inn with his grain to make oil. I stayed overnight in his barn, and then I paid him ten roubles, and he took me across the Galician border, seventeen miles away. After that, I was safe. Once you were in Austrian Galicia, they couldn't take you back. After that, I went to Lemberg, then Vienna, then and Trieste. In Trieste, I went to Sicily on a boat filled with nuts and wine, then on to New York.

'What happened to the wife I left behind in the old country? After I came to America, I heard she died of a broken heart. She'd had a baby boy, and he died too. I never saw him. She was a nice girl, but I didn't know her or her family very well. I was only with them for a couple of weeks. I came to America on her money. Her family gave me the dowry, around 500 dollars, so that's what I used.'

Chapter XXVI:
Svinich

What you don't see with your eyes, don't invent with your mouth.

Yiddish proverb

*F*alling snow obscures all. Surely no one will travel in such a blizzard. Even huge, snow-covered stray dogs curl desperately against the walls and doors of the central bus station. Take a look at the rusty minibuses with threadbare tires in the station yard: those motorised tin cans will never risk ice-covered, potholed roads.

I'm wrong, of course. I've spent too much time in places where people are easily upset by weather. This is Ukraine; snow is normal. The unheated can I board joins other cans, cars, horse-drawn carts, and off we go, gliding along as if nothing unusual is going on. Even the driver is not in the least troubled by high drifts. As we slalom merrily, left, right, centre, left, half-spin, centre again, he chats amiably to the woman sitting just behind him. Further obscuring the view, a special metal attachment just above the windscreen allows for his impressive collection of good luck tchotchkele: toy animals—two bears, a bunny, a puppy—a bouncing crucifix, an icon, several splendid sprays of plastic flowers.

Svyniukhy (Svinich) is now called Privetnoye, and it's some thirty kilometres away. On these bad roads, the trip there will easily take three or four hours, although I'm not certain about much of anything since I've also lost my modern road map and I can't understand anyone anyway. Outside, white hills swell gently, and despite the snowstorm, a heavy mist makes time inconsequential. Perhaps it's a curtain of sorts, one through which I must pass in search of the past. Yes, the countryside does resemble that of Ontario, still, there's something else out there, something quite unlike the New Country. Although Stalin ordered the collectivisation of smallholdings and the ploughing up of boundary brush, the traces of long strips, as narrow as the medieval past, are still stamped into the black earth by those long-gone serfs' toil. Old mud roads are here too, just wide enough for carts and horses, heading toward villages hidden by hills and coppices. And everywhere you look, those peasant women are there, drab, bulky, lumbering homeward.

People climb into and out of the tin can at strange places, without dwellings, signs, or indications of any sort. Sometimes we pause in tiny villages with today's usual jumble: decaying houses with tin roofs; traditional houses ruined by vinyl siding but possessing beautiful wooden terraces; ugly new shops in cement; brick bungalows lacking style and charm but with effective heating; beautifully tended ancient houses of adobe with small double windows and, sometimes, a sculpted entry. What I wouldn't give to be invited into a few of those for a gawk.

The driver, exasperated that I speak no Ukrainian, lets me know it, turning, looking at me pointedly, sneering, making snide comments to smirking fellow passengers, all of them flat-faced, blue-eyed folk. Let him have his fun, I don't mind in the least. I'm taking in the sight of the men and women trudging through the snow with straw baskets containing flapping chickens, or with heavy jute sacks. These tree-lined roads, carts and horses, unpaved mud streets, are visions from another time: yes, I have reached the other side of the curtain. What will I find in Svinich? Will I see the inn? Is there still a bench out in front? What about the river?

Two hours later, we are in Lokachi, a name I know from Ansky's post-WWI reports:

> *I stopped off in Lokatsh, an old Jewish shtetl with a brick portal and the ruins of an ancient castle...There were a lot of Jews here from Poretsk, Milyatin and other shtetlekh. And there was no money to help them. Cholera was more and more rampant, and there was no doctor at hand. One week earlier, a crew of homeless Galician gentiles had passed through, and had started a pogrom. The local Jews had appealed to the police chief, who angrily snapped, 'And you've paid me nicely for my protection?'*[198]

Lokachi is also a name synonymous with torture, humiliation, and massacre by Nazis and Ukrainian peasants in 1942: Jews from Svinich, Poritsk, all the surrounding towns and villages were brought to a ghetto here, then shot into a mass grave somewhere along this road where the forest starts.[199] It seems so far away, so impossible today. Did it also seem impossible back then?

It's market day and things are lively in the central square. The lumpy folk tumble out of the tin can, circulate between stands and shacks, go in and out of the inn in front of us—a building architecturally transformed to communist 'taste'. The market also lacks yesteryear's more colourful characters: the motley crowd of clamouring vendors, Jewish, Turkish, and Armenian; the crowds of resident Poles and Germans; the peasant women grilling maize cobs and roasting chestnuts. Once peasants sold pigs, bacon, tallow, sausages, carved pails, wooden spoons, troughs, yokes, shingles, and sacks of grain that, unless they fetched a good price, were lugged home

---

198 Ansky, *The Enemy at His Pleasure.*

199 Diment, *The Lone Survivor.*

again. There were meat and fish stalls, stands with silks, guns, knives, carpets, pottery, sandals, slippers, harnesses, baskets, sour milk, sugar, horses, and cattle. Sometimes wares were traded for flour and barley since tiny plots couldn't feed whole peasant families.

These days, no one haggles over old clothes, or sells rusty nails, battered tins of herring, a guitar with one string, a doormat worn to holes, an old saucepan, an ancient kerosene stove, a broken coffee grinder, rusty spring mattresses, or dogs. No one is seated at long tables eating sausages, pies, fish, pulling apart fowl and dipping the meat into a common tub of tomato sauce, and washing everything down with red wine. As for the cabbage pies reserved for the poor, a contemporary variety is present—sweet little buns filled with pickled cabbage that bundled up women sell in all bus stations. I devour them, and they're a treat. Shopping done, today's blue-eyed peasants, their baskets full with provisions, shove back into the tin can, and off we go again.

I have no way of knowing exactly where Svinich/ Privetnoye is, and no way of asking, so I sit, dream, stare out of the window. What am I thinking? That I'll somehow recognise the place through a call of the blood? Who cares? Life is easiest when passive and mellow.

Suddenly, I realise the driver has stopped the can in the middle of the road. He has turned to me and is asking something, but I can't make out what. I notice, for the first time, that, aside from the one woman still sitting behind him, I'm the only passenger left.

'Privetnoye?' I question. The driver only shakes his head with disgust, irritated by dull tools like me who venture forth with less than an idiot's grasp of the language. Then, with hands and feet, makes himself clear: Privitnoye is back there. Way back. The woman turns, holds up nine fingers, points in the direction from which we've come. So Svinich/Privetnoye has come and gone; there was no tugging of blood, no atavistic memory to apprise me of the fact.

The tin can's door opens. The driver motions for me to

get out. End of the line for me. Then he, the woman, the tin can, and all the bobbling good luck Schnick-Schnack weave merrily into white invisibility. So here I am. Alone. The snow is still falling heavily, quickly obliterating tracks on the road. Snow in front of me, snow behind, snow on either side: a landscape without accent and no sign of life. Nothing to do but head back, follow the blackened trees lining the vanished road. I think of the trudging peasants: if they can do it, so can I. This is the road ancestors took over centuries. Along here, a peddler great uncle once dragged his wares.

Occasionally a car slides past, occasionally a horse-drawn cart. Because of other people's warnings, I'm at first wary. But, in my shapeless old coat, my woolly socks, heavy boots, and baggy trousers, I'm as lumpy as any peasant. And am ignored.

After some time, I see two motionless dark shapes in the distance, and all the old stories come to mind. What could those forms be? Gnomes? Evil spirits? Souls of the dead? The Old Country crones my grandmother warned about? Genies? As I approach, the shapes transmogrify into two ancient women with headscarves and canes. If one is the sorceress Baba Yaga, her chicken-footed hut can't be far off. Perhaps they're just the usual run-of-the-mill witches who stand slack in fields or at the ends of tracks, waiting to lure unwary travellers into some netherworld. 'If an evil spirit addresses you, and you respond, death will shortly follow,' says ancient wisdom.

The crones stare at me warily—they probably think I'm the witch. But, very much a twenty-first-century real person, I march up to them, smile. They, very much twenty-first-century real people, smile back. We begin a conversation of sorts, using any half-understood word we can conjure up: one has a granddaughter in Ohio, and Privetnoye is only five kilometres further. Neither seems surprised to find a Canadian woman tramping through a snowstorm in backwoods Ukraine.

Finally, I arrive in Svinich, a village of mud roads snuggled into a mild slope of a valley. Two drunken peasants cross my path, arms slung about each other's shoulders for stability. Gold teeth flashing, they amuse themselves with what are, quite clearly, obscene propositions: they're the only truly vile people I've met so far.

Up and down, I prowl through the streets, ever on the lookout for a great uncle's smithy, for the family's old shenk at a crossroads—a shenk with double doors large enough to admit grain-loaded peasant's wagons. Here is a crossroad; here are two bars facing each other. One looks older, the other might be fairly new—or it has been much renovated. Could either have possessed oil presses? Across the main road, an abandoned building sits on a little hillock of sorts. It also seems to have been a bar...once upon a time, but it's only a communist creation, not what I'm hoping to find. The family inn probably disappeared long ago.

A car has been following me for a while. The driver, an older man, stops and opens the window, invites me for tea, coffee, a meal. A bottle of vodka occupies the passenger seat.

'No thank you.'

Ten minutes later, on another snowy street, here he is again. Again, he indicates I should get into his car; the vodka bottle is still there, rolling around on the seat. I hold up my plastic camera, show him I'm busy taking photos. After that, no matter what back street I'm on, he's here, his car slipping and sliding on the packed snow, the vodka bottle shimmying its drunken little dance.

Eventually, we do manage a truncated conversation, one with many gestures: what am I doing here? My grandfather was from this town? What was his name? (Surprising how well one can communicate without a common language). He contemplates. Again, tells me to get into the car; he wants me to meet someone.

With some misgiving (but, as usual, not enough), I shove the vodka bottle aside and climb in. And we're off, skidding merrily back through town then passing into a schoolyard. End of the line. He takes me inside, introduces me to Oxana, the school director, a former French teacher. What am I doing in Ukraine? Looking for lost relatives? Seeking a forgotten Galician poet?

She, a tall handsome woman with a strong personality and steady stream of chitchat, takes charge of me immediately. She presents me to the young and handsome math teacher (by his adoring looks, clearly a lover), decides I'm to speak to the classes, tell them I'm a Canadian, a Jew, a writer trailing an obscure, long-dead, nineteenth-century Ukrainian poet and singer; that my family was from this town, that those who remained were killed in the Holocaust. Some of the children speak English; for the others, Oxana will translate.

I'm dragged from one classroom to the next (all heated to boiling point and I'm still encumbered by my lumpy coat) like some show-and-tell object to be gaped at. Then photos are taken, and I'm bustled out into the street again.

No sign of the older man who drove me here; he was obsequious, even fearful, in Oxana's imperious presence, a mere serf. Who was he, I ask?

'Oh him. He's no one. Just owns a bar and restaurant.' With a wave of her hand, he is dismissed. 'How brave you are. Speaking no word of the language, coming here, travelling on local buses, staying in strange places without knowing a soul.'

'Why brave? Everything has been normal so far.'

'And without a map too.'

I want to explore the town some more, but Oxana has decided I'll not do it on my own. I've become her possession. She'll show me where the former Jewish houses were.

Passively, I follow my dictatorial cicerone through the streets. She knocks on doors, marches boldly into bungalow-type houses (whose interiors are like bungalow-type houses anywhere in the world). And after a great many inquiries, I'm hauled over to a snow-covered, vacant lot.

'A Jewish woman lived here years ago, but she died and her house has been pulled down.'

The tour comes to an end—Oxana doesn't want her fashionable, high-heeled boots muddied. We return to the crossroads with the two bars, enter the older one. It's a disappointing place with cutting-edge décor, much plastic, spotlights set into the ceiling, and pop music's whine—nothing like the sort of shenk I'm always looking out for. Oxana orders two cups of fairly vile coffee, talks about her husband, her young lover, and the desire to travel. Change the country, our stories are always the same. The cafe owner is also obsequious, for Oxana is an important person.

'Taverns? You say they used to be called shenks? Well, we always go to taverns, men, women, everyone. It's a tradition here in Ukraine. Taverns are centres of village life. We also have no problem going into each other's houses. Of course, like in villages everywhere, not everyone is friendly with everyone else.'

Then it's time to catch the late afternoon bus—she lives in Lokachi—and the driver is the one from this morning. Recognising me, he sniggers, tells Oxana of my nine-kilometre walk back to town. In turn, Oxana tells the other passengers who I am, what my family name is, what I'm doing here. Mentions the forgotten Ukrainian poet from Zbarazh...what was his name again? Velvel Zbarzher? Everyone's fascinated now; they lean forward in their seats. Some even stand to catch a better glimpse of me and to stare unabashedly.

'Do you have war monuments in France?' asks a man. 'And in Canada, too?'

But I feel frustrated. Sucked into Oxana's jet stream, I have been thwarted in my search for the family inn. I'll go back one day, I promise myself. One day. It's not much comfort.

***

*T*he next day, I do circle all the way back to Svinich. Without Oxana and her fine leather boots to hinder my progress, I can take the muddy road along the river. What is this odd-looking building? A shtibl? Perhaps a former chapel? It has been converted into a private home. I hang around for a while, wait for someone to appear so I can question them, but I'm alone out here—or almost: geese and chickens peck in the icy puddles, stray dogs sniff, play, trot briskly along the road as if they have important business to attend to and merry friends to meet. I search for a smithy, another inn on another crossroad. Find nothing.

The sky darkens a few tones. More snow? No, sleet. Discouraged, I retreat to the bar at the crossroads where, just yesterday, I sat with Oxana. Perhaps someone will tell me when the last bus leaves: heaven knows, I don't want to be stuck here. The same woman is behind the counter in the tavern, but she's not friendly, not like yesterday when, ingratiating, fawning, she catered to Oxana. I pay for my undrinkable coffee, go back outside, wait for the bus she insists is imminent.

The bus shelter is filled with rubbish: plastic bottles papers, plastic cups. There is no place to sit, so I contemplate the two bars across the road. Still nothing familiar, nothing that drums up an atavistic thrill. The bus doesn't appear. To the left, is the derelict building, that ugly communist cement structure set up on its hillock. To keep warm and stave off boredom, I walk towards it.

Something catches my eye. What I thought was a hillock under the building is, in reality, quite another building, long neglected, earthed over: a complicated and arched cellar in crumbling red brick. I descend the slope, circle, climb up onto the former tavern's cement veranda, and peer through dirty windows. Here are compartment-like nooks: a bar in the old style? I examine an outside wall where cement has shattered. Behind, is more brick. And here? Right here, there was a broad doorway, large enough for grain-filled carts... once upon a time.

This building is no communist structure: it's an ancient thing. How ancient? A few hundred years old? Was this Harry's former home, the shenk of my ancestors? Maybe. Who knows? Have I found it? Really? In the field behind, more shattered brick sprouts through the snow. Buildings once stood here, perhaps my great-grand-aunt's brewery. I follow the remains of a wall, and at the very end is the river, just where it's supposed to be.

I go back to the veranda, peer through the window again, mentally hack away the Communist décor, the cement, the entire twentieth century. Begin to nourish fantasies: what if I take the place over, this ancestral bar. Open it up again, create a shenk in the old style, a place where people can meet, talk, drink. I'd give those two video-clipping, spot-lit joints across the road a little competition, you can be sure of that.

People will come, I know they will; a Canadian woman running a bar? A Jewish descendant has returned? They'll come all right. Gawk. I'll learn Ukrainian, and they'll stay, listen to a few stories and some tall tales. Share. Perhaps some interesting people will show up: a few throwbacks, eccentrics, poets, even a songster, a Velvel Zbarzher who will exhort rebellion against the status quo, wean folk away from television, telephones, and pop's narcissistic lyrics. It could happen, couldn't it? Why not? What a fine idea, my starting a new life in an original, cranky way. Will I give it a whirl? Sure, I will. Honestly and truly? Do I have the guts?

Then I look to the left, see the tin can minibus bumping its way down the main road, and I race over the ice, reach the bus stop, flag it down, climb on. Lo and behold: it's the same driver again. He shakes his head dolefully—I'm a hopeless case—says something mocking to the other passengers. But I see there's a sort of affection to his mockery now. A hint of kindness, and indulgence. I think he's starting to like me.

Chapter XXVII:
Poritsk

Where's the little lane, where's the cottage?
Where's the lad that I so love?
The lane is gone, the cottage is gone,
The lad is gone, that I so love.

Yiddish Folksong[200]

*S*omewhere in the village of Poritsk, my maternal great-grandmother, still in her thirties, lay on her deathbed. Too poor to pay for medical help, she was at the mercy of quacks with magic formulae and nostrums against the evil eye. She died on an early spring day, and her last words were: 'It's so beautiful outside, and I'm going into the earth.'

I have a map of Poritsk, one drawn by a Polish immigrant after living for many years in Canada. How accurate can it be? I soon see there is no way to reconcile it with reality. Here, in the middle of the village, is a park of sorts where trees have, again, been brutally decapitated. Across the road are a few ramshackle booth-like shops with a gaggle of gaping

---

200 Vinkovetzky, Kovner, Leichter, *Anthology of Yiddish Folksongs.*

folk. And just barely visible is a distant hazy hill covered by a little forest. Is it the one mentioned by Ansky in his report of a pogrom launched by the retreating eighth division of the Russian army? In June 1915, one hundred and fifty Jews took sanctuary there, while local peasants and those from neighbouring villages, pillaged homes and shops. When the violence was over, the Jews came home and attempted to recover their property, but they were expelled by the police chief. Seeking help in the surrounding pillaged shtelech, most starved to death.

***

*T*hose who had run the roadside inns so valuable to drovers and travellers found their livelihood cancelled by the new rail network. After their revolt against the Russian government, Polish nobles had their lands confiscated, and the emancipation of serfs in 1861 (1864 in Congress Poland) caused the ruin of others. Thousands left for the cities, and some—or their descendants—became part of a new intelligentsia.[201] Left behind, were the Jewish middlemen and peasants formerly in their employ.

Emancipated but not yet adept at independent planning and exploitation of the land, former serfs were left to survive as best they could. They were crushed by redemption payments owed to their former 'owners' who still retained two-thirds of the land and kept the best acreage for themselves. Infertile narrow strips were sold off at over-inflated prices and, without savings, peasants applied to the state bank, landlords, local businessmen, middlemen, and tavern owners for loans, thus saddling themselves

---

201 One that included the poet Adam Asnyk, the writer and Nobel Prize laureate Henryk Sienkiewicz, aka Litwos, the author Eliza Orzeszkowa who wrote about the social conditions of her country and the relationship between Jews and the nobility. Others were playwright, theatre critic and actress Gabriela Zapolska; opera singer Solomiya Krushelnytska, Ivan Franko, poet, writer, literary critic and political activist. It was Franko who published a translation of Velvel Zbarzher's poem, *Messiah*.

with lifelong payments that passed down to their children:

> *Several peasants were standing around, dressed in ragged coats and straw hats...by a ramshackle fence, sat on a log Mikola Prots, himself—a tall man of about thirty-five, as thin as a matchstick, with a face haggard from poverty and illness. In his lap sat a five-year-old boy, clinging to his father and glancing fearfully at the strangers standing in front of the house. Next to him stood his wife with the younger child in her arms, wiping her eyes with her apron...*
>
> *'Any offers?' the bailiff urged, looking around.*
>
> *Shinder walked up to him, touched his left hand to his hat, and said, 'What for, Your Excellency? I'll give forty.'*
>
> *'Shinder gives forty; anyone wants to offer more?'...For his forty guldens, Shinder became the owner of the house and land estimated at 150 guldens and probably worth at least 200 guldens.*
>
> *'You foolish man,' Shinder said to Mikola. 'Didn't I tell you to make peace with me, give me half your land? And now, you see, I took the whole thing!'*
>
> *...A year passed. [Mikola's] heart pounded when he saw the large tavern on the edge of the village. Gathering the last of his strength, he rushed in that direction.*
>
> *'Good evening, Shinder!' he shouted on entering the tavern...'I have something for you.' Mikola pulled the bundle from his belt, untied it and set four tens in front of the innkeeper. 'Here! Now give me back my plot and my house.'*
>
> *'What, what, what?' the innkeeper exclaimed...'You want to buy a plot and house for forty guldens?...This land gives me three hundred guldens. I want four hundred, and the least I'll sell it for is two-fifty.'*[202]

To better their lot, the peasants began eschewing those vestiges of a feudal economy, the Jewish middlemen. They didn't need them: they could learn how to negotiate, sell

---

202 Franko, *Your Own Fault*, from *Faces of Hardship*.

the agricultural products they produced, form cooperatives, and set up shops. They could strike for decent wages, too, although there was no guarantee of success:

> *During the harvest time, peasants would arrive and cut the crops...the cutting would still be done by hand. The nobleman would pay them a very niggardly sum for their work. As much as he felt like paying...so all the workers got together and went to the nobleman demanding a greater price. The nobleman offered them a minuscule raise, which they would not accept, and so they began a strike. The nobleman didn't like this very much...He had never heard of such a thing. It smacked of socialism. Some miles distant, Cossacks were stationed. They were brought in for the express purpose of striking fear into the masses...*
>
> *When the peasants stopped cutting the grain, they hung around in groups, sitting on the ground, drinking vodka. A few Cossacks started badgering some of the peasants and...one of them, a striker, returned the blow. That's what the Cossacks were waiting for! In five minutes, they had all mounted their horses. They had a type of leather whip weighted with lead. They began to beat the peasants with these whips—whoever was in the street and looked like a worker. I saw how some jumped over the fence to get to the church and how the Cossacks on their horses also jumped the fence and whipped the strikers on their bare flesh as much as they could. Several leaders of the strike were arrested.*
>
> *On the second day, all the strikers went back to work for the wage the nobleman offered them. The nobleman was satisfied and the workers with welts on their backs had to work out of fear.*[203]

---

203 Levin, Ontario Jewish Archives.

***

I take the road leading out of town, pass the Polish cemetery with its martyr's memorial to the women and children massacred in the local church during an upsurge of Ukrainian nationalist violence. I turn back. Stop. All at once, things fall into place.

Here, at the edge of Poritsk are the same peasant houses, small barns, vegetable gardens, and broad fields that must have been here several hundred years ago. Those ugly low buildings in the centre are all that's left of the rows of Jewish shops. Across the street, in a little park-like area with smashed and rotted wooden tables, was the market square. On the left, stood the wooden synagogue before being burnt to the ground in 1942.

Alongside the empty lot of the former synagogue is a muddy back street with a few small houses. Negotiating puddles, I follow it. A stout woman, standing by her garden fence, gossiping with two others and watching me, calls out: 'The road leads nowhere. It ends in a field.' She makes the appropriate gestures, just to make sure I've understood. Somehow, she knows I'm foreign.

'I'm only having a look,' I answer. Searching for the dead who lived along this lane, for a meadow with a copse and wooden hut painted by an unknown artist. For the scent of a long forgotten romance.

By the time I pass her again, she has fetched her teenage daughter who has, supposedly, learnt English in school. But the girl, sulky and dull, can't speak a word of it, so conversation struggles on as best it can.

I point to the empty lot. 'That's where the synagogue stood, am I right?'

'That was a long time ago.'

'This street was once a Jewish street?'

She shrugs.

There's nothing else to discover. No ghosts are chatting to me.

***

*A*t her death, my great-grandmother left two daughters, Chantza and Machla, and several sons. Her husband remarried, and his new wife, disliking the daughters, treated them badly. Machla, no beauty and with no dowry, was an old maid at twenty-four, but this was 1909, and not all women were willing to accept the mockery and low status of such a designation.

Women had not participated in the Haskalah's battle, and the Maskilim had wanted to take women away from financial responsibility, tuck them safely in home nests. In this, they had failed. Women continued working in family shops and selling on the market square. Others, to escape poverty and gain independence, went to the cities and toiled in factories. Excluded from the religious sphere, unable to understand Hebrew texts, they had been free to read books in Yiddish, and those new works had helped spread ideas of secularisation, insubordination, and had underlined the harmful impact of early arranged marriages. For a successful relationship, the Maskilim had written, emotional and intellectual compatibility was a necessity; so was romantic love—although something quite so fanciful could hardly be counted on so early in the day.

> *Right outside our house, you could see the beautiful River Bug with three beautiful, tree-lined islands. All this smelled good, especially at night when the moon was shining. I used to take a boat and all alone would ride out to the islands and sing away. I was high spirited and cheerful. All I lacked was a girl... The scent of the trees and the water would fill all my limbs and made me constantly think of the future, of married life, which I so valued.*
>
> *I was always worried that I should, God forbid, fall into the hands of a shrewish wife. I very much wanted to know the girl who was going to be my wife, at least for a couple of years before the wedding. We should first be very much in love...I was against the practice of some who took dowries.*

How could such a thing as love and future happiness with someone you will share every morsel of food with, be equated with money?[204]

True, only the bravest women dared refuse traditional life, but there were enough of them to show it was possible to change one's destiny. Some fell in love with non-Jews; some became political radicals; some left for other European cities or took ships to a new life in America. Wherever they went, the search for economic independence brought many into the sweatshops. Underpaid, overworked, and sexually harassed, only the General Jewish Labour Bund (Association), founded in 1897, concerned itself with their condition.[205]

By the turn of the century, even the most hopeful Jews had lost faith in the Russian government, and disillusion had spawned new movements: Zionism with its promise of a homeland free of exclusion, Socialism, Marxism, Leninism, and Bundism. Machla became an ardent bundist, for the new ideas had even penetrated this village. So had dreams of romance.

To a cousin, Machla once hinted at a lover, an anarchist, a man she couldn't—or wouldn't—marry. Who was he? What happened to him? Did he influence her? Did the old painting have something to do with this story? How about that shed, the copse? I'll never know the answers.

Like any bundist, she espoused the secular life: religion was superstition; marriage was bourgeois. Yet, not quite so rebellious as she wished, she finally compromised: for the price of a boat ticket, she accepted an arranged marriage with a local man she'd never met—Harry, a widower, now living way up in the Canadian north. To make the compromise sweeter, she vowed to take her political battle to the New Country.

---

204 Levin, Ontario Jewish Archives

205 The General Jewish Labour Bund also organised Jewish self-defence units during the pogroms of 1903–1906. Although poorly equipped, those in the units were arrested and charged alongside the instigators: weren't Jews responsible for the pogroms? Didn't they exploit everyone else?

Part Four:
THE NEW COUNTRY

Isaac Matenko

Chapter XXVIII:
Pickering, Ontario

I love you, yes, but you fill me with disgust,
You're frivolous, and not someone I can trust.
When throughout the world there's suffering, a blight,
Your mind is fixed on what dress you'll wear tonight.
The cries and moans don't reach your little room
Where you are primping with powder, rouge, perfume.
A big fine house with new furniture adorned,
Such is your dream, to such a life you were born.

Mordechai Gebirtig [206]

*F*rom a child's point of view, the journey from Toronto
to the Workmen's Circle Colony in Pickering, Ontario
via the family Monarch was an epic one: a seemingly endless

---

206 A member of the Bund, Gebirtig created his lyrics and sang his melodies
while working in his brother's basement carpentry shop. The songs spread
throughout the Yiddish-speaking world. In 1942, knowing that death was
near he wrote: *The Jews are yelling. It is good. / The enemy, the wild one, / Walks
savagely and fast – / And ruins life.* While being led, with the other Jews of
Krakow, to the cattle wagons and deportation to the Belzec death camp,
Gebirtig began singing at the top of his voice and dancing. Refusing to be
silenced, he was shot by a German guard.

two-lane highway; a dull landscape of cultivated fields; sibling epithets flung back and forth; a slapping parental hand; and punctuation furnished by unreliable rubber tires.

These days, it's another trip altogether. That prime agricultural farmland has been covered by tract housing with bucolic monikers—Mulberry Meadows, The Hamlet, Forest Creek—quadruple or sextuple car garages, and treeless lawns, all interspersed with strip malls, vast parking areas, commercial zones, overpasses, highways, and strewed packaging. All the by-products of the Canadian Dream.

Leaving the train station behind, I trudge through Pickering which, after the redistribution of electoral districts in 2013, is now called Ajax. Passing lovely old wooden houses, newer un-lovely ones, I reach open fields and the river I knew as a child. It's still around, thank goodness, not yet drained, dug up, or cemented over, but far from treacherous, as Machla made it out to be; not violent and wild as I remember (it did carry off my yellow plastic duck). It's hardly even a river, merely a creek, Duffin's Creek, but its deep gully serves as a border between past and future—albeit a temporary one. Bulldozers are waiting just around the corner: any day now, these remaining fields of corn and scrub, home to wild animals and the world of imagination, will be buried under more cement and suburbia.

It has already encroached on *Yungvelt*, the Workmen's Circle's summer camp.[207] Those wooden buildings have been replaced by backyards, garden fences, gates, a smashed toy truck, two maimed plastic dinosaurs, and piles of rubbish. I knew the camp well although I never officially attended; during visits to my grandparent's cottage in the colony just across the creek, I would drift, ghost-like, through the camp in the off-season, lurk, poke around.

I return to the main road, now paved (back then, dusty gravel), cross the concrete bridge that is very different from

---

207 Founded in 1926, the colony lasted until 1971. The cottages were finally destroyed in 2016 to make way for a subdivision.

the stately truss structure my memory conjures up. Here is the white farmhouse, now divided into housing units, where we bought fresh corn and strawberries. Long ago, with Michael, the farmer's son, and his crony, Henry, we clambered onto the backs of heat-dazed cows and played out sluggish games of cowboys and Indians.

Turning left behind the half-derelict red brick farmhouse, once the caretaker's house and now the scene of a recent murder, I follow a weedy dirt lane. Here are the cottages, made of wood, irregular in shape and design. One after the other, they advance along the hillside. It looks...well...it looks rather like an Eastern European shtetl, but that was the only model the colony's founders had. They'd all come from the Old Country, these men and women, Yiddish-speaking bundists and anarchists, the Haskalah's revolutionary children and grandchildren.

I was last here in 1961, just before my grandfather's decision to leave for California. Machla wanted to remain, but half a century with self-absorbed Harry had softened her up. I had no idea the colony's buildings were still standing—my father, for reasons of his own, insisted they weren't—yet I must admit that the place has taken quite a beating.

Long abandoned, it is a ghost town, one visited by the curious who leave behind fast food wrappers, and by vandals who have burnt some cottages, destroyed the interiors of others, decorated all with bullet holes and graffiti obscenities in an ecstatic frenzy only they can understand. Today, thankfully, there's no sound other than that of the wind rustling bare stalks, making leafless branches scratch and pines hiss. I think I'm alone, but who knows? There could still be someone around, trigger-happy, observing me from some hidey-hole: a ghost town always comes equipped with thrills and chills.

Machla and Harry's cottage, the last on the left, is still standing. The evergreens Harry claimed he planted—only a hedge when I last saw them—untamed for over half a century, are as stately as they should be. The apple orchard has vanished: no sign of those caterpillar-munched trees. No trace of the old wooden outhouse; none of the vegetable patch where peas, tomatoes, cucumbers, potatoes, dill, and carrots once grew—all cottage residents had kitchen gardens, made pickles, pickled cabbage, and pickled beets. Of course, they did: Socialist-Territorialists[208] exhorted the Jewish proletariat to abandon small industry and craftsmanship and turn to agriculture. These bundists and anarchists obeyed the injunction more modestly.

Our cottage is boarded up; no trespassing signs are everywhere. I find my grandfather's old garden tools in the lean-to shed, then assemble enough rubble for a makeshift ladder. At the side of the house, I prise back the boards covering the main room's window and, finally, I'm inside.

They left so much behind: crocks, cloths, cutlery, and a copper oiling can. Did they think they would come back one day, pick up where they left off? Was the word 'forever' too frightening? In the bedrooms, beds with rusty springs, the mattresses on which my brother and I slept, are still in place. In the kitchen, the wooden icebox is gone, but that must have disappeared a long time ago, when the iceman and his huge blocks went out of style. Here are cups, glasses, the crystal lid of a long-vanished sugar bowl I can still remember.

'I've returned,' I say to the resident ghosts. 'You see? I'll bet you didn't think I would.' I wait, listen. Branches twitch against the ruined roof; loose clapboard snaps. Are they sending me messages?

'Hello? Anybody still here?'

In the main room, the dining table, the credenza, the sofa, all have been smashed into shards, but in fairly good shape is the light-coloured, heavy round wooden table where Harry wiled away afternoons, speaking the Yiddish I couldn't

---

208 The Jewish Marxist-Zionist *Poale Zion*, (Workers of Zion) was founded in Russia. Because of ideological conflict, there were many different trends and splits throughout its history. The Territorialists argued that the essence of Zionism was in its social and economic content, not in a link with Palestine.

understand, drinking tea and playing endless games of cards with his cronies.

That's what old guys did back then. No matter where they were, out here, or in a long-vanished candy shop/pickle barrel paradise in Toronto (on Dufferin? Spadina?), they slapped down cards, drank glasses of tea, schmoozed, and rolled out big ideas. Did they long secretly for the Old Country, the one they had known before it was wiped off the earth's surface? Did they still gossip about villages where the main square had been a familiar place, where they had known every peasant, every sound and smell, every dusky corner of the local inn?

***

*A*s a child, I saw the colonists in Pickering as older, passive folk. I had no idea they'd once been passionate radicals, bundists, socialists, free thinkers, and secularists. Began as a mutual aid society to help immigrants adapt to life in America, the Toronto branch of the Workmen's Circle, *Arbeter Ring*, was founded in 1908, and its members were committed to equality, social justice, and humanism.

How life in this colony must have jumped! Some women, no longer willing to accept the role of housewife with its attendant drudgery, numerous pregnancies, and subordination to males, joined the struggles for social reform: a few refused marriage to their lifelong mates. There were illicit romances, battles, and debates; there was (or so rumour said) a shooting in the 1920s. The most radical members went on to form Toronto's still functioning Jewish Labour League Mutual Benefit Society.

Activities were conducted in Yiddish, the one language all had in common. To imbue their children with Jewish culture and history, the Workmen's Circle merged with the Socialist-Territorialists and, in 1916, founded the I.L. Peretz School.[209] It was a touch-and-go operation at first. There was the usual external opposition from religious groups; there was, again, internal opposition from those insisting on Hebrew, not Yiddish. Yet, attendance went from forty to three hundred and thirty after the first year.

Part of the success was due to men like Isaac Matenko. Born in Russia in 1874, like any Maskil before him, Matenko received a traditional Jewish education but privately pursued secular studies in Yiddish, Russian, and French literature. In Canada, he went to work in a factory,[210] and when his shift ended, he came to the Peretz School to speak about Yiddish literature and read Yiddish stories to fellow workers and their children. Generous, modest, disliking conformists, he had no interest in the financial success of those around him. He found his pleasure in verses by Peretz, and in Sholem Aleichem's odd characters. Just think: I could have asked him about Velvel Zbarzher and he'd have known all the answers.

Matenko died in 1960. In his last years, he regretted that so little had been written about a time when Jewish life had held so much idealism. He was now old, he said, and unable to undertake such a task. Most of the old archives were gone— he'd collected them in a wooden chest kept in the Peretz School basement, but one icy winter when there was no fuel, a man named Blachman had burnt the chest and its contents.

---

209 Peretz (1852-1915) believed traditional Judaism had reached a dead end and that secular literature and culture had to replace religion. The school's founders were Matenko, Winesanker, Rhinewine, Bromberg, and Frumhartz. The school closed its doors in 1994.

210 He helped create the Worker's Union, which later affiliated with the International Ladies' Garment Workers' Union.

By now, Europe's intellectual world had been murdered. Those Old World traditions, literary depictions of shtetl conundrums and colourful characters were no competition for the New World's glittering commercialism.

'Who cared about those old stories?' said my father. 'Literary evenings in Yiddish? We were bored silly. We didn't want to hear about the Old Country. We were ashamed to speak Yiddish.'

Small tradespeople, sweatshop labourers, and members of the Workmen's Circle had struggled so their children would never work in factories. Those children pushed aside Old World idealism and social movements as they moved up in status and joined the middle class. Their toes tapped to foxtrots and swing jazz, not 'tuneless' old-fashioned klezmer.[211] Workmen's Circle membership declined: the old folks began dying off. Their offspring, now doctors, lawyers, dentists and businessmen, wanted nothing to do with this colony. Living in big suburban houses with sterile green lawns, belonging to golf clubs, dining clubs, squash and tennis clubs, they vacationed in Florida, bought bigger cars, bigger boats, and bigger summer cottages.

We, their children, were sent to expensive summer camps with an emphasis on sport and appearance—the preparatory steps toward economically successful mating. Raised in another world altogether, we missed out on the debates, the ideas, the history, and the literature.[212] No one mentioned the old stories.

I leave my grandparent's cottage, climbing back out of the window, hammering the wooden boards back into place,

---

211 Much of today's klezmer, a mixture of Broadway musicals, jazz, blues, rock and Hollywood film music, is only a vague memory of the old, perhaps rawer sounds.

212 Although small breakfast clubs within the community retained a memory of the past's camaraderie. I was lucky enough to have, alas briefly, participated in the now-defunct Eglinton Avenue breakfast club headed by the brilliant Dr Bill Goodman. There, as late as 2006, the shtetlekh and old affiliations were still evoked, although only one member had been born in Poland.

then go visit the cottages of others—places into which I was never invited as a child. Here, too, are glasses, cups, cutlery, tables, counters, kitchens, beds, shredded curtains, torn books, open school notebooks, pamphlets, dresses and shirts on hangers, photos, framed pictures on walls, waiting chairs, a sofa—all memorials to abandonment. Then I head up the dirt lane, still feeling watched, perhaps only by beady gopher eyes, or suspicious raccoons.

'I'll be back,' I shout out to the derelict colony's phantoms. 'I'll keep on coming back, too.' But this might be my last visit: new orange markers already designate the plots of a future subdivision. All physical trace of that old story will soon be gone.

***

*A*lthough I've tried hard to enter another epoch, it will always evade me. I'm old enough to have seen its pale tail end, but that earlier world, that which I've presented in this story, might be one the dead would never recognise.

Even Velvel remains an elusive figure. I've walked in his footsteps in Galicia and Romania, my fingers have caressed his on the copy of *Romanyah* that he sent with such hope to the Alliance Israélite, but he is always out of reach. No householder, sculptor, builder, or painter, he left no physical mark beyond his poems, and today, those are largely forgotten. Only occasionally does a verse appear in an anthology.

So here, Velvel the bard will have the last word, even though he's laughing at me, at us, at himself:

> *All around, people complain and whine*
> *And they're right*
> *These are hard times*
> *And things are going badly.*
> *And when they're tired out by whining*
> *When they've broken down*
> *The poet sings his happy song,*
> *A poet can't complain.*

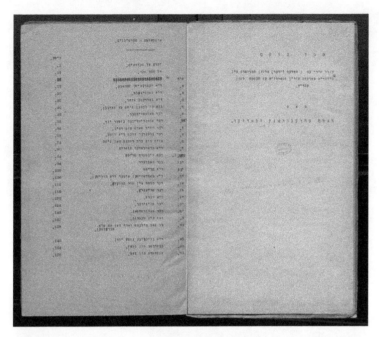

Makel No'am: Folk Songs in the language spoken by Jews in Poland and Moldavia, with copies in the Hebrew language, by Wolf Ehrenkranz Zbarzher. Below, in pencil, are the words: Including songs written in Lemberg in 1869.

Bibliography

Agnon, Shmuel Yosef. *Only Yesterday*, (Princeton: Princeton University Press 2019.)

Aleichem, Sholem. *On Account of a Hat*, translation, Issac Rosenfeld, (New York: Viking, Penguin, 2009.)

Aleichem, Sholem. *From the Fair: The Autobiography of Sholem Aleichem*, Translation Curt Leviant, (Lexington, Mass.: Plunkett Lake Press, 2012.)

Alroey, Gur. *Bread to Eat and Clothes to Wear: Letters from Jewish Migrants in the Early Twentieth Century*, (Detroit, Michigan: Wayne State University Press, 2011.)

Gebirtig, Mordechai. *Anthology of Yiddish Folksongs*, (Jerusalem: Hebrew University 2000.)

Ansky, S. *The Enemy at His Pleasure: A Journey Through the Jewish Pale of Settlement During World War I*, Translation: Joachim Neugroschel, (New York: Henry Holt, 2003.)

Ashby, Charlotte. *The Viennese Café and Fin-de-Siècle Culture*, (New York, Oxford: Berghahn Books, 2013.)

Assaf, David. *Untold Tales of the Hasidim: Crisis and Discontent in the History of Hasidism.* (Waltham, MA: Brandeis University Press, 2010.)

Bartov, Omer. *Erased: Vanishing Traces of Jewish Galicia in Present-day Ukraine.* (Princeton, N.J.: Princeton University Press, 2007.)

Beller, Steven. *Vienna and the Jews,* (Cambridge, UK: Cambridge University Press, 1958.)

Benjamin of Tudela. *The Itinerary of Benjamin of Tudela: Travels in the Middle Ages,* Translation Marcus Nathan Adler, (New York: Philipp Feldheim Inc., 1907.)

Bergelson, David. *When All Is Said and Done.* Translation Bernard Martin. (Athens: Ohio University Press, 1977.)

Berkovitsh, Israel. *Hundert yor yidish teater in Rumenye, 1876–1976.* (Bucharest: Kriteryon, 1976.)

Berkowitz, Joel. Henry, Barbara. *Inventing the Modern Yiddish Stage: Essays in Drama, Performance, and Show.* (Detroit: Wayne University Press, 2012.)

Blum, Jerome. *The End of the Old Order in Rural Europe.* (Princeton: Princeton University Press, 1978.)

Boileau, Charles Elliott. *The Great Empires of Austria, Russia and Turkey Volume 1,* (London: Richard Bentley, 1839.)

Burnand, Robert. *La Vie Quotidienne en France en 1830.* (Paris : Librairie Hachette, 1943.)

Castellan, Georges. *Histoire du Peuple Romain,* (Crozon: Editions Armeline, 2002.)

Dawidowicz, Lucy S. *The Golden Tradition: Jewish Life and Thought in Eastern Europe,* (New York: Schocken Books, 1984.)

Diment, Michael. *The Lone Survivor: A Diary of the Lukacze Ghetto and Svyniukhy, Ukraine.* Translator Shmuel Diment Yahalom, (Washington: U. S. Holocaust Museum, 1992.)

Dinezon, Jacob. *Memories and Scenes.* Translated by Tina Lunson, (Raleigh: Jewish Storyteller Press, 2014.)

Dynner, Glen. *Men of Silk: The Hasidic Conquest of Polish Jewish Society.* (Oxford: Oxford University Press, 2006.)

Dubnov, Simon. *History of the Jews from the Congress of Vienna to the Emergence of Hitler,* (London: Thomas Yoseloff, 1973.)

Dynner, Glen. *Yankel's Tavern: Jews, Liquor and Life in the Kingdom of Poland.* (Oxford: Oxford University Press, 2014.)

Eckardt, Julius. *Die Grenzboten,* (Leipzig: Duncker & Humblot 1870.)

Elliot, Charles Boileau. *Travels in the Three Great Empires of Austria, Russia and Turkey, Volume One.* (London: Richard Bentley, 1838.)

Eminescu, Mihai. *Iconostas si fragmentarium,* (Bucharest: Editura Tornada, 1872.)

Everdell, William R. *The First Moderns: Profiles in the Origins of Twentieth Century Thought,* (Chicago: University of Chicago Press, 1997.)

Franko, Ivan. *Faces of Hardship,* (Chambersburg, PA: Reprinted by TSK Group, 2016.)

Franzos, Karl Emil. *Aus Halb Asien.* (Berlin: Duncker & Humblot, 1876.)

Franzos, Karl Emil. *Der Pojaz.* (Berlin: Henschel Verlag, 1957.)

Gleig, G.R. *Germany, Bohemia, and Hungary, Visited in 1837,* (London: John W. Parker, 1839.)

Gnessin, Uri Nissan. *Beside and Other Stories,* (Milford, CT: The Toby Press, 2005.)

Gold, Hugo. *Geschichte der Juden in Österreich,* (Tel Aviv: Olamenu, 1971.)

Gordon, Mikhl. *Di bord un dertsu andere sheyne yidishe lider fun a groysen khosid (The Beard and Other Beautiful Yiddish Songs from a Great Hasid),* (Zhitomir: Shadau, 1868.)

Hapgood, Hutchins. *The Spirit of the Ghetto: Studies of the Jewish Quarter in New York,* (New York, London: Funk and Wagnalls Company, 1902.)

Herder, Harry. *Europe in the Nineteenth Century, 1830-1880,* (London: Longman, 1988.)

Heymann, Florence. *Le Crépuscule des lieux: Identités Juives de Czernowitz,* (Paris: Editions Stock, 2003.)

Hirsch, Marianne. Spritzer, Leo. *Ghosts of Home: the Afterlife of Czernowitz in Jewish Memory,* (Berkeley: University of California Press, 2010.)

Hödl, Klaus. *Als Bettler in die Leopoldstrasse,* (Vienna: Böhlau, 1994.)

Hogaş, Calistrat. *Pe drumuri de munte,* (Bucarest: Curtea Veche, 1914.)

Horodezky, Samuel Abba. *Religiöse Strömungen im Judentum, mit Besonderer Berücksichtigung des Chassidismus,* (Berlin, Leipzig: Ernst Bircher Verlag, 1920.)

Johnson, Sam. *Pogroms, Peasants, Jews: Britain and Eastern Europe's Jewish question 1867-1925*. (Basingstoke: Macmillan, 2011.)

Johnston, William M. *The Austrian Mind: An intellectual and social history, 1948-1938,* (Oakland: University of California Press, 1972.)

Kessler, David. *Memoirs of the Yiddish Stage*. (Queens: Queens College Press, 1984.)

Kletskin, B. *Studies in Philology, Second Volume*. (Vilnius: Vilner Verlag, 1928.)

Kotik, Yekhezkel. *Journey to a 19th Century Shtetl: The Memoirs of Yekhezel Kotik,* Edited by David Assaf, (Detroit: Wayne State University Press, 2002.)

Kuprin, Aleksandr. *Yama: the Pit,* (Paris: A&G Mornay, 1926.)
Lambrecht, Lars. *Osteuropa in den Revolutionen von 1848,* (Frankfurt am Main: P. Lang, 2006.)

Landis, Joseph. *Memoirs of the Yiddish Stage,* (Queens: Queens College Press, 1984.)

Liptzin, Sol. *A History of Yiddish Literature,* (Middle Village: Jonathan David Publishers, 1972.)

Maczak, Antoni. *Travel in Early Modern Europe,* (Cambridge: Polity Press, 1995.)

Manger, Itzik. *Velvl Zbarzher Shraybt Briv tsu Malkele der Sheyner* (Warsaw: 1937)

Margoshes, Joseph. *A World Apart: A Memoir of Jewish Life in Nineteenth Century Galicia,* Translated from Yiddish by Rebecca Margolis and Ira Robinson, (Boston: Academic Studies Press, 2008.)

Marrus, Michael. *The Nazi Holocaust, Volume 2, Part 6.* (Munich: K G Saur Verlag, 1989.)

McCagg Jr., William O. *A History of Habsburg Jews, 1670-1918,* (Bloomington and Indianapolis: Indiana University Press, 1989.)

Mintz, Alan. *Banished from Their Father's Table,* (Bloomington and Indianapolis: Indiana University Press, 1989.)

Mlotek, Chana. Mlotek, Joseph. *Songs of Generations: New Pearls of Yiddish Song,* (New York: Workmen's Circle, 1983.)

Mlotek, Chana. Mark, Slobin. Editors. *Yiddish Folksongs from the Ruth Rubin Archives,* (Detroit: Wayne State University Press, 2007.)

Oișteanu, Andrei. *Les images du Juif: Clichés Antisémites dans la Culture Roumaine: une Approche Comparative.* Translated by Stefanescu Pompiliu, (Paris: Non lieu, 2013.)

Onac, Iulia. *The Brustarosa Uprising in Romania, from Sites of European Antisemitism In the Age of Mass Politics,* (Waltham: Brandeis University Press, 2014.)

Orzeszko, Eliza. *An Obscure Apostle A Dramatic Story.* Translated by C.S. De Soissons, (London: Greening and Co. Ltd., 1899.)

Petrovsky-Shtern, Yohanan. *The Golden Age Shtetl, A New History of Jewish Life in East Europe,* (Princeton: Princeton University Press, 2014.)

Ashby, Charlotte. Gronberg, Tag. Shaw-Miller, Simon, Editors. *The Viennese Café and Fin-de-Siècle Culture,* (New York: Berghahn Books, 2013.)

Ravitch, Melekh. *Dos mayse-bukh fun mayn lebn, Zikhroynes,* (Tel Aviv: Michael Weichart, 1960.)

Reisen, Salmen. *Leksikon fun der yiddisher literature, prese und filologye,* (Vilna: Kletzkin, 1927.)

Rosenblit, Marsha L. *The Jews of Vienna, 1867-1914,* (Albany: State University of New York Press, 1983.)

Rosenstone, Robert A. *The Man Who Swam into History: The (Mostly) True Story of My Jewish Family,* (Austin: University of Texas Press, 2010.)

Roskies, David G. *The Jewish Search For A Usable Past,* (Bloomington and Indianapolis: Indiana University Press, 1999.)

Roskies, David G. Rubin, Ruth. *Voices of a People: the Story of Yiddish Folksong,* (Chicago: University of Illinois Press, 2000.)

Sachar, Abram Leon. *A History of the Jews,* (New York: Alfred A. Knopf, 1930.)

Sandrow, Nahma. *Vagabond Stars: A World History of Yiddish Theater,* (Syracuse: Syracuse University Press, 1995.)

Schwara, Desanka. *Ojfn weg schtejt a bojm: Jüdische Kindheit und Jugend in Galizien, Kongreßpolen, Litauen und Rußland 1881-1939,* (Köln: Böhlau, 1999.)

Shoberl, Frederick. *Austria; Containing a Description of the Manners, Customs, Character and Costumes of the People of That Empire,* (Philadelphia: C.S. Williams, 1828.)

Silberbusch, David Yeshaya. *Skizzen un Humoresken,* (Vienna: Lippe's Buchhandlung, 1921.)

Silberbusch, David Yeshaya. *Mi-Pinkas zikhronotai,* (Tel Aviv: Vaad Yovel Hashmonim 1936.)

Sincerus, Edmond (Schwarzfeld, Elias). *Les Juifs en Roumanie depuis le traité de Berlin,* (New York: Macmillan and Company, 1901.)

Slomka, Jan. *From Serfdom to Self-Government: Memoirs of a Polish Village Mayor, 1842-1927,* (London: Minerva Publishing. Co, 1941.)

Subtelny, Orest. *Ukraine: A History,* (Toronto: University of Toronto Press, 2000.)

Tung, Anthony M. *Preserving the World's Great Cities,* (New York: Three Rivers Press, 2001.)

Wachstein. *Velvele Zbarezhers briv zu zayn bruder Meyer: Loyt di originaln fun der bibliotek fun der yidisher kehile in Vin,* (Vilna: Bernhard Editor, 1928.)

Walkowitz, Daniel J. *The Remembered and Forgotten Jewish World: Jewish Heritage in Europe and the United States,* (New Brusnwick: Rutgers University Press, 2018.)

Wrawall, William. *Memoirs of the Court of Berlin, Dresden, Warsaw and Vienna in the years 1777, 1778, and 1779, Volume 2,* (London: Cadell and W. Davies, 1806.)

Wiener, Leo. *The History of Yiddish Literature in the Nineteenth Century,* (London: J. C. Nimmo, 1899.)

Winston, Hella. *Unchosen: The Hidden Lives of Hasidic Rebels,* (Boston: Beacon Press, 2013.)

Wisse, Ruth. *A Shtetl and Other Yiddish Novellas*, (Detroit: Wayne State University Press, 1986.)

Wolff, Larry. *The Idea of Galicia, History and Fantasy in Habsburg Political Culture*, (Stanford: Stanford University Press, 2010.)

Zamoyski, Adam. *The Polish Way*, (New York: Hippocrene Books, 1994.)

Bibliography (Articles)

Aus dem Leben eines judischen Volksdichters: Ein Einzelgänger des Getto,' (Vienna: Mittagblatt des Neuen Wiener Journals, Seite 8, November 27, 1917.)

Abraham Goldfaden, Obituary, (Czernowitz: Bukowinaer Post, January 14, 1908.)

Fried, Dr Moses. '*Biographisches Über Benjamin Wolf Ehrenkranz,*' (Berlin: Mitteilungen zur Jüdischen Volkskunde, 1917.)

Goldfaden, Avrom. '*Dor Haflagah,*' (New York: Folder 51 Collection RG 219, Series 1: Plays and Other Writings for the Stage, 1879-1906, YIVO Institute.)

Heinzen, George. '*Czernowitz,*' (Bonn: Rheinischen Merkur, February 1, 1991.)

Kirsch, Adam. '*Jewish Bride Has a Mole? Grounds for Divorce. Husband Smells Bad? Live With It. Inequality under the wedding canopy.*' (New York: Tablet Magazine, April 28, 2015.)

Singer, Isidore, Editor. *'Ehrenkrantz, Benjamin Wolf',* (New York and London: The Jewish Encyclopedia 1901-1906, Funk and Wagnalls, 1906.)

Streitman, Henric Stepfan. *'Wolf Zbarazher Ehrenkranz, Evocare,'* (Bucharest: Adam, 1938.)

Von Trimberg, Suskind. *'Why Should I Wander Sadly' from 'The Standard Book of Jewish Verse,'* (New York: Dodd, Mead and Co. 1917.)

Yudel, Mark. *'The Yiddish Language: its Cultural Impact' in 'Never Say Die! A Thousand Years of Yiddish in Jewish Life and Letters,'* (Berlin: Walter de Gruyter, 2010.)

Weissberg, Meir. *'Wölwel Zbarazer, der Fahrende Sänger des Galizisch-Jüdischen Humanismus,'* (Berlin: Mitteilungen zur Jüdischen Volkskunde, Heft XXXI, 1909.)

Bibliography (Online resources)

Bulletin de l'Alliance Israélite Universelle, (Paris: Correspondence, AIU Archives, 1882, FR_AIU_AH_FRA_D_52a-06.pdf)

Stern, Zehavit. *'From Jester to Gesture: Eastern European Jewish Culture and the Re-imagination of Folk Performance,'* 2011. *http:// digitalassets.lib.berkeley.edu*

Von Sacher-Masoch, Leopold. *'Der Alte Pfarrer,'* 1857. *https:// www.projekt-gutenberg.org/autoren/namen/sacher-m.html*

Bloch, Dr Joseph S. *'Errinerung aus Meinem Leben.' Vienna, 1922. http://sammlungen.ub.uni-frankfurt.de/freimann/content/titleinfo/1221248*

Jewish Heritage Europe. *https://jewish-heritage-europe. eu/2021/04/19/ukraine-great-synagogue-in-lutsk/*
Raisin, Jacob S. *'The Haskalah Movement in Russia,'* 2005. *https://www.gutenberg.org/ebooks/15921*

Soxberger, Thomas. *'Moderne Yiddische Literatur und Jiddischismus in Wien, 1900-1938.'* 2010. *http://othes.univie.ac.at/14408/1/2010-12-14_8604951.pdf*

The Jewish Virtual Library *https://www.jewishvirtuallibrary.org/*

YIVO *Encyclopaedia of Jews in Eastern Europe http://yivoencyclodepia.org*

Bibliography (Photos)

Part One	*Former Polish Castle*
Introduction:	*Poritsk, Ukraine*
Chapter I:	*Fernand Aaron, French Jewish businessman*
Chapter II:	*Roma children, Galicia, 1940 (Courtesy Attila Szabo)*
Part Two:	*Galicia, 1940 (Courtesy Attila Szabo)*

Chapter IX :   *Former Zbarazh synagogue*

Chapter XVII: *Jewish Soldiers, Vienna, WWI*
                     (Courtesy Yad Vashem)

Chapter XVIII: *Tarnopol synagogue (Courtesy Yad Vashem)*

Chapter XIX: *Hotel Zum Schwarzen Adler*

Part Three: *Former Synagogue, Lutsk*

Chapter XXIV: *Lev and Nathan*

Chapter XXVIII: *Isaac Matenko*
                     (Courtesy Ontario Jewish Archives)

Acknowledgements

*W*riters frequently become obsessed with people they'll never meet and epochs outside their experience. Since nothing discourages such lunacy, I am grateful to those who have gone along with my infatuation for Velvel Zbarzher and his world.

I am most deeply indebted to Irene Ehrenkranz Fishler, the sixth generation descendant of Velvel's father, Moshke Ehrenkranz. Without her archival research, her translations of many articles as well as Velvel's letters, her insights, wisdom, and great patience in answering all my questions, this book would have been a far inferior one. If I have made errors, I hope she will forgive me.

Many thanks to my wonderful publisher Katie Isbester for her encouragement, enthusiasm, and excellent suggestions, and Madi Simcock-Brown for her punctilious editing. I am equally grateful to Bernard Tisserand for his determination to make this book as lovely as possible, and to everyone at the Ontario Jewish Archives who, with their assistance and the reassuring Stephen Speisman Bursary, let me know that my nosy digging around just might yield something of interest.

I am also grateful for the help and encouragement of many others: Bill Gladstone who pushed me to begin the project and who kept in touch during one of my journeys through Ukraine and Romania, Stephen Glazer for his enthusiasm, and for obtaining papers from the Jerusalem archives, Mel Cederbaum and Dale Langbord Joffe at the Toronto Workmen's Circle for their reflections on Pickering, and the late Helen Glazer whose stories made the early days of the Pickering colony come alive.

I am equally indebted to my dear cousin, archaeological researcher Anna Iamim who rushed in with last minute translations from old Hebrew, to linguist Volker Dahm who helped with the translations of Zbarzher's poems, to Irene Baytsar for her company and insights, to Barry James who read through this manuscript and offered suggestions and, once again, to Bernard Tisserand for his patience and for his recommendations. Thanks to those who believed in this project and offered support, friendship, hospitality, photos, stories, or information: Robin Rogers, Judy Spring, Eva Samery, Penny Lynn Cookson, Attila and Paula Szabo.

Equally essential were those I met along the way. Some were indifferent, others amusingly awful, but many were patient with a lone and often incoherent traveller.

Permissions

Thanks to those who have allowed me to use photos from their archives: Yad Vashem, the Ontario Jewish Archives, Yosef Lustig of the Memorial Museum of Hungarian Speaking Jewry in Safed, Israel, and the most excellent Ehpes Blog (czernowitz.ehpes.com).

Many thanks to Matthew Charlton at The Academic Studies Press for the permission to use the poignant excepts from Joseph Margoshes' delightful, *A World Apart: A Memoir of Jewish Life in Nineteenth Century Galicia*, to the Ontario Jewish Archives for the many excerpts from Benzion Echiel Levin's fascinating unpublished memoirs, to Julian Marks for permission to use the excerpts from Ruth Rubin's *Voices Of a People*, and to Georges Borchardt Inc. for permission to use Joachim Neugroschel's translations of Ansky's The Enemy at His Pleasure: *A Journey through the Jewish Pale of Settlement during World War I*.

About the Author

*B*orn in New York, raised in Toronto, Jill Culiner, writer, social critical artist, and photographer has spent most of her life in France, England, Germany, Hungary, Turkey, and the Sahara. Her photographic exhibition about the First and Second World Wars, *La Mémoire Effacée,* toured France, Canada, and Hungary under the auspices of the French Ministry of Foreign Affairs and UNESCO. Her non-fiction *Finding Home in the Footsteps of the Jewish Fusgeyers* won the Joseph and Faye Tannenbaum Prize for Canadian Jewish History and was shortlisted for the ForeWord Magazine Award.

She presently lives in a former auberge in France that is so chaotic and strange, it has been classified as a museum:

http://www.jill-culiner.com

Blog:
https://jewish-histories.over-blog.com

Storytelling Podcast:
https://soundcloud.com/j-arlene-culiner

Claret Press

Claret Press shares engaging stories about the real issues of our changing world. Since it was founded in 2015, Claret Press has seen its titles translated into German, shortlisted for a Royal Society of Literature award and climb up the bestseller list. Each book probes the entanglement of the political, the historical and the everyday—but always with the goal of creating an engaging read.

If you enjoyed this book, then we're sure you'll find more great reads in the Claret Press library.

Subscribe to our mailing list at **www.claretpress.com** to get news of our latest releases, bespoke zoom events and the occasional adorable photo of the Claret Press pets.

CPSIA information can be obtained
at www.ICGtesting.com
Printed in the USA
BVHW070954071021
618410BV00007B/184